52 Ways to Wreck
Your Retirement

52 Ways to Wreck Your Retirement

... And How to Rescue It

Tina Di Vito, CA, CFP, TEP

John Wiley & Sons Canada, Ltd.

Library and Archives Canada Cataloguing in Publication

Di Vito, Tina
    52 ways to wreck your retirement : —and how to rescue it / Tina Di Vito.

Includes index.
Issued also in electronic formats.
ISBN 978-1-118-07609-5

    1. Retirement—Canada—Planning.   2. Retirement income—Canada—Planning.
3. Finance, Personal—Canada.   4. Retirement—Planning. I.   Title.
II.   Title: Fifty-two ways to wreck your retirement.

HG179.D58 2011   332.024'0140971   C2011-901788-1

ISBN 978-1-118-07609-5 (paper); 978-1-118-07839-6 (ePDF); 978-1-118-07840-2
(Mobi); 978-1-118-07841-9 (ePub)

Production Credits
Cover Design: Adrian So
Cover Image Credit: iStockphoto
Composition: Thomson Digital
Printer: Trigraphik | LBF

Editorial Credits
Executive Editor: Karen Milner
Production Editor: Pauline Ricablanca

John Wiley & Sons Canada, Ltd.
6045 Freemont Blvd.
Mississauga, Ontario
L5R 4J3

Printed in Canada

2 3 4 5 6 LBF TRI 15 14 13 12 11

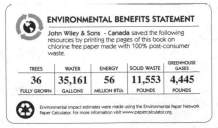

ENVIRONMENTAL BENEFITS STATEMENT

John Wiley & Sons - Canada saved the following
resources by printing the pages of this book on
chlorine free paper made with 100% post-consumer
waste.

TREES	WATER	ENERGY	SOLID WASTE	GREENHOUSE GASES
36	35,161	56	11,553	4,445
FULLY GROWN	GALLONS	MILLION BTUs	POUNDS	POUNDS

Environmental impact estimates were made using the Environmental Paper Network
Paper Calculator. For more information visit www.papercalculator.org.

CONTENTS

INTRODUCTION

WHY A BOOK ABOUT RETIREMENT? There are so many other, more interesting, things to read about. How about a book on ways to make millions in the stock market? For this one simple reason — I'm constantly hearing that Canadians haven't saved enough money, that they are not prepared for retirement or, worse, that they want to retire but they will never be able to. In order to have a successful retirement, you need to take action and make things happen. We spend one-third of our lives growing up and getting smart, one-third of our lives working and buying things, and one-third of our lives . . . *living off the money and other assets we've accumulated during our working years.* In essence, everything we do in the first two-thirds of our lives will affect the last one-third.

Canadians *can* achieve their dreams and to do that, they need some simple retirement strategies to help them transition into retirement with confidence and clarity. If retirement only lasted a few years, then you could get away with not having a retirement plan. But what if retirement were to last 30 years? Well, then we would need to pay some attention to planning for it rather than leaving it to chance. The way I see it, if you hope to have some control over this part of your life, you need to have a plan.

Too bad that last third of our life is called retirement. If you look in the dictionary for the definition of the word *retirement*, you will find words such as *withdrawal, privacy, seclusion,* and *overall end of usefulness* — it is not all that appealing. Is that what the rest of our lives will be about? No wonder so many people prefer not to think about it until the last minute. But retirement today is not the same as it was years ago. More and more are referring to this stage of life as the New Retirement — a new phrase to represent a new attitude, an active lifestyle, and a positive outlook on what the future could be, rather than the end of work, end of power, end of usefulness, end of life. These days retirement can mean slowing down and not working as much, working for only part of the year, focusing on a hobby, or volunteering. That's why some people say they'll never retire in the traditional sense of the word — they will always be actively doing something — it just might not be the same full-time job or career they've had during their full-time work years. Throughout this book I use the word *retirement* simply for lack of a better word, or lack of a word that is as well known as the word *retirement*. When I use the word *retirement*, I am referring to a time when full-time work for full-time pay ends, and pensions and withdrawals from savings begin.

Planning for retirement is not especially difficult; you just need to know where to start. And that's where we run into problems, because when it comes to personal finance, sometimes we just don't know where to start and, as a result, we procrastinate. So rather than starting with personal finances, start somewhere "fun." As you read through the chapters I want you to think about your retirement life. I want you to visualize what's around you, what you'll be doing, and imagine how you will be feeling when you have the freedom to do whatever you want.

The most important thing to keep in mind is that retirement planning isn't something that you do at a specific point in time or at a specific age. In fact, we are all affecting our retirement plans every day with every decision we make or don't make. You don't have to be retirement age, or even near it, to be affecting your quality of life in retirement. Everything we do or don't do in the second third of our lives in particular affects our retirement. For instance, deciding to buy a new car versus a used one, or accumulating large amounts of debt, will impact how much money is left over to set aside for retirement.

There are many simple things that we do or don't do that will impact our eventual retirement life. Even during retirement, there are a host of things that can derail even the best laid retirement plans. Here are some "retirement risks" to think about.

retirement risks:

1. Longevity risk — this is the chance that we'll live a long retirement. Sounds positive, doesn't it? But in reality, living a long retirement means that our savings will need to last a long time.

2. Inflation — inflation means that the price of goods goes up over time. While we're working, pay increases smooth over some of the inflation risk, but during what can be a very long retirement, inflation will erode our purchasing power, meaning our retirement nest egg will need to be even bigger to compensate.

3. Health risks — remember what I said about living a long retirement? The longer we live, the higher the chance that we'll need specialized health care at some point. Even though many medical costs are covered by provincial medical programs, many of the costs associated with long-term care are not.

4. Investment risk (market risk) — no one can predict the stock markets. A few bad years just as you are entering retirement and making withdrawals from your savings can mean that your portfolio will never recover, even though the market does.

5. Spending risk — as you enter retirement with limited resources, how you spend your money will impact how long it will last. If you spend too quickly, the long-term effect on your nest egg can be devastating.

6. Saving risk — if you don't know how much you'll need in retirement or where your retirement income will come from, you run the risk of not saving enough: under-saving. This is one of the main reasons those closest to retirement often decide to work for a few extra years.

7. Tax inefficiency risk — income taxes erode our earnings both during the working years and also during retirement. Minimizing income tax is one way to make your money go farther.

This book will give you the upper hand by arming you with the tools you need to better manage the financial and personal aspects of your retirement. It will take a close look at 52 ways we can wreck our retirement and provide strategies to help rescue it. Why are there 52 chapters? So that you can get your retirement on track within one year, and all you have to do is address one thing per week. Each chapter ends with a short to-do list for that week. In some cases, that aspect of your retirement plan may already be taken care of; in others, you may need to take action or simply start thinking about things in a different way.

So whether you're still many years away from retirement, whether it's just around the corner, or even if you're currently retired, this book can help you put the missing pieces in place for you and motivate you to take action. Of course, starting to think about retirement as early as you can is the best strategy, but starting today is the next best thing. I truly believe it's never too late to engage in retirement planning.

PART 1

starting to plan for retirement

CHAPTER 1

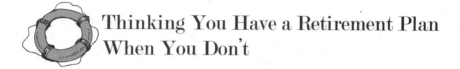 Thinking You Have a Retirement Plan
When You Don't

If you don't have a good understanding of what a retirement plan consists of, you may think that you are already doing everything you need to do to prepare for retirement, when you're not.

THERE IS A WIDESPREAD LACK OF UNDERSTANDING about what retirement planning is. The term *retirement plan* is often used loosely to describe very different things, such as a target retirement date, retirement savings, and investment strategies. There are many facets to retirement planning. It is important to understand the interconnected elements of a retirement plan, and then develop strategies to minimize your risks while maximizing the outcomes to achieve your goal — retirement. Having a retirement plan does not mean just making RRSP contributions or participating in a company pension plan. These actions represent just one facet of a retirement plan — saving for retirement.

what is retirement planning?

Retirement planning includes both lifestyle and financial considerations. It is the "what" and the "how much" of retirement — *what* you want your retirement to look like, and *how much* it will cost. The process involves selecting a potential retirement date, reviewing your current financial situation, identifying saving gaps, and building a plan to achieve the desired outcomes.

what is a retirement plan?

A retirement plan is a living document! It is just that — a PLAN. It can change from year to year, depending on your circumstances. It is a thoughtful organization of strategies and actions that will combine to help you reach your retirement goals.

A complete retirement plan consists of two distinct parts that I like to describe as the saving phase and the spending phase. The saving phase is made up of all the steps you need to take to get you to your retirement, and the spending phase is all about what you need to do to make the most of your retirement years.

During the *saving phase* the focus should be on growing your money, managing your spending, paying off debt, and so on. The overall goal is to accumulate enough money so you can live the lifestyle you want during retirement. On the other hand, during the *spending phase* the objective is quite different. Rather than focusing on saving for retirement, the goal here is to make sure your money will last you all through your retirement years.

starting the retirement planning process

What does retirement mean to you? This is very much an individual thing and no two people's retirements will be the same, so don't focus on what others believe retirement should be like — think about what it means for you. Think big picture first and consider how you want to live this part of your life and what your objectives or goals might be. Your views will likely change and become clearer the closer you are to your retirement. Regardless of how many years you are from retirement, it's important to think about:

- *when* you might want to retire
- *how* you might be spending your time

Let's take a closer look at each one of these considerations.

When do you want to retire?

This is a very important consideration, because this is the starting point in developing your retirement plan. Your age at retirement can affect how you will spend your time and how much money you will need to save. Don't worry if you change your mind about the actual date along the way; that's completely normal and is sometimes necessary to make the plan work. I'm not a big believer in having a set retirement date, but for planning to begin, it is important to think about when retirement might begin. In fact, virtually all retirement planning tools and calculators will ask you to select a retirement age as a starting point for planning.

How will you spend your time?

Sounds simple enough, but many people can't say what they'll be doing next week, let alone in 10 or 20 years. However, it is important to paint a mental picture of your future when creating your retirement plan. Start by thinking broadly before focusing on the day-to-day. Think about your hobbies, your aspirations, how much time you want to spend with your family and friends, and where you are planning to live. You need an idea of what you are saving for before you can come up with a plan to get you there.

planning your finances

Once you know what you are saving for, the next step is to determine how much money you'll need to accumulate during your working years to fund your desired retirement.

- Estimate how much your retirement will cost.
- Estimate your retirement income.
- Calculate how much you need to save.

How much will your retirement cost?

The farther away you are from retirement, the harder this might be to do. As a result, many people use an estimate based on their cost of living today. A common rule of thumb is to aim to replace approximately 70 to 80% of pre-retirement income. For lower income earners that replacement ratio might be closer to 90%, and for high income earners a replacement ratio of 50 to 60% might be sufficient. Keep in mind that some expenses will disappear upon retirement, such as work-related costs and mortgage payments, and others may arise, depending on your lifestyle. But remember, there is no one-size-fits-all approach to this. Therefore, knowing what you want to do in retirement should help you make a better estimate of how much money you'll need.

What will your retirement income be?

To determine how much you will receive as retirement income, you need to identify the income sources, such as government pensions, employer pensions, personal savings, etc., and estimate how much you will receive from each source. Keep in mind that a part-time job or a hobby can be another source of retirement income. Once you understand what your retirement income and expenses will be, you will know whether there is an income gap that needs to be filled.

How much do you need to save?

If there is a shortfall between your income and your expenses, you will need additional personal savings to fill the funding gap. The size of the gap will determine how aggressive your saving strategy needs to be. For instance, you may have a relatively small personal savings target if your total retirement income will cover most of your expenses. However, if your retirement income will cover only a small part of your retirement expenses, you will likely need to save more aggressively, unless you are willing to make some adjustments to your desired retirement lifestyle. Another consideration that will help determine how much you need to save is *how long* your retirement savings will need to last, because that will dictate how big your retirement nest egg will need to be.

value of a retirement plan

Ultimately, you have a choice as to how you approach retirement planning. You can play an active role, and be in control, or take a laissez-faire approach, hoping that things will just fall into place. Either you visualize your desired retirement and follow a roadmap to fund it, or you leave your retirement life to chance and let your savings dictate how you will live. Which alternative would you prefer?

rescue it!

To develop a retirement plan, follow these steps:

☐ Start thinking about what your retirement might look like.

☐ Think about when you might want to retire.

☐ Identify the sources of retirement income you will receive, including pensions.

☐ List your expected expenses/costs.

☐ Do a financial projection to see how much your savings will grow to by the time you reach retirement.

☐ Determine if your savings and pensions will be enough to pay for the kind of retirement you want to have.

Now you have the start of a retirement plan.

CHAPTER 2

 Being Fooled by Feeling and Looking
Younger than You Are

You may look and feel young, but don't let that fool you into
thinking you have lots of time to plan and save for retirement.
As the saying goes . . . time flies when you're having fun.

HOW OLD ARE YOU RIGHT NOW? How old do you feel? How old
do you look? How old do you tell people you are? In the past, our age
defined us rather rigidly. The terrible twos, the preteen and teenage years,
adulthood, middle age, and old age. These days our age no longer defines
who we are or what we are capable of doing. Some say the new middle age
is 50. There is a different state of mind around aging: we look, feel, and act
younger than our biological age.

One thing is certain: seniors today don't look like seniors from previous generations. Look at some of your old family photos. Wow, was Uncle
Bob only 40 in that picture? Why did everyone look and act so old?

These days the baby boom generation (those born between 1947 and
1966) is redefining what aging means. Even seniors are defying the age barriers: in June 2011, at the young age of 79, India's grand old marathon man
Ashis Roy completed his 110th marathon.

So how could feeling and looking younger wreck your retirement? One
simple word — procrastination. If you feel younger than you are, you *don't*
feel any sense of urgency about planning or saving for retirement. How can
you possibly be motivated about something that is a long way away?

when should you start saving for retirement?

The best time to start saving for retirement is when you first start working. In other words, the earlier the better. But when you're young, you don't think about retirement; it's the last thing on a 20-year-old's mind. After all, retirement is for old people, not for someone just starting out in life! However, if you fail to plan and save early enough, you miss out on one key ingredient in the retirement formula — **time**.

Start Today

Although the ideal time to start saving is early in life, other competing financial priorities often get in the way. If you're long past 20, when is the next best time to start saving for retirement? That's simple — today!

The importance of starting now cannot be ignored, because you want to make the most of the *compounding growth* of your savings, for as long as you can, since **time** is the single biggest influence on how much money you can accumulate.

Let's take a look at two scenarios. An annual RRSP contribution of $5,000 growing at 5% per year over a 30-year period results in total savings of $348,804. The total contributions were only $150,000, so 57% of the total savings accumulated came from the growth in the account.

Now let's look at the effect of a shorter saving period. Take the same annual contribution amount of $5,000 and the same 5% return, but over a 20-year period. The total savings accumulated after 20 years is only $173,596. The difference in total savings between the two scenarios is $175,208, which represents $50,000 less in contributions and $125,208 in lost growth from compound interest.

Of course, fewer years of contributions will mean a smaller account, but not by the same proportion. Growth over time plays a big role in how much is accumulated.

Years	Savings	Contributions	Growth
30	$348,804	$150,000	$198,804
20	$173,596	$100,000	$ 73,596
Difference	$175,208	$ 50,000	$125,208

increased contribution amount

Some may argue that they can make up for lost time by making larger contributions later in life when their income is higher and other financial obligations are taken care of. Using the same example, to achieve close to the same total savings of $348,804, contributions would have to increase substantially. If you have only 20 years to save, the required contributions would have to be approximately $10,000 per year, which is double the amount if you save for 30 years ($10,000 versus $5,000), and with a 10-year saving period, contributions would have to be approximately $26,500 per year.

As you can see from this example, it is possible to make up for lost time by increasing contributions later in when some expenses such as mortgage payments are gone. Even if you should be able to manage the bigger contributions based on your cash flow, the reality is that having more disposable income may result in a change in current spending habits, for instance buying a more expensive car or going on more lavish vacations rather than diverting the extra cash to saving for retirement. In a recent study, researchers put this theory to the test. A study of empty-nesters examined what participants did with the extra money once their kids moved out. The results showed that, rather than increasing savings, they used the extra money to buy more things.[1]

Think about what you did the last time *you* received a pay raise or a bonus. Did you save more, or use the extra money for something else? Waiting to start saving until you have more money may make sense *in theory,* but it's not a good strategy in reality.

get motivated

What would help motivate you to start planning for retirement? If you had a crystal ball and you could see your older self — perhaps in poorer health — would it motivate you to start saving? Apparently the answer is yes. Researchers conducted a study to determine how people's attitudes

[1] Center for Retirement Research at Boston College – November 2010. Children and Household Utility: Evidence from kids flying the coop. Norma B. Coe and Anthony Webb.

around saving for retirement might change if they could see themselves in the future. In the study, half of the participants saw a digitally aged image of themselves, and the other half saw their current image. Both groups were then asked to consider how much they should save for retirement. Those who saw the image of their aged future self were motivated to save more than twice as much as the group that saw themselves without aging.[2]

A picture can evoke many emotions: fear, excitement, disappointment. If you don't have the benefit of a digitally aged photo to motivate you, try to imagine some of the activities that you'll want to do in retirement and how much they will cost you. Let's say you want to golf once or twice a week. How would you feel if you had to give up golf entirely during retirement because you couldn't afford it? It may not take the fear of future disappointment to motivate you to start saving; just thinking about all the things you want to do in the future may be enough to get you started.

rescue it!

☐ Take a trip to the future! Start by imagining what activities your future self will do during retirement.

☐ Start saving now! Establish a regular savings routine and watch your savings grow.

☐ Divert a portion of any future pay raise or bonus to retirement savings.

---

[2] Hal Ersner-Hershfield et al., "Increasing Saving Behavior Through Age-Progressed Renderings of the Future Self," *Journal of Marketing Research*, in press.

CHAPTER 3

 Not Using Your Common Sense

There are simple commonsense money management strategies that are old standards but still valid today — but we are not following them.

COMMON SENSE TELLS US THAT it's important to "look both ways before you cross the street"; "chew before swallowing your food"; "say please and thank you"; and so on. Common sense also tells us that good money management includes saving, not over-spending, and investing carefully. Then why is it that we are experiencing financial distress? The truth is, we are not exercising common sense — we're not saving enough, we're spending too much, and we've accumulated huge amounts of debt. Perhaps it's time to go back to basics!

pay yourself first

This is still one of the most basic money management rules you will hear. You work hard for the money you earn, but before you know it, half of your paycheque is gone. Some goes to the government in the form of income taxes, some goes to payments on loans or mortgages, some goes to dining out, buying a new pair of shoes, and so on. No wonder it is so difficult to save! Obviously, if you try to save for your future after everyone else has taken their share, you won't have much, if anything, left over. But by turning this around and paying yourself first, you're making saving a priority, while at the same time limiting how much of your paycheque you allow yourself to spend.

Your future should be higher on the priority list. No matter how old you are, it's always a good idea to save a bit of money with each paycheque for the future or for a rainy day. How much do you need to put aside? As a starting point, you should aim to save at least 10% of what you earn for your retirement. For those starting to save later in life, savings should be closer to 20%, or even higher. And don't forget to increase how much you save each time you get a pay raise or a bonus, as we discussed in chapter 2. Regardless of what level of income you are earning today, it's important to remember to pay yourself first!

a penny saved is a penny earned

What you don't spend today is there for you tomorrow. During your working years, if you need more money, you have the option of working more; however, there will come a time when you no longer earn an income. Therefore, it is important not to spend everything you have while you are working. If you earn a penny and spend it, it's gone; but if you earn a penny and save it, it is still a penny. And if you're smart about it, that penny you saved will grow over time and be able to provide you with more money to spend. This is part of the classic theory behind saving and budgeting, making a conscious decision about how much you are spending today versus how much you have set aside for a rainy day or for retirement. There are many ways to save money. For example, reducing interest charges or fees you pay is like earning money.

live within your means

Don't spend more than you earn. We have become accustomed to buying without using our own money, but borrowing comes at a price. Borrowing has become so commonplace that by the end of 2010, Canadians had accumulated debt equal to 148% of their disposable income.[1]

---
[1] Statistics Canada. December 13, 2010.

It's a fact of life that you will need to borrow for some big purchases, such as your home. In addition, tempting offers such as "no money down" may sound appealing to you because you don't have to come up with the money to pay for it now. However, if you can't afford to buy the item today, how do you know that you will be able to pay for it in the future? While you may have all the best intentions to save up for your purchase, unexpected things may come along that will undermine your ability to repay the debt. Worst still, if borrowing becomes a habit, it can significantly impact your financial well-being, both before and after retirement.

slow and steady wins the race

It's the fable of the tortoise and the hare. The way we apply this fable to money management common sense is that you need to stay the course and be focused. Once you have established a savings plan, stick to it! This is not to say that you should not make adjustments to your plan if necessary. Rather, the idea here is to follow your strategic plan, avoid distractions, minimize risks, and keep your final goal in sight.

buy low, sell high

Everyone knows that in order to make money on an investment, you need to sell it at a higher price than you paid for it. However, we can never predict the market, and our emotions often get in the way of good investment decisions. We tend to wait for some indication that the stock market is rising before we jump on the bandwagon to take advantage of the upswing. This is referred to as the herd mentality — chasing the trend and following the crowd. Oftentimes, it's too late by then to make money. And having waited for the upswing, when the market begins to decline, we often rationalize that it's a temporary event and delay selling until it's too late, because we develop an emotional attachment to a particular investment. Clearly, this behaviour goes against common sense and often leads to stock market losses.

Think back to the fall of 2008 and early 2009, when the stock markets around the world were tumbling. How did you react? Were you eager to sell investments regardless of the fact that the values were at all-time lows, or were you interested in buying opportunities? It would take nerves of steel to actually invest during a market decline — but if you follow the buy low and sell high theory, that is actually what you should have done.

if it's too good to be true, it usually is

A fool and his money are indeed soon parted. It is important to take the time to understand the opportunities being presented before you make a financial decision. For instance, common sense tells us that promises of high returns with little or no risk are highly unlikely and opportunities for quick wins can often turn into quick losses. If something does not make sense, it's better to say "no" and take the chance that you might miss out. Take the time to do some research and get all the facts before you make any decisions.

rescue it!

☐ First and foremost, exercise common sense.

☐ Be informed before you make a financial decision.

☐ Don't just say it — do it! Set up an automatic contribution plan to pay yourself first.

☐ Don't spend more than you earn. Try to save for your purchases instead of borrowing.

CHAPTER 4

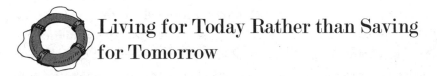 Living for Today Rather than Saving for Tomorrow

As our day-to-day lives get more and more complicated, time and money are at a premium. Why should we not have the best in life for ourselves and our family today, when who knows what tomorrow will bring?

THERE ARE SO MANY COMPETING PRIORITIES in our lives today (kids, mortgage, loans, luxury toys, vacations) that we usually don't make saving for retirement a priority.

priorities

Think back to the last time you made a to-do list. The list was probably prioritized, with the items that were the most important to you and your family at the top of the list. Any items that could be deferred to tomorrow were relegated to the bottom, or even fell off the list completely, as new priorities appeared. When it comes to deciding how to spend money, activities that provide the highest level of immediate gratification are usually at the top of the list. So it stands to reason that if retirement is viewed as an event that will happen very far off into the future, it will not be at the top of our to-do list.

now or later?

Most people work to earn money. The money we earn allows us to live today, and to set some money aside so we can live tomorrow. If you want to live *big* today, you will have less money for the future. What happens if you choose to live bigger than you should today, and you find yourself spending more than you earn? Some people feel they can just work more or work longer to pay off debts and accumulate savings. But what will happen later in life or during retirement if you are no longer able to work to earn more money? It's relatively straightforward — the money you live on should come from your personal savings that you've specifically set aside while working, just for this purpose. Then why is it so hard to save for the future? Quite simply, when we live for today, we value things we can have right now more than those we will enjoy later. When you consider that saving is all about delayed consumption and delayed gratification, it makes sense that we'd rather use and enjoy the money today, live our lives to the fullest right now, and not worry too much about the future. This is exactly what gets people into financial difficulty.

willpower

In financial planning, the words *budgeting* and *saving* evoke the same emotions as *dieting, exercising,* and *quitting smoking.* We generally know smoking is bad for our health, and we're reminded of it every time we see a package of cigarettes — the package is like an ad for a horror movie. But knowing that smoking is unhealthy doesn't always lead to quitting. Similarly, we know that watching what we spend and saving for the future are *good* for our financial health — we know there are long-term benefits — so why do we struggle to get started and, even more important, *why can't we stick to the program?* The reason may very well lie in a lack of self-control. Lack of self-control is not influenced by the amount of information we have; it's due to the fact that short-term desires compete for our time and money. For example, let's say a goal is to lose 10 pounds by the end of the month, and to do that, ice cream has to be completely removed from our diet. Seems simple enough to do, but let's say we eat some ice cream right now. We know it will affect our diet goal, but we can satisfy an immediate need — we get to enjoy the ice cream right now. Simply put, we value the pleasure of eating the ice cream right now much more than we value losing weight by the end of the month, because the end of the month seems a long way away. We may even rationalize that we'll eat even less tomorrow, to make up for the ice cream treat today. Whether we will actually eat less tomorrow is another story.

Now, when we compare a diet to a retirement savings goal, we see many similarities. Both usually take a long time to achieve; both require discipline and delayed gratification. While we know the benefits of saving, we also know that we don't save nearly as much as we should. Knowledge is not the obstacle; it's following through (like the ice cream and the diet). The farther away the end goal is, the more attractive other, more immediate spending decisions appear. After all, we've got 20 years to make up for the lack of saving today, right?

how much?

How much should you set aside? Is the right amount 10%, 20%, or perhaps even more? To give you a general idea of how much you need, think of it this way: if you need a pre-tax income of $20,000 at the beginning of each year on top of any other pensions you might be getting (e.g., OAS, CPP, employment pension plan), and you think you'll need it for about 20 years, you should have a $400,000 nest egg. This figure assumes that the initial withdrawal amount of $20,000 is increased each year by the rate of inflation, assumed to be 3%, and that you pay tax at a rate of 40% on investment earnings of 5%.

So how do you get there, and what changes do you have to make to your life today? I'm sure you're familiar with the concept that if you just save $5 a day, which really isn't that much, you'll be rich.

Well, let's take a look at that:

Saving just $5 per day for 365 days over a 20-year period means you've set aside $36,500. If you can earn 5% on your savings, they'll grow to $63,000. So that's not bad, but you're not rich!

To give a big boost to your savings, you need to give a big boost to how much you save! How about saving $20 per day? That's $7,300 per year, and adds up to $146,000 after 20 years. Again, if you earn 5%, those savings will grow to $253,000. Now, that's better!

automatic saving

One thing is for certain, the more money we earn, the more money we spend. One way to make your savings grow is to put saving on autopilot. Payroll deduction is the easiest way to save because the savings are automatic — since you don't see the money, you don't have the opportunity to spend it. Another good strategy is to increase your savings rate every time you get a raise, so while you may start small, your original $5 contribution per day would grow with your paycheque.

Remember: the longer you wait, the larger your contributions will need to be to make up for lost time.

rescue it!

- ☐ Set goals that are shorter term — start with a monthly goal to save a certain amount so you can celebrate your progress along the way.

- ☐ Start small if you have to, but not too small — remember, to give a big boost to your savings, you have to give a big boost to how much you save.

- ☐ Put savings on autopilot by having your employer or bank make automatic withdrawals from your paycheque or bank account to help maintain the discipline of regular savings. (For instance, banks will take a set amount from your bank account every week or month and put it into an RRSP.)

CHAPTER 5

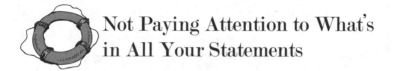 Not Paying Attention to What's
in All Your Statements

Not paying attention to the valuable information in your
statements to catch potential mistakes can be costly to you.

STATEMENTS ARE SUMMARY DOCUMENTS that you receive annually, monthly, or even weekly, through the mail or electronically. These days we get statements for almost everything: payroll, bank accounts, credit cards, investment accounts, etc. Often we simply glance at them without paying close attention to the details, but by taking a more careful approach, you'll find opportunities to protect your money.

find the errors

It's important to check your statements for errors on a regular basis. Pay attention to information such as spelling mistakes to your name or address, missing deposits, withdrawals you didn't make, cheques you don't remember writing, unusual ATM withdrawals, credit card charges for items you did not buy, and interest charges that you were unaware of. These could be simple errors, or could indicate that someone else has used your personal information to engage in fraudulent activities that can seriously jeopardize your finances. So it's important to have errors investigated and corrected as soon as you become aware of them.

know what you're being billed for

Before automatic bill payment services were introduced, we had to look at the balance to make a payment. But when bill payments are put on autopilot, there is less reason to look at our statements. While it is a good idea to set up automatic bill payments for reasons of convenience, it is still important to pay close attention to your statements, because you could be paying too much without even knowing it. For instance, you need to make sure you are not paying for services you didn't order, or being charged for services that you have cancelled. Every year we hear stories on the news of people who have paid for cancelled services for a decade or two without realizing it. Don't be one of them!

Whenever you have automatic bill payments coming out of your bank account, you should pay close attention to the billing cycle. You don't want to get caught in an overdraft position and be penalized with fees if your bill payment is due before your paycheque is deposited. In some cases, you can be put on a different billing cycle so that overdraft situations are avoided— be sure to ask.

verify your take-home pay

Even if employees know the amount of their gross earnings and take-home pay, they often can't recite all the deductions that are being made. For starters, when you look over your pay stub, you might want to see how much income tax is being withheld, to find out what income tax bracket you are in. Your tax bracket determines how much tax you'll pay on investment income, and the amount of tax savings you'll generate by making RRSP contributions. You also want to review how much is being deducted for health or dental coverage, and life and disability insurance. Check to determine whether you have the appropriate coverage and if the deductions are correct. If you are participating in an employer pension plan, you want to make sure the correct contribution amount is being deducted. If you are expecting a pay increase, check to make sure it is properly reflected, and made effective from the correct date.

Employees who receive a physical paycheque have no excuse not to look it over and make sure everything is correct. People whose pay is automatically deposited to their bank account still need to make an effort to review their pay stub. Some companies have introduced "green" payroll systems, where pay information is made available for employees to view online and no paper documents are produced. Once again, while going green is evidence of good corporate citizenship, employees must remember to check this information on a regular basis.

reduce fees

Looking carefully at your bank account statements can help identify opportunities for you to save money. Know how much you are paying in banking fees and what they are for. If you find yourself paying significant fees for service charges such as issuing cheques, making debit card purchases, withdrawing from ATMs, and making bill payments, you should check with your bank to see if there is any other type of account that meets your needs better. For example, many banks offer accounts with a flat monthly fee for unlimited transactions or no fees on an account where a minimum balance is maintained. Some even offer low- or no-fee accounts for seniors. Take advantage of reduced fees whenever you can.

In addition to monthly fees, take a closer look at your withdrawal habits for patterns that are costly to you. For instance, using another bank's ATM can cost as much as $2.50 per transaction, and this can add up over time. Essentially, you are paying for convenience. So, minimize the use of other banks' ATMs as much as possible by planning ahead and knowing how much you will need. Every little bit counts!

manage your debts

When you look at your credit card or loan statement, you want to take note of your outstanding balance, the interest rate, and how long it will take for you to pay off what you owe. It is also important to pay attention to payment due dates and to make your payment on time, so you don't incur additional interest charges or service fees. Late payments will also appear on your personal credit rating, which can impact your ability to get financing in the future.

Unknown charges on credit card statements should be reported as soon as possible; otherwise, you may be liable to pay for purchases you did not make. It is basic money management to keep track of how much you owe, what your payments are, and to pay on time.

beneficiary designations

Certain accounts and plans — such as RRSP, RRIF, TFSA, your company pension plan, and life insurance — allow for beneficiary designations. Naming a beneficiary other than your estate results in the funds passing directly to that person upon your death and bypassing your will. A review of your statements can tell you who is named as a beneficiary, so you can determine if it is correct and still appropriate. If your statement does not show this, contact the provider and ask them to confirm who is named as beneficiary on the account or plan.

Years ago I worked part time in a local bank branch and I recall the first time I had to deal with an RRSP of a deceased client. The surviving spouse came into the branch with all of her paperwork in hand — death certificate, probated will, and a list of all of the accounts her husband had with the bank. Things were going about as well as you can imagine in such a situation, until it came to dealing with the RRSP. This is where the discussion became complicated. The widow was the client's second spouse; however, the person named as beneficiary on the deceased client's RRSP was — you guessed it — the first spouse. Perhaps it was the client's intention to keep his first spouse as the beneficiary, perhaps not. In any case, always review your beneficiary designations at least once a year, or whenever there is a change in your personal circumstances, to confirm that they are what you want them to be. Further discussion on beneficiary designations can be found in chapter 48.

rescue it!

☐ Take time to review your statements when they come in; check for unusual transactions and look for ways to reduce interest and fees.

☐ Set up a reminder to check electronic statements.

☐ Report any errors and unusual activities as soon as you spot them.

☐ Pay your bills as soon as they come in — if you use your bank's online bill payment method, you can postdate your bill payments to the due date.

CHAPTER 6

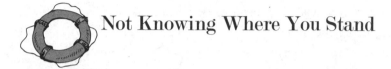 Not Knowing Where You Stand

Not knowing where you are today makes it impossible to determine your current net worth and to develop a retirement strategy for tomorrow.

IN THE PREVIOUS CHAPTER, WE LEARNED that it's important to review all of your statements: to identify errors as well as to determine how much you're paying in interest and other fees. The next step is to take all your statements and put them together to form a snapshot of your net worth. Without knowing where you are today, how will you know what steps you need to take to reach your retirement goal?

what is net worth?

A net worth statement is a type of personal balance sheet. It is a summary document that shows all your assets (what you own), minus your liabilities (what you owe), at a particular point in time. The choices you make during your lifetime that affect your financial situation can be seen on a net worth statement. A net worth statement should be the starting point for all financial decisions, because it shows how much you have in investments, the value of your home and other personal property, how much debt you have, and the interest rates you are paying, and it can show where there is room for improvement. However, few people consider their net worth when making retirement planning decisions.

what impacts your net worth?

Every decision or lack thereof in your life has a financial consequence. While some of your decisions will get you closer to your goals, others may take you farther away from your goals. For instance, buying a house means you'll likely have a mortgage payment that will consume a big portion of your pay and can take you many years to pay off. While this decision will impact your current cash flow and lifestyle, it is nevertheless a smart saving strategy, because you are building up one of the biggest assets in your net worth, and investing in something that will increase in value over time. A home is an asset that can be sold to provide cash or can be lived in during retirement. Now let's look at a different decision, such as going on vacation. While there is nothing wrong with taking a vacation, the reality is that this decision will have a negative impact on your net worth, which will ultimately impact how much you will have for your retirement. Even a seemingly small decision such as having a specialty coffee every day will impact your net worth. This is because the $3.50 coffee over a 20-year period will cost you approximately $30,000. As you can see, every decision — big or small — will impact your net worth.

putting it all together

The first step to create your net worth statement is to take the information from all of your various statements and combine it into one document.

Begin by listing your assets — that is, everything you own. List all your liquid assets, such as cash in bank accounts and other short-term investments that are easily accessed, especially in case of emergency. Then list your long-term assets, including RRSP/RRIF accounts, investments such as stocks and bonds, and other investments that cannot be easily cashed. Finally, list your personal use assets, such as your home, furniture, car(s), vacation property, and so on, separately from your investment assets.

The next part shows liabilities. Make a list of all your debts, such as loans, mortgage, line(s) of credit, and credit card(s). Next to each debt, show the interest rate you are paying on it, and whether the interest is tax-deductible. This step is important, because it may highlight opportunities to reduce interest costs. If you are married or in a common-law relationship, you should also prepare a net worth statement that shows who owns what. That is, you want to list everything you own and owe personally, everything your partner owns and owes personally, and everything you and your partner own and owe jointly. It's important to know who owns what from a tax and estate perspective. For instance, having too many investments and retirement savings in one person's name rather than the other's could mean that income splitting opportunities are being missed. Listing the assets held in joint ownership and those with beneficiary designations will give you an idea of how your estate would be distributed on the death of one of the partners.

why is it so important to understand your net worth?

From a planning perspective, a net worth statement tells it like it is and may reveal more than you think you know. For instance, you may think you have built substantial net worth because you have a $400,000 home; however, if you take your mortgage plus all of your other debts into consideration, you may be surprised to find that your net worth is much lower than you thought. This knowledge can alter your future decisions about taking on more debt. A net worth statement also provides a starting point for making financial projections to determine how much your investments might grow by the time you retire. A better understanding of your net worth can motivate you to take action to pay off debt sooner or to increase your savings. Or it may show that your savings goal isn't far off after all. One additional important thing to keep in mind is that some of your assets (such as RRSPs and RRIFs) have a future income tax liability. This means that when they are withdrawn or sold, taxes will have to be paid, and the value of these assets will be reduced by the amount of the tax that has to be paid, thus reducing your net worth.

rescue it!

☐ Gather together all your recent statements and prepare a personal net worth statement. The personal net worth statement will be referred to throughout the rest of this book and will help you determine what action you need to take to rescue your retirement.

- [ ] Examine all your assets to see what will be available to fund your retirement.
- [ ] Review your liabilities (debts) and the related interest rates. Think about which debts will be entirely paid off by retirement and which ones you need to concentrate on first. You'll learn more in chapter 15, where we review debt, and also chapter 16, where we discuss mortgages.

Personal Net Worth Statement As at: _____	You	Spouse	Joint
Liquid assets:			
Bank accounts	$	$	$
Short-term investments			
Other			
Long-term assets:			
Investment accounts including TFSA	$	$	$
RRSP/RRIF			
Locked-in RRSP/RRIF			
Employer pension plan			
Life insurance cash surrender value			
Other			
Personal use assets:			
Home	$	$	$
Vacation property (location)			
Car(s)			
Boat or other vehicle			
Furnishings			
Total all assets	$	$	$
Liabilities (interest rates):			
Credit card(s) (%)	$	$	$
Personal loan (%)			
Mortgage — home (%)			
Mortgage — vacation property (%)			
Line of credit (%)			
Investment loan (%)			
Total liabilities	$	$	$
Net worth (Assets less Liabilities)	$	$	$

CHAPTER 7

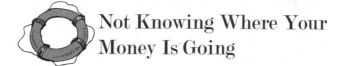

Not Knowing Where Your Money Is Going

If you don't know how you are spending your money, how will you know if you're spending too much?

HAVE YOU EVER FOUND YOURSELF THINKING, "I had $100 in my wallet on Friday — and here it is Monday morning, and it's almost all gone. Where did it go?" You're not alone! Many of us have felt the same way. Few people keep track of their spending or have a budget. That word — **budget** — everyone dreads it and tries to avoid it. In some circles, the word *budget* is a lot like the word *diet* — best not to mention it in public. Nevertheless, having a budget is important at all stages of life, because it helps you to keep from overspending. But before you can make a budget, you need to get a handle on where your money is going, especially when the timing of your money inflows doesn't match your money outflows.

where does it go?

Very few people keep good records of where their money is going. Without this important first step, there is a lot of trial and error involved in putting together a budget and figuring out how much you should be spending on certain items. I recall having a conversation with one couple who couldn't seem to find money to save for their retirement. To help them understand where their money was going, I challenged them to track their spending for one month. At the end of the month, they were surprised at how much they spent on certain items, and were especially concerned with how much they spent on food. It turns out that most of their food costs related to eating in restaurants, and reducing spending in this area alone would have a big impact on their ability to save money. Once they knew where their money was going, they were able to create a budget to help them decide how they should spend their money.

personal budget

What is a personal budget? A personal budget is a thoughtful consideration of how much money you're expecting will come in at some time in the future, and what portion of this income you intend to spend or save. It is a forecast, or a plan; something you're committed to achieving. Unfortunately, as with all plans, sometimes things don't turn out exactly as we expect. We might have to spend more on items that come up suddenly, or we might lose a job and not have as much income as we thought we were going to have. There are many things that can cause a plan to be altered. What's most important is to review the personal budget regularly and make adjustments where necessary, before things get out of hand and we spend too much.

why do we overspend?

Before credit and debit cards became the norm, we lived in a cash society — it was a time when you could touch the money, hold it in your hand, and appreciate all the hard work it took for you to earn that money. When your wallet was full, you had money; when your wallet was empty, you were broke. You knew how that worked, and you accepted it. In fact, when you got down to your last $20, it was not all that easy handing over the money to someone else for a purchase. When you have limited resources, you take more time to consider whether each purchase is really worth it. You tend to be more cautious, because you may need that money tomorrow for something more important. I recall as a child going to the bank with my mother on a weekly basis and watching as she did the family banking. She would take my father's pay-cheque, pay whatever bills were due, deposit some money into their savings account, and take out some cash for the week's daily expenses, such as grocery shopping. Either she knew instinctively how much money she needed in cash for those weekly expenses, or she made sure she didn't spend more than she had. Essentially, they lived on a weekly budget, which for my parents included saving some money each week.

These days, with debit and credit cards, automatic pay deposits, and online bill payments, you don't need to physically hold money at all. We've evolved to the point where we know that if we don't have enough money in our wallet for a certain something that catches our eye, no problem, we just pull out our debit card or credit card and the purchase is completed. Using plastic instead of paper money has given us more confidence to spend more than we have in our wallet — but how much more? Numerous studies have been done around spending and credit card usage. The research shows that people are willing to pay anywhere from 50% more to 200% more for an item when they are told they can purchase the item using a credit card! That's not all — did you know that people leave larger restaurant tips, are faster to make a spending deci-sion, and are more likely to make a purchase when they use a credit card? Researchers have coined the phrase "the credit card premium"[1] to describe this phenomenon. Hmmm . . . have you ever wondered why casinos prefer that we gamble with chips or casino cards instead of cold hard cash? The chips don't even look like real money — they're colourful and shaped like coins instead of the $10, $20, and $100 they represent.

back to basics with money jars

I'd like to retell an interesting story about money jars, and two now very famous actors who weren't so famous way back when this actually hap-pened. It's a story about two friends, Dustin Hoffman and Gene Hackman. As the story goes, Hoffman asked his friend Hackman if he could borrow some money for food. Hackman agreed to lend him some money, but then

---

[1] Prelec, Drazen, and Duncan Simester, "Always Leave Home Without It: A further investigation of the credit-card effect on willingness to pay." Sloan School of Management, MIT, June 2008.

noticed a row of Mason jars on a shelf in Hoffman's kitchen. The jars all had labels, such as rent, books, etc., and some even had money in them. So he asked why Hoffman needed to borrow money for food when there was money in some of these money jars. "Well," Hoffman told him, "there is no money in the food jar!"

It may seem odd to treat money that way, but doing this sort of mental math has its advantages. The money jar method may prevent you from spending more on a particular item than you had planned, but it has another, more important result. With the money jars, you realize that what you *think* you spend is not always what you *actually* spend. For instance, if you place some money in a money jar for spending on takeout meals, only to run out of money in just a few days, it highlights a common problem — we tend to underestimate how much we spend on certain items. In most cases, we underestimate how much we spend on those items that we have the most control over.

You don't need to use Mason jars, or jam jars, for this: you can use envelopes, or separate bank accounts, to achieve the same result. For instance, you can have your paycheque deposited to a savings account, and then transfer your spending money based on your weekly personal budget into a chequing account, and that's all you can spend for the week. Many financial institutions now offer free access to online budgeting and spending tools that can help you to categorize your transactions so you know how much you're spending.

how flexible is your spending?

Now that you know how you are spending your money, if you need to cut spending, where do you start? Once you know your spending habits, it's easier to make such a decision. First, list your spending for basic needs — things that you cannot do without — and for discretionary needs — those "nice to have" purchases that you can do without or reduce if you have to. You can even list spending for luxury items — things that are special treats.

A simple way to visualize this is with an adaptation of Maslow's hierarchy of needs pyramid as it applies to personal spending (see the illustration below). The most basic needs would be the first to be satisfied. Once the

Figure 7.1: Hierarchy of Personal Spending

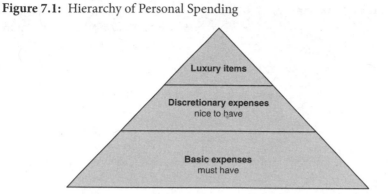

basic needs are covered, money can be spent on discretionary items. These items may be very important to you, but they are things you can do without if you have to. For instance, food is a basic need, but going out for dinner is a discretionary choice of how we receive food. Finally, the luxury items are the dreams that we hope will one day be a reality, once all of our other needs are taken care of. In this case, a vacation might be a discretionary need, but taking a six-month trip around the world might be seen as a luxury. Remember that a personal budget may be disrupted, for instance if there is an illness that prevents you from earning income, or unplanned costs such as a major home repair. Those unexpected costs would be funded from accumulated savings (remember the rule to pay yourself first, which would result in establishing a savings plan as part of discretionary needs), or perhaps insurance policies, and not with your personal budget.

If we let our emotional mind (I need it) take over our rational mind (I can't afford it), we may move more and more items from the luxury section of the pyramid into the basic needs section, as we rationalize that we absolutely need it. A new car becomes a "must have," an all-inclusive vacation is no longer just nice to have, and that's how we end up spending more than we should.

Knowing where your money is going is one thing — making adjustments to your spending habits is another. Understanding how you are spending your money today will give you a sense of how you might be spending your money in the future. But that's just one part of it. It will be just as important for you to know where your money is going during retirement, because your spending patterns may change and the timing of when you receive pensions and other incomes may not always match the timing of your expenses. Getting into the habit of tracking how you spend your money is a good money management skill to have both now and during retirement.

rescue it!

☐ Track your spending for one month to determine how you are spending your money.

☐ Determine your basic, discretionary, and luxury needs, and establish a budget for spending.

☐ If you're really bad at sticking to a budget, try the money jars!

PART 2

mistakes around investing

CHAPTER 8

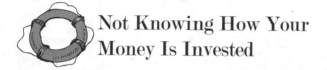 Not Knowing How Your
Money Is Invested

On the one hand, not knowing how your money is invested can cause sleepless nights, but on the other hand, it can have you believing that your money is earning more than it actually is.

BACK WHEN THERE WERE ONLY A HANDFUL of investments to choose from, investing was easy. These days, the options are endless. With thousands of choices, and new products popping up every day, we have unprecedented access to different types of investments. Complex products, changes to income tax rules, and access to international markets for your investments, all make financial matters more confusing than ever. Thanks to the Internet, we are living in an era where information about investments, stock markets, and economic conditions is everywhere and easily accessible 24/7. You would think that this would help us be smarter about the investment choices we make, wouldn't you? But having more access to more information doesn't always result in better decision making. Instead, it can result in information overload — it's too time consuming to go through everything to figure out what's relevant and what isn't. It's too difficult to interpret what we read and decide whether a particular investment fits our personal situation. Rather than making us better investors, all this choice can cause anxiety and paralysis. Research has shown that the more choices we are given, the less likely we are to make a decision. This is just what happened at a gourmet food store that set up a display of imported jams for customers to try. One day the store displayed six different jams; on another day there were 24 different jams to try. What they found was that the display with the 24 jams attracted more customers, but those who saw a much smaller display with only six jams were 10 times as likely to buy a jar of jam.[1] So, just like the customers who saw the displays of jam, rather than making better investment decisions when we have more choices, we make no decision at all, or we make investment decisions based on what's familiar rather than what's best, or we let the actions of others sway us. When it comes to saving and investing for retirement, we need to take back control and understand just how our money is invested and how it is expected to perform.

In July 2009, I spoke to a retired woman who was well aware of the market turmoil, because it was constantly in the news, and was convinced that she had lost a great deal of her retirement savings. A quick review of her account showed the entire amount in her account was invested in a product that provided a 100% principal guarantee. Not only was all of her money safe, but she was earning a decent interest rate. Of course, she was relieved to hear the good news, but it was clear that she had formed a complete misunderstanding of how the market collapse would affect her personal investments. This is not unusual — many people don't fully know or understand how their personal savings are invested and, as a result, make decisions based on assumptions rather than fact. This is another area where beliefs and actions don't align. Research shows that 92% of people agree it is important to do research before they invest, but 49% don't actually do any homework regarding their investments.[2]

how is your money invested?

Rather than trying to learn everything there is to know about every product out there, understanding some of the most common products available can help you make better decisions and achieve investment success.

---

[1] Sheena Iyengar, *The Art of Choosing*. New York: Twelve, 2010.

[2] *Moving Forward with Financial Literacy*, Financial Consumer Agency of Canada, September 2008. www.fcac-acfc.gc.ca/eng/publications/surveystudy/reachhigherconf/pdf/reachhigher-eng.pdf

The first thing to understand is that there is a difference between *loaning money* to a company and expecting to receive all of it back plus interest, and *investing* in a company and taking the risk that, while you might make a lot of money, you might lose some or all of your money.

Many products have similar characteristics but provide different results. This section is a primer on different types of investments and is by no means an exhaustive list or description of all available investments. However, it should provide some of the basics you need to know about the most common products available to consumers. Focus on understanding these products and then build your portfolio from there.

Guaranteed Investment Certificates (GICs)

Despite the word *investment* in the name, this is a *loan* to the issuer (usually a bank), which carries an interest rate. There are a variety of GICs available today, but the premise is the same for all — certain elements are guaranteed, such as the interest rate you will be earning and the principal amount of the investment. Terms can extend from days to years, and the interest rates will vary depending on the term selected. Some GICs are locked-in for a certain period of time, while others carry a cashable feature that allows you to either withdraw your money prior to the maturity date or re-invest it in another product. Products with a cashable feature generally offer a lower interest rate, which effectively means you are paying a premium for the added flexibility. Some GICs are linked to certain investments ("market-linked") and have the potential to pay a higher rate of return than what is guaranteed. These products provide an upside potential without any of the downside risk. As a result, even if the investments that are being tracked have negative returns, the minimum interest rate stated for the GIC is still guaranteed.

One other important fact to note is that the Canada Deposit Insurance Corporation (CDIC) insures GICs with terms of up to five years, which means you get your original investment back even if the issuer goes bankrupt. CDIC covers up to $100,000 invested in your name, plus provides additional coverage of $100,000 for your RRSP or RRIF account, and another $100,000 for any joint accounts per financial institution.

Principal Protected Notes (PPNs)

Like GICs, these are debt instruments (loans), but they *may not* be insured by CDIC. The principal is guaranteed by the issuer and, while the PPN pays interest income, it also has the potential to follow the stock market and provide higher returns in the form of capital gains. As with the market-linked GICs noted above, the returns won't necessarily be the same as the equity investments that the PPN is tracking, but total returns may be higher than the stated interest rate.

Bonds (Government and Corporate)

Bonds are longer-term loans, issued by all levels of government (federal, provincial, municipal), as well as corporations. Bonds pay either a fixed interest rate for the duration of the bond, or the interest rate may increase based on inflation. Those that increase the interest rate based on inflation are called "real return bonds."

Because you can buy or sell a bond after it has been issued, the price that is paid may be more or less than the face value, and can result in a capital gain or a capital loss when the bond is sold or redeemed. This is the main difference between a bond and a GIC. The price of the bond fluctuates based on prevailing interest rates. For instance, let's say a $100,000 bond is issued last year with a 5% interest rate, so it pays $5,000 per year in interest. If interest rates today are 7%, then last year's bond is paying considerably less than what an investor could get in the market today by investing $100,000. He would only be interested in buying last year's bond if the $5,000 per year interest income is equivalent to a 7% rate of return. As a result, he would offer the seller less than the $100,000 face value to buy that particular bond. If the seller agrees to the offer, she may realize a capital loss if she paid more for the bond than the amount she is now selling it for. As for the purchaser, if he holds onto the bond until the maturity date, the issuer will pay him the full $100,000 face value, even though he did not pay that much for the bond. At that point, he will realize a capital gain. The important lesson is that you can buy and sell bonds before their maturity date and, depending on prevailing interest rates, you may have a capital gain or capital loss on the sale.

Equity Investments (Stocks or Shares of a Corporation)

Buying shares is a direct investment in a company, *not* a loan that pays a set amount of interest income. The shares may or may not pay dividends, and may result in capital growth or a capital loss for the owner. There are two types of shares: common shares and preferred shares. With common shares, *the amount of the investment is not guaranteed.* The shares may be sold for much more than the original cost, resulting in a capital gain, or much less, resulting in a capital loss. Rather than interest income, the shareholder might receive income in the form of dividends. Preferred shares are an interesting investment — some view them as an investment in the company, and some consider them to be more like a loan to the company. Although preferred shares represent ownership, they do not generally appreciate with the value of the company and are typically sold on the open market or redeemed by the company at face value. However, they *pay a stated dividend rate* to the holder.

Mutual Funds

Mutual funds are a form of investment that allows many investors to pool their money together to invest in a wide variety of investments. Each fund invests in specific types of investments, from government and corporate bonds to stocks of large and small corporations, including international corporations. The level of risk will depend on what the mutual fund invests in. All investment decisions are made by a portfolio manager based on the mandate of the fund. Depending on the investments held in the mutual fund, your return can be in the form of interest income, dividends from Canadian or foreign corporations, or return of capital, and may result in a capital gain or a capital loss. Mutual funds that are set up as corporations provide tax efficient distributions and allow you to move from one fund to another fund in the same *family* without realizing a capital gain until you sell out of the family. Other options to consider are Exchange Traded Funds (ETFs) and index funds, which track an index, a commodity, or a basket of assets. These funds are considered to be managed passively because, rather than relying on decisions made by the portfolio manager, they simply replicate the index. They also tend to have lower management fees than an actively managed mutual fund, which can save you money in the long run.

Segregated Funds

An investment that has two distinct parts: an investment portion that produces a return, and an insurance policy that covers the risk. There is also a guarantee attached that protects the investor's principal from sudden market declines. The guarantees range from 75 to 100% of the principal. Another feature of this product is the ability to name a beneficiary. If a beneficiary other than the estate is named on the segregated fund, the investment passes directly to the named beneficiary, bypassing the will, and can therefore avoid probate. Since a segregated fund is considered an insurance contract, it also provides the holder with creditor protection: it protects the investment from creditors.

monitoring your investments

It's important to go over your investment statements to understand how your money is invested, and to pay attention to how your investments perform. You should be able to answer questions such as: What is your rate of return? Does the value of your investments fluctuate from month to month, or is it relatively stable? What kind of income is the portfolio earning; is it interest income, dividends, capital gains, or return of capital? *Different types of income* are taxed at different levels of income tax, and this will impact your after-tax return.

Is there cash in your investment account that is not invested? Don't be alarmed if there is, as this sometimes happens if your investments pay out interest, dividends, or other distributions that are not automatically re-invested. If you don't need the cash from the distributions for current expenses, you might want to speak to consider setting up an automatic re-investment plan to keep as much of your money as possible invested at all times.

Are there any investments, such as a guaranteed investment certificate (GIC), that are coming up for renewal that you will have to make a decision about soon? Is your money locked-in or is it easily accessible in case of an emergency? For example, a certain GIC may not be accessible until the maturity date, whereas a mutual fund can be cashed in, in whole or in part, at any time.

Are there any charges you didn't expect? Are there foreign income taxes that have been withheld from interest or dividends received on foreign investments? Did you even know you owned foreign investments, and are they appropriate for you?

rescue it!

What you need to ask about your investments:

☐ Are any of my investments covered by CDIC insurance, and are they within the insurance limits?

☐ How will fluctuations in the stock market affect my investment?

☐ When can I access my investment? Is it considered locked-in for a period of time?

☐ Is there a penalty or fee for withdrawing before the maturity date?

☐ How often can I expect an income payment?

☐ What *kind* of income do my investments pay (interest, dividends, or capital gains)?

☐ Is the rate of return guaranteed?

☐ How will income paid from my investments affect my tax situation?

☐ What fees am I paying to buy and sell my investments?

☐ Do the investments align with my investment objectives?

CHAPTER 9

 Not Knowing How Much Risk
You Can Tolerate

If you don't know how much risk you can tolerate, how can you make appropriate investment decisions?

UNDERSTANDING YOUR RISK TOLERANCE can make you a better investor. Not necessarily because you'll earn a better return all the time, but because you'll make investment decisions that are suited to your personal situation. Many books have been written on the topic of risk and investing. A common thread that runs through many of them is the idea that we overestimate our tolerance for risk. People tend to feel overconfident about their investment knowledge and, as a result, make decisions that they later regret. Imagine chatting with some friends about a topic such as bungee-jumping. Your friends are all enthused about this activity. The idea seems exciting, invigorating, and well, why not? "I'll do it!" you all say . . . then the time comes to jump off a bridge with only some thick elastics holding you up. Suddenly you realize you aren't as sure about this as you thought! For you, the physical risks may be much more important than the potential satisfaction one gets from completing such a task. The fact is, everyone looks at risk differently.

As investors, we may give inaccurate responses to certain questions when it comes to how much risk we're willing to accept in our investment portfolios. This came to light in the 2008 market crash, when thousands of

Canadians realized that they had taken more risk than they were comfortable with, and that risk did indeed mean that the value of an investment could go down considerably.

what is risk?

The way I like to explain risk is that the outcome is not guaranteed. When there is risk, there's a chance that things will turn out worse than they are right now, or they might turn out better than they are. In other words, it's a game of chance. And the reason we play the risk game is for the chance that things turn out better. In fact, we are excited about the possibility that things will turn out much better than they are today. That's why we buy lottery tickets — for the chance to win. That's why we play the slot machines — for the chance to win. There is some element of risk in all investments. So when one investment is considered more risky than another, do we really understand what that means? An investment that is considered higher risk will have higher volatility of returns than one that is considered very low risk. In other words, an investment that is likely to experience a wide range of fluctuating annual returns would be considered more risky than an investment that has a narrow range of annual returns.

Figure 9.1 shows the hypothetical volatility of two fictitious investments. The one that is considered higher risk due to its higher volatility can produce returns as high as 14% and as low as negative 12%. The other investment is much more stable and as a result is considered lower risk.

Figure 9.1: Volatility of Returns

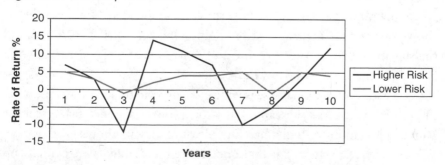

The average rate of return for the lower-risk investment over the 10-year period shown is 3%. Can you guess what the average rate of return was for the higher-risk investment? It was the same: 3%. When we are told that the value of an investment can fluctuate anywhere from positive 14% to negative 12%, do we hear only the positive part and hope for the best?

how much risk are you willing to take?

Is it possible to be risk-averse in some areas and a risk taker in others? Absolutely! The point in time when you will need access to your money will impact how much risk you should be willing to take. Look at your investments as if they were on a timeline. Money that you will need in the short term should be invested more conservatively, because you don't want to take the chance that there will be less money there when you need it. Money that you don't need for several years could be invested in more risky products, because over time, the fluctuations smooth themselves out. One solution to reducing or smoothing out risk in your portfolio is to simply lengthen the timeframe. But a longer timeframe can have the opposite effect on your short-term lower-interest-rate investments, because inflation erodes their purchasing power over time. That's why the recommendation for younger investors with a long time horizon tends to be more aggressive and heavily concentrated on equity investments, whereas the recommendation for those closer to, or in, retirement tends to be more conservative and includes more short-term investments.

do you feel loss aversion?

Are you more willing to be safe than sorry? Test yourself. Take your most recent investment statement — now scratch out the actual market value as shown on the statement, and write in a number that is 20 to 30% less. Put the statement back in the envelope and don't look at it for at least a week. Now open the statement. How do you feel?

A person who is loss-averse is willing to forgo an opportunity for a gain, rather than risk a loss. Research has shown that investors tend to feel the pain of a loss more strongly than any pleasure they might get from a gain. What's even more striking is that once retired, individuals are actually up to five times more sensitive to losses than the average person.[1] With few years to recover from a loss and with few options for working longer or saving more, the only alternative for those already retired would be to cut back on their spending. It's no wonder retirees are more sensitive to losses than others.

your blueprint for investing

How much risk should you take at various stages in your life, and particularly at retirement? An investment policy statement (IPS) is a clear blueprint that will help you build and manage your investment portfolio. An IPS identifies your investment objectives, time horizon, and the contributions or withdrawals you will make over time. It also addresses risk tolerance, and how often and under what conditions a portfolio will be reviewed and rebalanced. During retirement, your investment policy statement would also consider how much income you need from your portfolio, and when you need it.

If the biggest mistake individuals make is to adopt the herd mentality, or to become too emotionally attached to their investments, then having an IPS will help them stay the course and resist overreacting to changes in market conditions. You can make your own IPS using one of many free online tools, or it can be completed with your financial advisor.

Depending on your savings and pensions, you may have enough income that you do not need a high rate of return on your investments to achieve your retirement goals. If that is the case, why chase returns while trying to time the market and take on more risk than you need to?

rescue it!

☐ Assess and understand your risk tolerance level by completing an investment policy statement.

☐ Go over your investments with your financial advisor to make sure they are in line with your IPS, and rebalance if necessary.

---

[1] Eric Johnson, Columbia University. American association of Retired Persons (AARP) & American Council of Life Insurers (ACLI), 2007.

CHAPTER 10

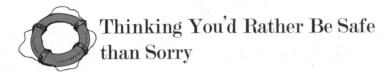 Thinking You'd Rather Be Safe
than Sorry

Being too conservative in your investment approach actually
adds additional risk and could cause you to run short of
money sooner.

AS WE DISCUSSED IN THE PREVIOUS CHAPTER, loss aversion toward investing means you would rather be safe than sorry — essentially, you don't want to make an investment that might cause you to end up worse off than you are now. Some people who have incurred a loss advocate this approach and, in fact, consider it a mistake to invest in the stock market! But is this strategy a safe way to hold all your money?

In the long run, keeping all your money in cash or short-term investments (or even under your mattress) increases the risk that your money will not grow over time, and might even shrink. This is a bad recipe for a retirement fund.

impact of inflation — the silent investment killer

No matter how "safely" you want to be invested, being too safe may mean you're not keeping up with inflation, and over time this will greatly reduce your buying power and hence the common reference to inflation as the silent investment killer. Whenever there is negative volatility in the stock market, a lot of advice about safe investing surfaces. It's not uncommon to hear that the safest place for money is under your mattress, where there is no chance to lose any more money on a bad investment decision. But this is not a good strategy to use if you are trying to avoid making a bad investment decision. Putting money under the mattress can actually shrink the value of your money, which is the same as having an investment loss. For instance, if inflation is 2%, the decision to not invest your money at all results in a 2% loss. While you expect to minimize risk by being very safe, you actually lose 2% because of inflation.

tax — the other silent killer

Even if you do invest and earn a rate of return equal to the inflation rate, you may still not be making any headway. At first glance, it appears that this investment strategy would allow you to maintain your purchasing power. That is, until you calculate the income tax that you owe on the investment earnings. The chart below shows the impact that inflation of 2% and a tax rate of 25% will have on various investment earnings.

Earnings after tax and inflation			
Rate of return	0%	2%	4%
Less income tax	0%	(.5%)	(1%)
Less inflation	(2%)	(2%)	(2%)
Net earnings	(2%)	(.5%)	1%

As you can see, when you invest, you need to earn a rate of return that is higher than inflation plus income taxes if you want your money to grow. If your investments are in a tax free savings account (TFSA), RRSP, or RRIF, there will not be any income taxes on the income earned in those plans.

is it ever OK to be too safe?

Sometimes I do believe it's better to be safe than sorry. In fact, I had to do that very thing myself, at a point in time when I felt I couldn't afford to take on any risk. My husband and I had just sold our house and weren't going to be taking possession of our new one for six months. So the proceeds from the house sale had to be kept safe. I wasn't worried about inflation, because we had already bought the other house, so any income this money earned was going to be a bonus. We took the safe route and purchased a guaranteed investment. It just so happened that over that six-month period our return would have been far higher if we had invested in equities, but since hindsight is 20/20 and we weren't willing to risk any of the down payment, we chose to be safe!

earn 1% more

If an investment portfolio can earn just 1 or 2% more over a long period of time, it will have a significant positive impact on total savings. The chart below shows how much $30,000 today will grow to at various rates of return.

Rate of return	3%	4%	5%	6%	7%
Value after 10 years	$119,806	$127,270	$135,205	$143,636	$152,592
Value after 15 years	$130,541	$142,487	$155,450	$169,519	$184,788

For those who prefer to be safe, there are ways to increase return without taking on significant additional risk.

buy an escalator

Safe investors tend to prefer investments that guarantee the principal invested plus pay interest, such as a GIC as mentioned in chapter 8, even though these investments provide the lowest liquidity, due to the fact that they are usually locked in for a period of time. The interest rates offered by these products are based on the length of time the money is invested for. A one-year term usually carries a lower rate than a five-year term. So how do you take advantage of these different rates to create a low-risk investment strategy and gain that extra 1 or 2% without locking in all your money for a long period of time? I use the term *investment escalator* to describe a strategy where a series of investments are purchased with maturity dates ranging from one to five years. I don't suggest GIC type investments that go beyond a five-year term, because they are not CDIC insured.

Here's how it works. Divide your money into five equal portions, to purchase five individual GICs with different maturity dates. The GICs that mature in one or two years give you access to some of your money if you need it, while those with three- to five-year maturities provide you with a higher rate of return. Imagine each step on a very slow moving escalator representing an individual GIC ranging in duration from one to five years. The one-year GIC is at the top of the escalator, and the five-year GIC is at the bottom. Each year, one GIC will mature as it reaches the top of the escalator, and this money becomes available for re-investment, or you may decide to cash it in. In order to keep the escalator going, you would buy a new GIC with a five-year term, and put it at the bottom of the escalator. If you continue with this re-investment strategy, after the first year, all subsequent GICs purchased will be for the longest possible term of five years, and so you would be getting the highest possible rate at that particular time.

Let's look at an example that compares three different strategies: buying a one-year GIC and renewing each year; buying a five-year GIC, and finally, using the escalator strategy, where one-fifth of the initial investment is used to invest in each of five individual GICs that mature each year over the five-year period. The chart is based on an initial investment of $10,000, and assumes constant interest rates as follows:

Interest rates for various terms

1 year	1%
2 year	1.5%
3 year	2%
4 year	2.5%
5 year	3%

Comparison of the value of $10,000 after 5 years

	Buying a 1-year term	Buying a 5-year term	Buying an escalator
First year	$10,100	$10,300	$10,200
Second year	$10,201	$10,600	$10,441
Third year	$10,303	$10,900	$10,713
Fourth year	$10,406	$11,200	$11,009
Fifth year	$10,510	$11,500	$11,321

Note: With the escalator, you purchase five separate GICs for $2,000 each that have a term from one to five years, earning interest as noted above. After the first year, the one-year GIC that was earning 1% has matured and is re-invested into a new five-year GIC with a 3% interest rate. This is repeated each year as one of the GICs matures.

Compared to renewing a short-term GIC every year or having your money locked-in for a long time, this investment escalator strategy increases your overall rate of return while providing some liquidity each year as one of the GICs matures. This strategy works even better during a period when interest rates trend upward because renewals are made at increasingly higher rates instead of the constant 3% as assumed in this example.

These days, there are some products on the market that already have the escalator feature built in, so you don't need to figure this out on your own.

Wanting to feel safe with your money is normal, but being too safe will cause you to be sorry. While you're saving for retirement, every little bit helps, and failing to keep up with inflation and taxes will cause your retirement nest egg to shrink.

rescue it!

☐ Keep as much of your money as possible invested at all times, even if it is just keeping up with inflation.

☐ Hold investments that pay interest income in accounts such as a tax free savings account to eliminate income taxes.

☐ Create an investment escalator to get a higher return with some flexibility in a low-risk environment.

CHAPTER 11

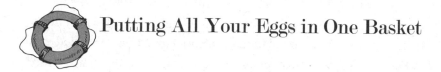 Putting All Your Eggs in One Basket

Can you have too much of a good thing? When it comes to your personal balance sheet, the answer is yes.

IT'S OFTEN SAID THAT HAVING TOO MUCH of a good thing can be harmful to you. This is true with many things in life. For instance, a plant needs water to live, but give it too much water and it will die. From a financial perspective, it's important to diversify so you don't put all of your investment eggs in one basket. But even with diversification, something that is known to be good for your investments can be bad if there's too much of it.

what does it mean to diversify?

In very simple terms, diversification means buying different investments that complement each other so that you can spread out the risk. Imagine that you have some money to invest and you decide to buy shares in just one company because you feel it has the best prospects. The rate of return in your portfolio will depend entirely on the results of that one company. If the value of the shares rises, your entire portfolio will grow by the rate of return. However, if the value of the shares falls, your entire portfolio will suffer by the rate of loss. So, by adding shares of other companies into your portfolio, you can reduce the risk. In fact, research shows that by adding more companies to your portfolio you can not only reduce risk but also even out (or smooth out) returns, and possibly even earn a higher rate of return. This is because some investments may increase in value while others may decline in value and, on average, both volatility and risk are reduced.

If you are a self-serve investor and want to build a diversified portfolio to minimize risk and maximize returns, experts suggest that you should include approximately 40 different investments. But trying to follow so many investments will be virtually impossible unless this is your full-time job. That's why the use of mutual funds, including index funds and Exchange Traded Funds, has become so popular among average investors. Mutual funds provide both instant diversification and professional money management.

different basket, same eggs

When it comes to diversification, what you see is not necessarily what you get. While investing in one mutual fund will provide you with a diversified investment, having more mutual funds doesn't always increase diversification. As a result, you may think you have a well diversified portfolio but in reality you don't — it's just a mirage.

It's important to understand how your money is invested, and also just what is in your mutual funds. If you take a look at a couple of Canadian equity mutual funds, you'll probably see a lot of duplication. This is almost unavoidable, because the Canadian equity market is very small: it represents only about 3% of the world market. So buying several different Canadian equity mutual funds from different money managers doesn't necessarily increase diversification — you may just be buying more of the same investments. I reviewed the top 10 holdings of three Canadian equity mutual funds managed by three different companies, only to find that they weren't very different at all. At the time when I compared the holdings, two out of the three mutual funds owned virtually the same investments. In total, nine out of the top 10 holdings were the same for those two funds. The third mutual fund was the most different, but even then, four of the top 10 holdings matched those in the other two funds. Again, because the Canadian market is so small, it's difficult to avoid duplication of holdings, so while you think you have a diversified portfolio, all you are doing is buying the same investments over and over again.

Another common problem occurs when there is a deliberate attempt to diversify with different types of investments. For instance, let's say you own a money market fund, a bond fund, and an equity fund, which in aggregate represents your optimal asset mix. By definition, you may have created a balanced portfolio perfectly suited to your needs and goals. So what additional benefit would you receive if your next investment decision is to buy a balanced fund? This purchase would be irrelevant for two reasons. First of all, the balanced fund might hold many of the same investments your other three funds already own, so there's the issue of duplication of investments again. Second, depending on the asset mix in the balance fund, you may be straying from your optimal asset mix when all of the investments are looked at as a whole. For example, the balanced fund may hold more low-risk, low-return investments than you should have in your portfolio.

And finally, if you try to diversify by buying just about every type of fund out there so you have exposure to as many different companies and asset classes as possible, you might be better served by buying an index fund or Exchange Traded Fund, both of which simply replicate a particular index.

employer programs cause the same concern

Some employers provide enhanced savings opportunities to employees by offering programs that include buying company stock. Whether the programs are stock purchase plans, defined contribution plans, or stock options, there is one common element — the employee acquires shares in their employer. While these plans provide an attractive savings option, here too you can have too much of a good thing. Over the years, employees can accumulate a sizeable amount in these plans, which puts them at risk of being under-diversified. What's more, employees often wait until just before retirement to make investment decisions about the shares they own in these employer plans. You may recall the story about Enron's employees losing massive amounts in retirement savings. These employees had retirement savings plans that invested mainly in their own company's shares, and when Enron collapsed, their retirement savings evaporated. The lesson to be learned here is that if you wait until retirement to diversify, you run the risk that the value of those shares may go down just at the time you were planning to sell them, leaving you with a lot less savings than you expected to have. And to add another wrinkle to the diversification puzzle, if you work for a large Canadian company, chances are quite high that balanced or equity mutual funds will also hold shares in your company. Once again, you have too much of a good thing.

One final thought about diversifying your personal balance sheet: this has to do with real estate holdings. Your home is usually the largest asset on your personal balance sheet. And if you buy more real estate, such as a vacation home or rental property, then you may find that once again, you have too much of a good thing. So when it comes to retirement savings and investing in funds or other investments that have a return based on real estate, be aware that you may already have a large portion of your personal net worth already invested in this asset class.

rescue it!

☐ Review all of your investments, including individual holdings in your mutual funds, to see exactly how your money is invested, and determine if you have duplicate investments.

☐ If you are part of an employer plan that allows you to buy shares in your employer, keep track of how many shares you own and rebalance when necessary. Review the rules around making withdrawals from your employer plan to determine when and how often you can withdraw or sell shares without penalty or additional costs.

CHAPTER 12

 Thinking That Retiring Means
You Stop Investing

*Since retirement can last for as long as 30 years, your
accumulated retirement savings still have time to grow, even
after you retire.*

WHEN IT COMES TO INVESTING, a common theory has been used
to guide people's thinking as to what a reasonable asset allocation should
look like at various stages in their life. It is a very simple concept to understand and remember. Basically, you take 100 minus your age, and that's
how much you should have in equities, with the balance in less risky
investments. Using this simple formula, you would have a larger portion
of your savings invested in equities in your younger years and a smaller
portion in your later years. For instance, at age 35 you would have 65% of
your money invested in equities. At age 70, a reasonable allocation would
be 30% to equities. In other words, more of your money is allocated to
asset preservation rather than asset growth.

We have learned that equities provide the best protection against
inflation and that, over a long period of time, a portfolio with a higher
allocation to well-diversified equity investments will outperform a portfolio with more conservative investments. We also know that retirement
can last 25 to 30 years and our savings need to continue to grow by more
than inflation and taxes — so then why is there so much reluctance to

include equities in a retirement portfolio? It comes down to one thing — the amount of volatility a portfolio can withstand during retirement and, more specifically, volatility when there will be regular withdrawals being made from the portfolio.

how volatility can wreck your retirement portfolio

To show the impact that volatility of returns can have on a retirement portfolio with annual withdrawals, we compare two sample portfolios. The two separate portfolios each begin with $200,000 in them, invested entirely in equity investments. Annual withdrawals of $10,000 are made each year. Portfolio A earns a steady 3% each year (after tax and inflation); portfolio B earns negative 12% for the first two years, then positive 15% for the next two years, and this pattern is repeated throughout the retirement years, so there is an average rate of return of 3% (after tax and inflation).

Results: After 19 years, Portfolio B runs out of money and does not have enough to make the full $10,000 withdrawal. Portfolio A still has $99,533 after the $10,000 withdrawals is made in the 19th year.

The reason Portfolio B runs out of money sooner is that the negative returns occur at the beginning of the retirement period. After just two years of withdrawals during two years of negative returns, the portfolio is worth only $136,080. If the sequence of returns for portfolio B had been the opposite, i.e., positive 15% for two years and then negative 12% for two years, with this pattern repeated, the portfolio would have $39,322 in it at the end of 20 years. So to minimize the risk that volatility adds to your portfolio during retirement, many advocate holding a low-risk portfolio. This was an extreme example of how volatility affects a portfolio because it assumes the entire portfolio is invested in equity investments.

Another common approach would be to divide the portfolio into individual portions of money based on when you need it. For instance, if you need $10,000 per year, then you would need to set aside $50,000 for the next five years. This money would be invested in short- to medium-term investments to minimize volatility, because they would need to be cashed in over the next five years. You could even consider the investment escalator mentioned in chapter 10. The rest of the money (i.e., $150,000) can be invested with more of a long-term approach, which would include a higher proportion of equity investments. This approach may require more frequent rebalancing to ensure that enough funds are moved from long-term investments to short-term investments over time, so that the annual withdrawal can be made when needed while providing some flexibility as to when rebalancing will occur. For instance, if the stock market is in decline, you can delay transferring those investments that have gone down in value and wait until there is a recovery.

retirement is not a short period of time

When you consider you may only be saving for 25 to 30 years, and retirement can last 25 to 30 years, it's common sense to expect to continue to earn income on your investments during retirement. Unless you are independently wealthy and focused solely on wealth preservation, you will need your savings to continue to grow after tax and inflation so that you can make the withdrawals you require for the rest of your life. In the example above, portfolio A still held $92,519 after making $10,000 annual withdrawals for 20 years. At this point, the entire original savings of $200,000 have been withdrawn, and the $92,519 remaining in the account represents growth in the portfolio. Without the growth, the money would have run out after 20 years.

rescue it!

During retirement years:

☐ Ensure that you have a minimum of five years' worth of withdrawals invested in low-risk, easily accessible investments.

☐ Keep a long-term view for the balance of your retirement savings.

☐ Avoid or minimize withdrawals from a declining portfolio by delaying expenses that are not absolutely necessary.

CHAPTER 13

 Watching Your Investments Too Closely

The more you pay attention to how your investments are performing, the more you will want to try to time the market and the more you will make impulsive decisions that you will likely regret later.

LET'S FACE IT — THERE'S SOMETHING ALLURING about the stock market and all the fortunes that can be made. It's quoted on the daily news, and any time there are big fluctuations, everyone is talking about what happened and beginning to look for trends and patterns. Even though news reports announce what has happened in the past ("the stock has fallen 10%"), investors assume that the stock will continue to fall in the near future.

If you've invested in the stock market, your investments will fluctuate over time. It is common knowledge that no one can predict the stock market performance with any kind of certainty. The only thing that can be predicted is that sometimes the stock market will go up and sometimes it will go down.

Have you ever tried to follow an individual stock even for just one day — or one hour? Try it and I'm sure you will be both surprised and exhausted. Imagine trying to keep track of an entire portfolio. The price of a stock can change every time it is bought and sold. Over a 10-year period, the average rate of return might be 7%, but the returns in each of those 10 years could be very far from 7%, with some very good years and some very bad years. So which approach is best — following an "active trading" model, or a "buy and hold" model? A study released in March 2011 showed that investing in the S&P 500 over a 20-year period ending in December 2010 would have resulted in a 9.14% rate of return, but the average equity investor had a return of only 3.83%.[1] The study cites investor behaviour and specifically too-frequent trading as the main reasons why returns are lower. Investors don't all behave the same way. When comparing men and women, men tend to be more overconfident about their investment abilities than women, and as such trade their accounts almost 50% more often than women.[2]

Numerous studies have shown that by missing just the best 10 or 20 days of the year, your net growth could be significantly less. This was very true in the time between the fall of 2008 and the summer of 2009. After significant market losses, investors panicked and abandoned the stock market for the safer haven of cash and short-term investments. Deciding when to re-enter the market proved to be a difficult decision, and waiting too long resulted in missing much of the recovery.

Investors cannot make completely unemotional investment decisions, and watching their investments too closely adds fuel to the fire. If you find yourself in this position, ask yourself why you are watching your investments so closely.

- Are you nervous or anxious about how it might perform, based on a hunch, some research you've done, or a rumour you've heard?

- Are you waiting for the right time to sell, and looking to spot a trend?

- Is it a hobby, that is, are you investing with what I call your "play" money rather than your life savings?

common mistakes

Herding

Copying what others are doing simply to join the crowd for fear of being left out. As a result, you tend to buy too late and pay a higher price, or sell when everyone else is selling and risk losing money.

---

[1] Dalbar Inc., *2011 Quantitative Analysis of Investor Behaviour*, March 2011.

[2] Barber, Brad M. and Terrance Odean, "Boys Will Be Boys: Gender, Overconfidence, and Common Stock Investment," *Quarterly Journal of Economics*, February 2001.

Impulsive Reactions

Overreacting to news stories in the media (either positive or negative) without doing proper research.

Optimism

Believing good things are going to happen from this point onward as a result of studying trends or looking at past history. Just because a stock has gone up in value over the last week does not mean it's going to continue to do so.

Overconfidence

A little bit of knowledge can be dangerous when it leads you to believe your skills and abilities are better than they are.

Regular Review of Your Investments

How often should you be checking your investments? What do the experts say?

I was being interviewed by a journalist and she asked me that very question, so I in turn asked her when was the last time she checked — it had been over a year. I told her that's not often enough — a lot can happen in a year. Both to your investments and to you personally. I would suggest reviewing your investment statements, as a standard rule, as soon as you get them. If you have any questions or concerns, contact your investment advisor to discuss whether your investments are behaving as expected, and if not, what might have caused the fluctuation. If you are a do-it-yourselfer, you may prefer to review your holdings more frequently, such as once a week.

what causes stock prices to move?

If you are doing all your own research, you may want to watch for some key types of news items that could affect the investments you own:

1. World events, such as the attacks on the World Trade Center on September 11, 2001, and the Japanese tsunami disaster on March 11, 2011 — both events caused stock markets around the world to fall.

2. Economic data, such as the unemployment rate, the inflation rate, and the value of the Canadian dollar, will all have an effect on stock prices.

3. Company earnings will impact company stock prices, of course, but can also impact an entire industry if investors assume other similar companies will report similar results.

4. Mergers and acquisitions — the departure of senior executives or a company founder may impact the stock price, as investors may believe the company's performance will change.

5. Corporate milestones, such as loss of a contract, winning a new contract, launch of a new product, or having to defend against a lawsuit, can have a significant impact on the company's revenue, and may also impact competitors.

There's a lot to be aware of — no wonder there are news networks dedicated entirely to business news. Once you spend some time watching these programs, you'll realize that even the experts can't agree on what stocks to buy. So while it's important to be aware of any news, it's equally as important to not overreact to what you hear without doing additional research to determine if any adjustments actually need to be made to your portfolio. Pay attention to your investments — don't neglect them, but don't watch them like a hawk, either.

rescue it!

☐ Ignore the day-to-day changes and focus on your long-term investment objectives.

☐ Complete an investment policy statement, and whenever you are tempted to rebalance, review it to remind yourself why your portfolio is structured the way it is.

☐ Check your investment statements regularly so you know how your money is invested and can determine if any adjustments need to be made.

CHAPTER 14

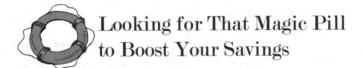 Looking for That Magic Pill
to Boost Your Savings

The closer you are to retirement, the more likely it is that you
will want to rely on your portfolio's rate of return to do the
heavy lifting to get you to your savings goal.

FALLING BEHIND IN SAVINGS can cause a feeling of desperation and, as a result, some investors become too aggressive with their investment portfolio to try to make up for lost time or a bad year or two in the market. Once you have established a retirement savings goal, what should you do if you're not on track to achieving that goal? Unfortunately, there is no magic pill to boost your savings.

trade-offs are needed

Three factors play a role in reaching your savings goal:

1. Time
2. Contributions
3. Rate of return

If you change any one of these inputs, the others will be impacted. Consider which input you have the most control over, and work with that.

1. Time

It's no surprise that starting to save early in life can make you a millionaire. It's true — just save $125 every two weeks in an RRSP from age 20 to age 65, earn 7 to 8% on those savings, and by age 65 you'll have $1,000,000. Unfortunately, not only do few if any 20-year-olds make saving for retirement a priority, but in general people don't get serious about retirement savings until later in life. While it's impossible to turn back time, you can increase the amount of time before retirement by retiring later; however, that's not an option everyone can take or would want for themselves.

2. Contributions

How much and how often you contribute is largely within your control. In fact, most would agree that it is our responsibility to contribute to our savings, rather than relying entirely on government and employer programs. Since contributions are under our control, that should be the first place to look when we want our savings to grow. Imagine a $1,000 investment that earns a 5% rate of return — after one year, you have $1,050. Now consider the result if you were to add an additional $100 in savings to your portfolio. After one year, the $1,100 investment that earns 5% will be worth $1,155. You'd have to earn a 15.5% rate of return on the original $1,000 to have the same amount saved up after one year.

By making an additional contribution, you've grown your portfolio without taking on any more risk. Unfortunately, you can't always rely on being able to increase contributions.

Another way to have an impact is to make regular contributions, regardless of market conditions.

Dollar Cost Averaging

Investors' fears about stock market fluctuations can be paralyzing. It was clear during 2008 and 2009 that investors preferred to keep their money in cash and wait out the turbulence before making any investment decisions. Continuing to invest can be one of the hardest things to do during market

volatility, but it works in your favour. By continuing to make regular contributions, you will benefit from *dollar cost averaging* and when the market
improves, and history tells us it will, you will reap greater rewards than if
you stopped contributing. This is because, in periods of market decline,
dollar cost averaging (continuing to invest) means you will be able to buy
more units or shares with the money you're investing, and since the price
of what you're buying is lower, it reduces the total average cost for your
investments.

For example, if you invest $200 this month in a mutual fund that is
priced at $10 per unit, you will buy 20 units. Next month, if the value of
the mutual fund is $5 per unit, your $200 investment allows you to buy
40 units, not 20 like in the previous month. Therefore, after two months,
and $400 of investment, you own a total of 60 units (20 from the first
month and 40 from the second month). If in the third month the mutual
fund returns to a price of $10 per unit, your $400 investment will be valued at $600 (60 units at $10 each). You've earned a 50% return on your
original $400 investment. As long as your investment strategy was and is
still appropriate for you, it's often best to continue to invest even during a
market decline.

3. Rate of Return

The third factor in how much your money grows is the rate of return. No
one knows how the market and our investments will perform, and we
certainly can't control it. Even with investments that provide a guaranteed return, we cannot control the rate that is available for that particular
investment. We might like the guaranteed investment to pay 10%, but at
the time we purchase it, the rate may only be 2%. When you rely on the
rate of return to boost your savings, the common approach is to take on
more risk by investing more heavily in equities, in the hope that the returns
will be high enough to get you to your savings goal. In the examples above,
what risk would you have to take with your portfolio to generate a 15.5%
rate of return? Or what about a 50% rate of return? Is that risk appropriate for you, based on your risk tolerance and time horizon? Even if you
could earn 15.5% this year, how realistic is it to expect that kind of return

year after year, given historical market returns? Investments that have the potential to generate higher rates of return are considered more risky and are more volatile, which means the value can fluctuate from year to year. Are you willing to take the chance that your portfolio could experience a significant decline in value just before your retirement?

how do the trade-offs work?

Now that you know the three inputs that are key to growing your savings, it's clear that, with more time, larger contributions and a higher rate of return you will accumulate more money.

Figure 14.1: Maximizing inputs results in more savings

Now let's look at how alternative strategies get you to the same savings goal (for the sake of simplicity, income taxes are ignored in this example).

1. *Time* is on your side — save $2,000/yr for 30 years and earn 5%. Total contributions of $60,000 and $79,522 of growth, for a total value of $139,522.

2. With less time, increase *contributions* — save $4,000/yr for 20 years and earn 5%. Total contributions of $80,000 and $58,877 of growth, for a total value of $138,877.

3. With less time, increase *rate of return* — save $2,000/yr for 20 years and earn more than 10.3%. Total contributions of $40,000 and $99,048 of growth, for a total value of $139,048.

In these examples, starting 10 years later and saving for only 20 years instead of 30 means you have to earn a rate of return that is 5.8% higher. Alternatively, staying with a return of 5%, contributions would have to double from $2,000 to $4,000 per year, just because you're starting 10 years later! Perhaps you can save more later in life, once other obligations such as your mortgage are paid off, or perhaps you can't. This is the trade-off that must be made when retirement savings don't begin until later in life.

Greed and desperation often cloud common sense and cause people to make investments that are outside their comfort zone. Those who have fewer years until retirement and haven't saved as much as they should have may be enticed by promises of quick results.

a word of caution

The number of financial scams out there is impressive. There are scams to avoid income tax (like the investing scam that promised tax-free withdrawals from your RRSP or RRIF); those that promise huge tax deductions (like the charitable gifting scam that promised donation receipts equal to three or four times the actual amount donated); and those that promise unheard-of returns (like those by Gary Sorenson or Bernard Madoff or Bertram Earl Jones — these men allegedly swindled investors out of millions of dollars).

There is rarely a quick fix to get your portfolio to the level you think it should be at. It's not practical to rely solely on portfolio performance to make up for the fact that you haven't saved enough or didn't start early enough, or to get back on track after a market decline.

rescue it!

☐ Set savings targets and milestones that are achievable.

☐ Don't focus only on rate of return to grow your portfolio.

☐ Cut expenses and increase contributions.

☐ Increase time by working a few more years.

PART 3

mistakes around debt

CHAPTER 15

 Thinking That All Debt
Is Created Equal

Some debt is considered bad, while other debt is considered good. Knowing the difference can help you save money.

OVER OUR LIFETIME WE WILL BE FACED with many situations where we will have to borrow money — buying a car, paying for a higher education, buying a home and furnishing it. The list goes on and on. As a result, we will accumulate different kinds of debt and some will take longer than others to pay off. One thing is certain: sometimes it makes sense to borrow and sometimes it doesn't. Preparing for retirement is not only a matter of building savings; paying off loans so you can retire debt-free is equally important.

I'm continually amazed at what fantastic bargain shoppers we have evolved into. Everyone is keenly aware of where to go for the best price — we not only shop around, but expect price matching! So if we're so price-conscious at the time of purchase, why are we willing to pay so much more for the product as a result of borrowing? By using credit cards, loans, pay-later schemes, and so on, the true and final cost of the item we're getting is actually a lot more than it says on the price tag. When we borrow, we are faced with having to pay the money back with interest. The interest charge is the "extra" price we pay (a premium) to have something now rather than waiting to buy it at a later time when we have enough money and don't have to borrow. While this chapter discusses types of debt, a discussion about how to pay off your mortgage faster is found in chapter 16 and a discussion around credit card debt is found in chapter 17.

good debt, bad debt

First of all, having *too much* debt, so much that it becomes difficult to manage the payments, is a bad thing no matter how you look at it.

When it comes to the debt we have, we often hear that there's good debt and there's bad debt. Isn't all debt bad? It depends on how you look at it. In general, financial advisors follow two general rules to determine if a particular debt is considered good or bad.

1. Borrowing for something that's going to increase in value over time (like investments or a home) is a good debt; borrowing for something that doesn't go up in value or declines in value (like electronics or a car) is a bad debt.
2. A loan where the interest paid is tax-deductible is better than one where the interest is not tax-deductible.

good ways to use debt

If the interest you are paying is tax-deductible, then it's usually considered good debt. If a loan meets certain specific criteria (described below), the interest payable on the loan is tax-deductible and, as a result, it's the equivalent of paying a lower rate of interest on the loan. This is because the interest you are paying is reduced by the income tax savings generated by the tax deduction. Let me explain: let's say you borrow $10,000 and the interest on the loan is 6%. To keep things simple, assume you're making just the interest payments on the loan. After the first year the loan has cost you $600 in interest. When you prepare your annual income tax return, you can take a deduction equal to the $600 you paid in interest and subtract it from other income you've earned in the year. This reduces your overall taxable income. If your marginal tax rate is 40%, then the $600 deduction saves you $240 in income taxes! In effect, the loan cost you only $360 and not $600. This is like paying interest of 3.6% rather than 6%.

Sound too good to be true? Remember, I said only loans that meet certain criteria qualify for tax deduction on the interest paid. The income tax rules allow a tax deduction for interest costs incurred for the purpose of earning income from a business or property. One point that does require special mention is that interest paid on a loan whose sole purpose is to earn capital gains with no expectation of ever earning income does not qualify as a tax deduction, because a capital gain is not considered income for tax purposes. Therefore, if you are borrowing money to invest in common shares, the interest cost is generally tax-deductible. If you buy an investment with a fixed dividend (such as a preferred share), then you can deduct interest only up to the amount of the dividend that is included in your tax return, which is generally 144% of the actual dividend you received. If you buy an investment with a fixed interest rate, you generally can deduct interest costs on the loan only if the loan interest is less than the fixed rate of return the investment will pay. The rules around interest deductibility are very complex. If in doubt, it's best to speak to a tax advisor to determine if your particular loan qualifies for tax-deductibility.

leveraged investing

Borrowing money to make portfolio investments is called leveraged investing. Before getting into the complexities of leveraged investing, it's important to note that anyone with a home mortgage has used leveraging to buy a more expensive asset than they could otherwise afford. This section will review how you can use leveraged investing as a strategy to build an investment portfolio faster than using only your accumulated savings. If you use a loan to invest in the stock market and your investments go up in value or pay income such as interest or dividends, you can earn substantially more money than without the loan. On the other hand, if markets decline, you may find yourself with a loan that is larger than the value of your investments. This is why leveraged investing is considered a risky strategy. There is potential for a very large return, but also a very large loss.

Example #1

	No loan	Loan
Original investment	$ 10,000	$ 10,000
Loan	$ —	$ 40,000
Total invested	$ 10,000	$ 50,000
Income earned (10%)	$ 1,000	$ 5,000
Less: Loan interest (5%)		($ 2,000)
Total account value	**$ 11,000**	**$53,000**
Payback of loan	$ —	($ 40,000)
Total account value	**$ 11,000**	**$ 13,000**

This simple example shows how borrowing to increase the amount invested can help your money grow faster when rates of return are positive. After one year, borrowing $40,000 at a cost of 5% and earning a rate of return of 10% on your total portfolio results in having $2,000 more money after the loan and interest are fully paid off. Taxes are ignored for simplicity, but remember that investment income is taxable at your marginal rate, and the loan interest would likely qualify as a tax deduction.

Example #2

	No loan	Loan
Original investment	$10,000	$ 10,000
Loan	$ —	$ 40,000
Total invested	$10,000	$ 50,000
Loss of 20%	($ 2,000)	($ 10,000)
Less: Loan interest (5%)		($ 2,000)
Total account value	**$ 8,000**	**$ 38,000**
Payback of loan	$ —	($ 40,000)
Total account value	**$ 8,000**	**($ 2,000)**

The results are very different if there is a decline in the market. After one year, borrowing $40,000 at a cost of 5% and losing 20% on your total portfolio results in losing all of your money. To close out the transaction, you still have to pay the interest cost of $2,000, as well as the full amount of the loan. Not only is your original $10,000 gone, but you're in the hole for the $2,000 interest cost. It is clear that leveraged investing magnifies a loss and is a risky strategy.

Hopefully the decline is temporary and you can wait it out until the market recovers. Most people will panic and make rash investment decisions in this situation. If you cash out during a decline in the market it will be impossible for your portfolio to fully recover, even when the market goes up in the future. If you were to do this during retirement or within five years of retirement, and the markets experience a decline at a time that you will be making withdrawals, it can quickly erode your retirement savings.

When interest rates are low, leveraged investing looks even more attractive for anyone wishing to give their portfolio a boost. While leveraged investing used to be a strategy reserved for high-net-worth individuals, it has now become more commonplace. Nevertheless, it should be approached with caution and by seeking the advice of an investment advisor or a tax professional.

student loans

What about student loans? Is that good or bad debt? There are two sides to this story. First of all, education is an investment in the future earning potential of the student, and one could argue that the purpose of such a loan is to invest in an asset that will increase in value once the education is completed.

Second, the interest on certain student loans may be eligible for a 15% non-refundable tax credit. The credit is available only to the student, even though the parent may be the one who actually makes the loan payments. The result is similar to other tax-deductible interest in that the tax savings from the credit reduce the actual cost of the loan. Only loans received under the *Canada Student Loans Act,* the *Canada Student Financial Assistance Act,* or similar provincial or territorial government laws for post-secondary education are eligible for the non-refundable tax credit. If the student has very little income while in school, the interest paid can be carried forward for up to five years in the future, to when the student is earning sufficient income to use the credit. It's important to note that interest paid on personal loans or lines of credit, regardless of whether they are in the name of the student or the parent, do not qualify for the tax credit.

RRSPs

What about borrowing to make an RRSP contribution? Many people procrastinate and wait until the last minute to make their RRSP contribution. This can make it much more difficult to come up with a lump-sum amount of money for an annual RRSP contribution. People who want to contribute by the deadline may find that the only way to do so is to borrow. Financial institutions offer a variety of RRSP loan options specifically for this purpose. However, although the loan is being used to make an investment in the RRSP account, the interest on the loan is not tax-deductible. The reason for this is that the investments are in a tax-deferred account and are not taxed the way ordinary investment income is taxed. When the investments and related growth is withdrawn from the RRSP, the withdrawal is taxed as ordinary income and not investment income. But this shouldn't discourage you from considering an RRSP loan, because the contribution to the RRSP is tax-deductible! So in effect, you *are* getting a tax deduction as a result of the loan. And if you play it smart, you can use an RRSP loan to bump up your contribution, and then use your tax savings to pay off the loan. For example, if you have $3,000 to contribute to your RRSP and borrow an additional $2,000, your total tax-deductible contribution will be $5,000. If you're in the 40% tax bracket, your tax savings (which usually result in a tax refund) will be $2,000! This is just enough to pay off the entire loan. The fact that the numbers matched perfectly was not a coincidence. It's based on a simple formula that you can use to give you an idea of how much you should borrow so that the resulting tax savings can be used to pay off the entire loan. Here's the formula:

$$\frac{\text{Cash to contribute}}{(1/\text{tax rate} - 1)} = \text{amount to borrow}$$

If you file your tax return electronically, you'll likely get the tax refund within a month, so you'll pay minimal interest on your RRSP loan. This formula assumes that the full RRSP contribution will generate a tax refund. If you earn other income that is not subject to source withholdings, such as interest, dividend income, capital gains, rental income, and so on, or have asked that the withholding tax on your employment income be reduced because of your regular RRSP contributions, then this strategy will reduce total taxes owing but may not generate a tax refund.

My general rule for RRSP loans is *do not borrow if you cannot repay the entire loan within one year*. Otherwise, you may find yourself borrowing again and again each year to make your annual contribution. If you do borrow to make your RRSP contribution, here is a simple strategy that will help you to avoid having to borrow in future years. Make payments sufficient to pay off the loan within six months (not one year), and then for the following six months, make the same payments directly to your RRSP for the current year. That way, when the deadline comes, you've already made your annual contribution and you don't have to borrow.

rescue it!

☐ Pay off non-tax-deductible loans first.

☐ Use RRSP loans wisely and use the tax savings to pay the loan off quickly to minimize non-tax-deductible interest charges.

☐ Don't go overboard and borrow what you can't afford to pay back.

☐ Speak to a tax professional when considering a loan to make portfolio investments.

CHAPTER 16

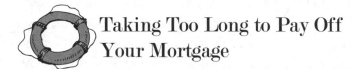 Taking Too Long to Pay Off
Your Mortgage

Making regular mortgage payments is a big drain on cash flow.
One of the best strategies is to enter retirement mortgage-free.

MANY CANADIANS DREAM OF OWNING their own home. A home represents who you are, it's a place to create memories, and it is a solid financial asset. Buying a home is a significant commitment that requires time, patience, and a major investment — searching for the perfect home, accumulating a significant down payment, and years of making regular mortgage payments. Think about your family and friends — almost everyone has had a mortgage at some point in time. Your home is likely the largest purchase you'll ever make, and unless you've won the lottery or inherited a sizeable amount of money, no matter how debt-averse you are, you likely had to get a mortgage to buy it. And given the fact that your first home is not likely to be your last, there's a high probability that your mortgage amount may be increased once or twice along the way to accommodate your new and often more expensive home. While you have control over buying and selling your home, what you can't control over the duration of the mortgage is the interest rate. And that's one of the main factors that will determine how quickly you can pay off the mortgage. Paying off your mortgage as quickly as you can will free up cash to save and invest for retirement. And don't forget about your net worth statement described in chapter 6 — reducing your debt improves your net worth.

Over the years, mortgages have evolved significantly, and understanding how mortgages work is the key to paying them off faster and, at the very least, before retirement.

fixed or variable rate

How much risk are you willing to take with your mortgage? Deciding on what kind of interest rate to select is similar to making investment decisions. You never know what the future will bring and, therefore, there is an element of risk when deciding between a fixed, variable, or blended rate of interest. A fixed rate is generally higher than a variable rate, but with a fixed rate you are assured that your payments will not change for the duration of the mortgage term. With a variable rate, there is no guaranteed interest rate — it may move higher or lower than when you entered into the mortgage, depending on market conditions. If you are willing to accept the risk of not knowing exactly what the interest rate will be, it may pay off in the long run. Studies show that selecting a variable rate mortgage can save thousands in interest costs over the duration of the mortgage, leaving you with more money to save for retirement.

open, convertible, and closed mortgages

If you have what's called an open mortgage, you have full flexibility to do what is best for you within the term of the mortgage. You can pay it off entirely, renegotiate with your current financial institution, or move the mortgage elsewhere. This is a handy feature if you feel interest rates will be falling and you want the flexibility to renegotiate at a lower rate. With a convertible mortgage, you can convert it to a closed mortgage with the same financial institution without any interest penalty. A closed mortgage limits your prepayment options and you will be charged an interest rate penalty to renegotiate to a lower rate or to pay off the mortgage.

Added flexibility comes at cost — interest rates for an open mortgage tend to be higher than for a closed mortgage.

what term to choose?

The *term* of the mortgage refers to the contract period for the interest rate. For instance, a one-year fixed-rate mortgage at 4% means you'll pay 4% interest on the outstanding mortgage balance for one year. At the end of that year, you have the option to renew the remaining mortgage amount for whatever term you choose and at the market rates at the time of the renewal. Some financial institutions offer terms of up to 10 years or more.

interest rates will fluctuate

How long of a term should you choose? If you choose too long a term and interest rates fall during the term, you might find yourself locked into paying a higher interest rate than the current rate. Looking back over the years, mortgage rates can change dramatically. Let's say you bought a house in January 1991 and locked-in for a term of five years at a time when the average five-year rate was approximately 12.13%. Mortgage rates can change very quickly and just one year later, in January 1992, the five-year rate had fallen to 9.71% — a full 2.42% lower. What's more, during the five-year period from January 1991 to January 1996, the five-year rate had fallen to as low as 7.33% in January 1994. If you had chosen a variable rate mortgage you would have benefited, since your rate would have been automatically adjusted as the rates fell. In fact, selecting any term shorter than five years would have given you an opportunity to renew at a lower rate.

Rates for 5-year terms as of January	
Year	Rate
1991	12.13%
1992	9.71%
1993	9.47%
1994	7.33%
1995	10.60%
1996	8.02%

Interest rates have been fairly stable and at record lows between 2006 and 2011 — one might argue that they can't really fall much lower. In fact, there's a good chance they'll go up in the future. As you approach retirement, you may be faced with deciding whether to lock in your rate for a longer period of time so you'll know exactly what your payments will be, or to go with a variable rate and hope that interest rates will continue to fall so you can pay off the mortgage faster. No one knows what future interest rates will be. Remember, if you can't pay off the mortgage before retirement, you might want to reduce the risk that renewing at a higher interest rate in the future will make your mortgage unaffordable during your retirement years. Read on for how to do that.

amortization is key

The amortization period for a mortgage is the time it will take to pay off the entire amount. The amortization is based on many things, including the interest rate on the mortgage and the size of the mortgage payments. If the interest rate goes up during the amortization period, and the payment does not increase, then it will take longer to pay off the mortgage. Conversely, if the rate goes down, and the payment is kept the same, then it will be paid off much faster because a larger portion of the mortgage payment is reducing your principal. A common amortization period is 25 years, but you can select a shorter term as low as 5 years or a longer term of up to 30 years. In January 2011, the federal government introduced rules that tighten mortgage availability and payment terms by increasing the minimum down payment amount required to buy a house, and reducing the maximum amortization time from 35 to 30 years. While these rules may make it more difficult or even impossible for some would-be buyers to qualify for a mortgage, from a retirement planning perspective, the message is a good one for Canadians. A shorter amortization means much less interest is being paid on the mortgage and, hopefully, more and more Canadians can enter retirement debt-free.

With a 30-year amortization, starting a mortgage at the age of 35 means the final mortgage payment will be made just as you enter retirement at 65. Not bad, you might say. And in fact, that is pretty good, considering the number of people who now admit they may be entering retirement with a mortgage. But if you've chosen to forgo saving for retirement and instead focused on paying off your mortgage, you'll find that you may be house rich and investment poor as you enter your retirement years. Your options may be to sell your home or take out a reverse annuity mortgage, as discussed in chapter 31, to generate the cash flow you need. On the other hand, if you could pay off your mortgage 10 or 15 years sooner, then you could use those mortgage-free years to make large contributions toward your retirement savings.

how can you pay off your mortgage faster?

Many mortgages allow you to make accelerated or extra payments during the year, such as allowing an extra 10% of the original principal as a lump-sum payment each year, or simply increasing regular monthly payments by up to 10%. If you can afford it, the better strategy is to make accelerated or higher payments on a monthly basis, rather than waiting for the anniversary date to make a large lump-sum payment. This is mostly because good intentions don't always pan out and you may not have the extra savings available when it comes time to make the one-time payment. Paying off a mortgage as quickly as possible, and especially before retirement, is ideal and the best way to do that is to make it as painless and automatic as possible — that way there is no option to spend the money on other things.

Example: A 30-year-old has a $150,000 mortgage amortized over a 25-year period with a 4% interest rate and makes monthly payments of $789. Remember, this means it would take 25 years to pay off the entire mortgage if the interest rate and payment were to stay the same during those 25 years. With these assumptions, the mortgage will be fully paid off by age 55. But the goal should be to pay the mortgage off even sooner. One strategy that has worked for many is to select the payment amount you know you can afford to pay, and then see what the amortization works out to be. So in this example, if the individual can afford a payment of $906 per month (only $117 more), the entire mortgage will be paid off in 20 years, which saves more than $18,000 in interest. Now that the mortgage is paid off five years sooner, the $906 per month can be directed into an RRSP, TFSA, or other savings account earmarked for retirement. After 10 years of making those same contributions, the retirement savings account would be over $141,000, assuming a 5% pre-tax rate of return. After 15 years, the savings would grow to over $243,000.

To recap, if the mortgage started at the age of 30, by age 50 it would be totally paid off and by age 65 there would be $243,000 in retirement savings, by just taking the mortgage payment that you are accustomed to making and continuing to make it directly into an investment account once the mortgage is paid off.

Another way to pay off a mortgage early is to convert from a monthly payment to a bi-weekly payment structure: this will reduce your interest charges and pay down the mortgage faster. When you choose a bi-weekly payment structure, you make the equivalent of 13 months of payments instead of 12 each year. While this doesn't put a big strain on your cash flow, it will help to be mortgage-free sooner. The impact of this strategy will vary depending on the interest rate you are paying on your mortgage — the higher the interest rate, the greater the interest savings.

your house is not an ATM

As you diligently pay off your mortgage and your home increases in value, you build additional equity that will be a valuable asset during retirement. Home equity represents the part of the home that you own outright. If you were to sell your home, the home equity would be available to you after paying off the remaining mortgage, if any, as well as any other selling fees such as legal costs and real estate commissions. Over the years, homeowners have been able to access their home equity without actually selling their home by using a homeowner equity line of credit. While a line of credit is similar to a mortgage, it is not exactly the same as a mortgage. Instead, it's considered a pre-approved loan based on some portion of the available home equity that you can access when you need it. The interest rate on a homeowner equity line of credit is generally lower than that of an ordinary unsecured loan or credit card. Interest is charged only after you access the funds. Unlike a mortgage, the required payments on a line of credit are usually interest only. This can be a concern, because unless you make a concerted effort to pay back the principal, you won't be paying off the loan balance.

It's important to understand that it can be dangerous to have both a mortgage and a fully used homeowner line of credit, because it leaves little if any wiggle room if house prices fall and you choose or are forced to sell your home. For instance, in the U.S. many people borrowed to buy their houses with little if any down payment, and then, as the value of their houses went up, they borrowed against the growing equity in their houses for renovations such as pools, new high-end kitchens with granite counter-tops, and other luxuries. Unfortunately, most of these renovated homes did not retain their value during the U.S. mortgage and home market crash of 2009. As a result, many Americans found themselves selling their homes at prices that were more than 40% less than their *perceived value* and therefore significantly below the combined value of the outstanding mortgage and line of credit on the property. An important lesson from this story is to avoid treating your home like an ATM that you can draw against at any time.

Having a fully paid-off home during retirement should be one of your top financial goals.

keep payment constant

When interest rates are going down, resist the temptation to make lower mortgage payments! A good rule to follow is to not reduce your mortgage payments unless the payments are no longer affordable. Keeping the mortgage payment the same even though the interest rate is lower will help save you thousands of dollars in interest charges over the term of the mortgage. Not paying off your mortgage before entering full-time retirement can put an extra strain on an already reduced cash flow, especially if interest rates go up during your retirement years. You may have no choice but to pay a higher monthly amount, or you may have to increase your amortization, which means it will take you even longer to pay off the mortgage.

Whenever interest rates are low, the focus should be on paying off mortgages faster and be mortgage-free by retirement!

rescue it!

☐ Review your mortgage agreement — look for the maturity date, the interest rate, and your payment amount — ask your lender to explain anything you don't understand.

☐ If you can afford to make a larger payment — do it! Increase your payments up to the maximum amount you can afford and within the limits allowed in your mortgage agreement and pay off your mortgage years sooner.

☐ If you have a home equity line of credit, pay both interest and part of the principal each month.

CHAPTER 17

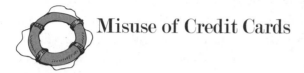 Misuse of Credit Cards

The way we use credit cards today, it's hard to imagine life without them. But when credit cards are used as long-term loans, they can easily wreck retirement.

THE FIRST ALL-PURPOSE CREDIT CARD issued in Canada was called the Chargex card. It came on the market in August 1968 and has since changed our lives forever. The popularity of credit cards can be attributed to convenience — there is no need to carry around large amounts of money to make a purchase, and they are widely accepted around the world. Credit cards also offer additional safety and security measures as compared to carrying around cash. If the card is lost or stolen, it can be replaced, and you won't be liable for any fraudulent charges. Credit cards have also made buying on credit socially acceptable — there is no longer a negative stigma to buying with a credit card.

They are so popular that, according to a recent estimate, there were an estimated 72 million credit cards in circulation in Canada in 2009.[1]

Having a credit card has become a necessity. Many people have more than one credit card in their wallet. Having multiple credit cards may lead you to feel "wealthy" — especially the gold or platinum cards — but the cards don't represent wealth, they represent debt.

---

[1] *Euromonitor International*, January 2010.

plastics are not all evil

Credit cards can work in your favour if you use them wisely. When you are paying for a purchase with a credit card, you are paying with the credit card company's money — and as long as you pay off the entire balance by the payment due date, you will pay little or no interest. From a planning perspective, that allows you to defer payment of a purchase and better manage your cash flow. This is especially important during retirement, when you may be receiving your income once a month and not weekly or bi-weekly. It's also an efficient way to help you better track and budget your expenses, because your purchases are summarized for you each month, and some credit card companies even provide an annual summary. From a retirement planning perspective, understanding where your money is going is one of the hardest things to do. So a credit card statement can be viewed as an efficient way to keep track of how much you are spending and where.

be aware of interest rates and fees

Interest Charges

How do credit card companies make money? They charge a fee to the retailers who accept the card as payment, and they charge you interest on unpaid balances. At the time of writing, interest rates charged by credit card companies averaged around 20%, with some lower-rate cards charging under 10%. Department store credit cards tend to charge more than the average. As you can imagine, using credit card debt as a long-term loan is too expensive to be taken lightly. If you actually stopped to see how much it costs you to use your credit cards, you might not be so quick to make purchases that you can't pay off quickly.

Annual Fees

Some types of credit cards charge an annual fee just to have the card in your wallet. In return for the fee, you receive additional benefits, such as points accumulation, travel insurance, and cash-back features.

One benefit worth mentioning is that some credit cards provide a doubling of the warranty on purchases made on the credit card for up to an additional year. This can come in handy and save you from buying expensive extended warranty coverage on products such as electronics and home appliances. While you may save money by paying one all-encompassing fee for all these benefits, most of the time you aren't able to take full advantage of all the benefits offered, either because you have multiple cards that offer the same benefits or because you have access to a similar benefit under a different program. For instance, if you are a member of CAA, you may have access to certain travel benefits through that membership and may not need the benefits provided by your credit card. Having more than a couple of cards in your wallet means you have to make a decision each time you use a credit card, as you try to remember which one offers the benefit you need. For instance, some cards provide insurance on car rentals, while others don't. Next time you rent a car and waive the insurance, make sure you're paying with the card that carries the insurance benefit! Many cards also allow card holders to collect points or "miles" and if you use several cards, it will take you longer to accumulate a large enough amount on each card to be able to take advantage of the perk.

Cash Advance Fees

When you use your credit card at an ATM or your bank branch as if it were a debit card, there is either an additional fee that you will be charged for the cash advance or the interest charges on the cash advance may be higher than what is charged for purchases. In fact, the cash advance is treated like an immediate loan made by the credit card company and, as a result, interest is charged from the day of the cash advance (rather than from the payment date, like with purchases). If you use the blank cheques from your credit card company to pay off a balance from another card, ask what interest rate you will be charged on the transaction.

Foreign Exchange

If you travel outside Canada and use your Canadian-dollar credit card to make purchases in a foreign currency, the credit card company will charge you a foreign exchange fee, which is usually embedded in the exchange rate it applies to the purchase (so you may not notice it). This results in paying more for the purchase than you might have thought. If you do a lot of travelling, for instance to the U.S., you should consider applying for a U.S.-dollar credit card. When your monthly bill comes in, you pay it off in U.S. dollars at the rate in effect at the time. A U.S.-dollar credit card can be particularly cost-effective for Canadians who spend lengthy periods of time across the border. Just make sure any annual charges for the card don't outweigh the benefits of reduced foreign-exchange-rate costs.

pay off balances quickly

It's common sense to pay off credit card balances quickly to minimize interest rate charges. A recent study indicates that 59%[2] of Canadians regularly pay off credit card balances in full every month, and as a result pay no interest at all. Unfortunately, some struggle to pay just the minimum amount each month. This is often the case if you use your credit card to finance large expenses such as a child's education or to pay for an expensive car repair or family vacation. But when you pay only the minimum amount, the interest on the purchases just keeps adding up, and it will take you a very long time to pay off the balance.

The 2009 market meltdown raised the issue of the growing debt load among Canadians and that has prompted the Canadian government to introduce some new rules to help consumers understand and better manage their credit card debt. Credit card companies must now provide details directly on the statement as to how long it will take to pay off the current balance if only minimum payments are made. The best way to show how long it could take to pay off a credit card balance when only minimum payments are being made is with a simple example. If there is a $2,000 balance on a credit card that charges an 18% interest rate, by making only the minimum required payment (the standard minimum payment is the greater of $10 or 3% of the balance — in this case $60), it would take almost 14 years to pay off the entire $2,000. That's if you don't add any other purchases

---

[2]Genworth Financial Canada and Canadian Association of Credit Counselling Services, *The Financial Fitness Survey*, August 2010.

to the card! Here's the big shock — just paying off the $2,000 over the 14 years would cost $1,798.88 in interest charges. That should be incentive enough to try to do whatever you can to pay off the amount sooner. In this example, if the monthly payment was increased to $500 per month instead of just the minimum amount, the credit card debt would be paid off after just five months — 13 years and five months sooner. After the credit card is paid off, the $500 amount can go to pay off other debts or make additional contributions to your retirement savings plan. If you have an outstanding credit card balance, you can go online to see for yourself how increasing your payment will help you pay off the balance sooner.[3]

reduce the interest

If you use credit cards to buy something you can't afford right now, but then take too long to pay off the balance, it will end up costing you a lot more than just the price of the item.

Credit cards charge different rates of interest and fees. If you have several cards, take the time to check what the interest rate is on each. If you carry a balance on more than one card, think about directing extra cash to paying off the card with the highest interest rate first. Then stop using that card. You will feel a certain sense of accomplishment once you scratch that debt off your personal balance sheet, and you will be motivated to eliminate even more debt.

There is another solution to eliminating high credit card interest costs — get a debt consolidation loan from your bank. These loans will carry a lower interest rate and will help you manage your cash flow because you will have only one payment to make. The caveat is that you must stop using your credit cards until the loan is paid off; otherwise, you enter a vicious cycle of adding more debt to what you currently have.

rescue it!

☐ Limit the number of credit cards you own. Get rid of the high-interest cards and those that charge a fee for services you don't use or need.

---

[3]Credit card calculator used: www.fcac.gc.ca/iTools-iOutils/CreditCardCalculator-eng.aspx

☐ Accumulate points wisely — having fewer cards means points will accumulate faster on the remaining cards.

☐ Pay on time — don't pay late, because high interest rate costs can add up quickly.

☐ Don't use credit cards as if they were long-term loans — consider debt consolidation to reduce interest costs and simplify your money management.

PART 4

saving
for retirement

CHAPTER 18

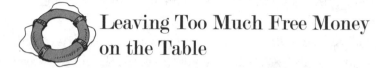 Leaving Too Much Free Money
on the Table

It's hard enough to save on your own, so when there's someone else willing to offer a hand and some money, it would be wise to accept the offer.

SOME SAY THERE'S NO SUCH THING as a free lunch. But when it comes to taking advantage of all of the benefits your employer provides, many of us leave lots of free money unclaimed. In some cases, employees don't know what's available to them; in other cases, employees know what's available, but don't do anything about it. Your employer benefits are part of your total compensation package — they are valuable to you while you are working, and your decision whether to take advantage of these programs or not will impact your retirement lifestyle.

employer pension

If your employer offers a registered pension plan, such as a Defined Contribution pension plan (DC) or a Defined Benefit pension plan (DB) or group RRSP, you should join as soon as you are eligible. If you're not sure whether your employer offers a pension, what kind of pension plan it is, and when you might become eligible to join, ask! Even if you work part time, you may be surprised to find that you can join the plan.

One significant benefit to joining an employer pension plan is that the employer will generally provide a matching contribution. This is free money to you that could easily double the amount of pension savings you accumulate.

However, to be entitled to the employer contributions, which is referred to as "being vested," you must be a member of the pension plan for a minimum time period. There is no vesting requirement if you participate in a group RRSP.

Although the vesting period for registered pension plans varies from province to province, it's usually a minimum of two years. Should you leave your employer or cease being a member of the pension before the vesting period is up, you will get back any contributions plus interest for a DB plan, or you will be entitled to the current market value of your investments if you belonged to a DC plan. Even if you don't stay in the pension plan long enough to be vested, it's still a great structured savings program. Over the years I have emphasized the importance of joining employer pension plans. Canadians who have not joined their company plans would often cite affordability or say that they're too young to think about retirement. These days the more common excuses are "This is my second career — I already have a pension from my previous employer so I don't need to join another one" or "I don't think I'll be working here very long, so it's not worth it to join." BUT if there is an element of matching contributions from your employer — free money — you are short-changing yourself by not taking advantage of it. I've seen too many situations where employees have decided to pass on joining the pension plan, only to find themselves regretting it later on.

What if you were eligible to join years ago but didn't? If you're part of a DB pension, in some cases you might be able to buy back some pension entitlement — which is like turning back the clock and catching up on your missed contributions. Even if your employer were to allow you to buy back pension entitlement for years when you were not part of the plan, it will cost you much more to do that today than if you had joined originally. Buying back pension years is a big decision, and you should speak to a financial advisor to determine if the benefits of an increased lifetime pension outweigh the cost of the buyback.

insurance programs

Large and small employers may offer a variety of group insurance policies that can be very cost-effective for the employee. Typical plans that are offered include life insurance, disability insurance, and health and dental insurance. Some plans share the cost between the employee and employer; others provide a minimum amount of coverage paid for by the employer, while employees pick up the additional cost of more extensive coverage. In either situation, you save money by taking advantage of reduced insurance costs. If you need more insurance, always consider buying the additional coverage through your employer group plan, and be sure to confirm whether you can continue to carry the coverage into retirement. Some employers will even pick up the cost of some minimum amount of life insurance coverage during retirement years for their pensioners.

health and dental plans

Many employees that have access to these plans don't use them to the fullest or are paying for benefits that are covered by a spouse's plan. Often we review the plan booklet when we join the company and don't pay much attention to benefits other than the coverage rates for prescriptions and dental coverage, so you might be paying for services that are covered by your benefit plan that you are not using. For instance, does your plan cover services such as massage, acupuncture, or a naturopath? Will the plan reimburse you for the cost of joining a fitness centre? When it comes to retirement planning, reducing your spending today will make more money available for retirement savings. If the company you work for will cover or subsidize the cost of services that you would have been spending money on anyway, then why not claim the benefits and save the money?

Benefit plans have become quite elaborate and, given the fact that many services once covered by provincial medical plans are no longer covered, many group plans pay partial or full coverage for the services. Most provincial medical plans cover the cost of eye examinations only for those under 18 and over 65. If you're between 19 and 64 and would like your eyes checked, you might find yourself having to pay for the examination. If you don't know what your health and dental plan covers, you may be paying for services that you can claim from your plan.

stock purchase plan

Being able to buy shares in your company is an attractive employee perk. Although you won't get to buy shares at a discount price, because you'll have to buy at the market price, you likely won't have to pay commissions on the purchase. Also, if your company provides any kind of matching, you'll get more shares as a result. For instance, if your company's stock purchase plan provides a matching of 20%, then for every $100 you contribute, your company would contribute $20. Even if the stock price does not go up in value, your total savings have gone up by 20%. To look at it another way, even if the shares were to go down in value by 16.6% you'd still break even.

Over a 20-year period, the growth in the value of the shares plus any dividends received on those shares can add considerably to your net worth. A word of caution here — you should review your personal net worth statement to determine how much of your total investment portfolio is in your company stock. Remember, you can have too much of a good thing (see chapter 11).

employee assistance program

Does your employer offer other services in addition to the standard health and insurance plans? Some companies offer what's referred to as an Employee Assistance Program (EAP), which provides a variety of services to employees. Some of the more common services include access to emergency child care, referral to medical experts for a second opinion, general information on healthy living and dealing with stress, and access to counsellors. The benefit of EAP programs is that they are usually free or offered at discounted rates to employees. If you don't take advantage of these services through the program when you need them, you are leaving free money on the table.

employee discounts

Employee discounts can extend beyond products and services offered by your own employer. In fact, many large companies and professional associations provide their employees and members with discounts on everything from mobile phone charges and computer purchases to hotel costs and car rental.

When saving for retirement, don't ignore opportunities to get extra money from your employer. Matched contributions help you accumulate money faster, but so does free access to services and employee discounts, because not having to pay for these things yourself will help you keep more of your money, to be used to pay off debts or save for the future.

rescue it!

☐ Ask what kind of pension plan your employer offers and how much it will contribute on your behalf. Find out when you are eligible to join. Then join!

☐ Review your benefits, such as health and dental benefits, and determine what services are available now and what services will be available during your retirement years.

☐ Join all employer plans that offer matching contributions.

CHAPTER 19

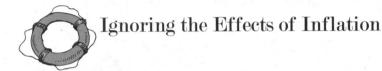 Ignoring the Effects of Inflation

Beware of the devastating effects that even a low rate of inflation has on your spending power over a 20- or 30-year retirement period.

WE ARE NO LONGER ACCUSTOMED to the double-digit inflation seen in previous years. In the last few years, the inflation rate has been relatively low, and so we've largely ignored it. In the spring of 2011, inflation began to rise, causing everyone to start to take notice of increased costs for fuel and energy. But how long can low inflation continue, and is it really as low as we're told it is?

what's inflation?

Inflation is an economics term that is used to describe a rise in the price of goods and services. Statistics Canada calculates the Consumer Price Index (CPI), which measures inflation for a set basket of about 600 goods and services, including food, housing, furniture, transportation, clothing, health care, and recreation. The percentage of those individual items in the total basket reflects the spending of a typical consumer. For instance, a bigger weighting is placed on food than on clothing. The CPI takes into consideration changes in the basket of goods as new products enter the marketplace.

It is beneficial to look at how prices have gone up over time to understand how inflation can impact our standard of living during the retirement years. Over the 20-year period from 1990 to 2010, while inflation averaged just 1.95% per year, purchasing power over that time was cut by 32%. In 2010, for every $10 worth of lifestyle spending, you would only get $6.80 worth in 1990 terms. If your disposable income during that period did not go up by inflation, the basket of goods you purchased in 1990 would not be able to be purchased again in 2010.

Impact of inflation[1]
$100 in 1914 — would cost $1,926.23 in 2010
$100 in 1955 — would cost $827.46 in 2010
$100 in 1990 — would cost $147.06 in 2010

Before we get too fixated on that, we need to consider one important point. The items in the CPI do not all go up by the same amount. You see, some of the products and services you buy may go up by less than the CPI average, and others may go up more than the CPI average. Let's look at the price of laptop computers. When they first became something a typical consumer would buy, they cost approximately $10,000. Today, laptops are no longer considered a luxury item, but are viewed as a basic item, like a pen and a calculator used to be. It's not unusual for a family to have more than one laptop computer, and since the price of a laptop can be as low as $500, one can correctly state that it's a case of price deflation, not inflation. Deflation on the price of the laptop means you have more disposable income left over, because you are only spending $500 on a computer, and not $10,000. However, the cost of other goods rises, and if the total price of your basket of goods goes up and your income is not keeping pace with inflation, you either have to reduce your spending or dip into your savings.

Understanding inflation and how it will impact your retirement lifestyle is critical in retirement planning. But the CPI represents inflation for a set basket of goods for a typical consumer, and does not necessarily reflect

---

[1] An inflation calculator can be found on the Bank of Canada Web site: English www.bankofcanada.ca /en/rates/inflation_calc.html and French www.hanqueducanada.ca/fr/taux/inflation_calc-f.html

what *your* basket of goods might look like. How similar to the typical consumer do you think you might be today? How about during your retirement years? Everyone has a personal inflation rate that is NOT exactly the same as the CPI. It's personal. And it's based on what you buy (different basket of goods), and how much of it you buy (different proportions). Your personal inflation rate will change over your lifetime, depending on how you spend your money.

different basket

Let me give you an example. First, assume the CPI is 2%. Now, we know that there are over 600 items in the CPI basket, but what if it only contained four items, weighted equally in the basket — education, health care, electronics, and food? If we assume that the price of education went up by 5% and health care went up by 8% and electronics went down 10% and food was up 5%, for an overall 2% rate of inflation, how would this impact your spending? Would you have more money to spend this year or less? It all depends on how you are spending your money. A family with children and high education costs would be quite concerned to find tuition fees up by 5%, but if they are buying electronics for the family, they may find lower prices than last year. That same family might not be so concerned with health care, because they have health insurance through their employer plans, and they're young and healthy anyway, so they don't spend much on health care. Alternatively, an older family who does not spend any money on education or electronics may be very concerned about the fact that health care costs are 8% more than last year.

Different-Sized Baskets

Even if two people buy the same things, they may not buy them in the same proportions. For instance, when I go grocery shopping I have to consider not only what items need to be on my shopping list but also the quantities of food two active teenagers might consume — one of whom is a 17-year-old boy. My son and daughter and husband enjoy eating steak.

On the other hand, my neighbour has two young children so our grocery lists will be quite different.

What if you do buy the same thing as your neighbour, but in a different proportion? How would that impact your personal inflation rate?

Item	Inflation rate	Family A	Family B
Education	5%	$ 50	$ 400
Health	8%	$ 700	$ 50
Electronics	10%	$ 50	$ 150
Food	5%	$ 200	$ 400
Total spending		$1,000	$1,000
Actual inflation rate		6.35%	2.9%
Additional money needed next year to be able to buy the same goods:		$63.50	$ 29

As you can see, even if you buy the same basket of goods, but in different proportions, you have a different inflation rate.

why is inflation such an issue?

Inflation will impact both how much you have available to save for retirement after paying your bills, and how much you can afford to spend during your retirement years. Inflation is a concern for you if the price of the goods and services that you buy go up by more than your after-tax income. In the above example, family A has to come up with an additional $63.50 after tax to buy the same basket of goods; otherwise, they will have to either cut back their spending or reduce the amount they are directing to savings.

During the working years, a pay raise or bonus might be enough to make up the difference. But that's not always the case. Ever wonder why, even though you get a raise, you don't have a lot more disposable income?

In retirement, increased costs mean you either spend less or dip into your savings at a much faster rate. Unfortunately, you can't rely on getting a pay raise.

Inflation can significantly impact your retirement lifestyle even if you have plenty of income coming in when you first retire. For instance, if your company pension is not inflation-adjusted, over a 20- and 25- and 30-year period, even a low inflation rate of only 2 or 3% will have a devastating effect on your purchasing power — it can cut it in half. So what may have once been considered a generous pension payment at the start of retirement won't go very far in 20 years if it's not adjusted to inflation.

Pensions such as CPP/QPP and OAS are inflation-adjusted based on the CPI, but we've just reviewed how the CPI may not be representative of what you'll be spending in retirement.

As for your investments, you need to be concerned with what's called the time value of money. Money will lose its value over time because of inflation eroding its purchasing power. That's why we invest our money so that it grows, and hopefully by more than the rate of inflation. In the very first example, if you didn't earn at least 1.95% after tax each year over a 20-year period, you would not have been able to buy the same basket of goods. That's why it's so important that your investments continue to grow even during your retirement years.

rescue it!

☐ Know how you are spending your money to better understand how inflation will impact you, both now and in retirement.

☐ Even though inflation is relatively low now, incorporate an inflation rate of 3 to 5% when projecting what your retirement spending might be (see sample inflation table at the end of this chapter) and adjust the projection when inflation increases above your estimates.

☐ Review your retirement savings and aim to earn at least the same as, and preferably more than, inflation on an after-tax basis.

☐ Determine if your employer pension is inflation-adjusted, and by how much, to understand how inflation might erode your pension during retirement.

Inflation table

This table shows what the price of $100 of expenses today will be in the future at various rates of inflation. Amounts are rounded.

Number of years	Inflation rate			
	2%	3%	4%	5%
1	$102	$103	$104	$105
5	$110	$116	$122	$128
10	$122	$134	$148	$163
15	$135	$156	$180	$208
20	$149	$181	$219	$265
25	$164	$209	$267	$339
30	$167	$215	$278	$356

CHAPTER 20

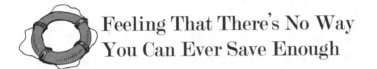 Feeling That There's No Way
You Can Ever Save Enough

*The big question is — how much is enough for YOU? I bet you
don't need $1 million.*

SAVING FOR RETIREMENT TAKES DEDICATION and motivation.
Feeling there's no way you can ever save enough won't help you get closer
to your goal and may lead you to give up on saving entirely.

Why is it that Canadians *in all income brackets* feel they'll never be able
to save enough to retire? No matter what group I'm talking to, not having
enough money to retire is always the number one concern. Pay attention
to the headlines in the news — I have yet to see one that says the majority
of Canadians feel they have saved enough for retirement.

There's a lot of pressure on us to *save enough.* But how much is
enough? How large a nest egg do you need to accumulate before you can
live the kind of retirement you want? That's the million dollar question!
But I bet you don't need a million dollars. There is no one-size-fits-all
solution.

Let's put it in perspective. If you were to live 5 years in retirement,
then you would need to have saved a lot less than if you were to live
30 years in retirement. But what if, in those 5 short years, you require
significant medical care? How much would you need then? That's a different number altogether. If you have a very generous defined benefit

pension plan that is fully indexed, you may not need a lot of other personal savings to meet your income needs. But if you don't have a pension plan at all, it's all up to you.

How much you will need to have saved for your retirement years is based on your lifestyle and a bit of luck. Take a look at your life today. How much is it costing you? Where is your money going? What might you not have to pay for in the future (such as kids, mortgage), and what new costs might arise (health care, travel)?

When determining how much to save, financial planners make recommendations based on the general desire to maintain your current lifestyle during your retirement years.

Ask yourself — could you continue to live the same kind of lifestyle that you are living right now if your only source of income is from your pensions and personal savings? Remember, you could be spending almost a third of your life in retirement — will your money last that long? It depends. Do you want a basic, simple retirement where you're content to live within your means, do you want to maintain your current lifestyle, or are you hoping for a deluxe, supersized retirement, where you can do all the things you've always wanted to do but never got a chance?

Even the best-laid plans require some additional contingency planning. There are a lot of unknowns that can arise and are difficult to plan for, such as:

- Living a long time — your nest egg has to stretch for more years.

- Inflation — your purchasing power can be eroded, which means you'll be spending more money each year without buying more.

- Health care needs — even a few years of ill health can greatly reduce your savings.

- Stock market declines — making withdrawals from your investments during periods of declining markets will chew up your savings faster.

- Helping others — children or grandchildren may need financial support.

- Where you live — living in a more expensive city rather than a smaller town can impact your cost of living.

determining the size of your nest egg

There are many free calculators on the Internet that you can use to determine how long your nest egg will last, and they all use very different assumptions. The main thing is that it's a good idea to have an estimate — a ballpark amount that you need to have saved so there are no big surprises when you reach your retirement. Here's a quick way to come up with a saving goal:

If you need to withdraw $20,000 per year from your personal savings to supplement your pensions for 25 years (age 65 to 90), you should have a nest egg equal to approximately $500,000, assuming a 5% initial withdrawal rate. If you delay your retirement date, your savings don't need to last as long, so to be able to withdraw $20,000 per year for 20 years, you only need to have saved $400,000 assuming a 5% initial withdrawal rate.

If the amount you need is much lower, say $10,000 per year for 25 years, you should have a nest egg equal to $250,000 with a 4% initial withdrawal rate. When doing a ballpark calculation, a rule of thumb which uses a hypothetical initial withdrawal rate of anywhere between 3 and 5% is quite common.

The closer you are to retirement, the better you will be at predicting how much you'll need, at least in the early years.

working toward your savings requirement

Step 1 — How much annual income do you need from your personal savings, over and above income from government and company pensions, during your retirement years? (Review chapters 1 to 3.)

Step 2 — How many retirement years do you need the income for? It is customary to plan to age 90, though none of us ever know how long we will live.

Step 3 — How much money do you need to have saved at the start of retirement so that you can withdraw your annual income need? You can find a financial calculator on the Internet to do this, or you can ask your financial advisor to help you calculate it.

Step 4 — How much money have you saved so far?

Step 5 — How many years are you from retirement or, in other words, when (how soon) do you want to retire and start making withdrawals from your personal savings?

Step 6 — Calculate how much you need to save between now and retirement, and what kind of return you need to earn to get you to your savings goal. Again, you may want to use a financial calculator to do this, or ask your financial advisor to help you calculate this amount.

incorporating your hidden pension

When we looked at the retirement income need, we ignored pensions such as CPP/QPP, OAS, and your employer pension. That is to say, we looked only at the income that was going to come from your personal savings. At one end of the spectrum, you have no pensions whatsoever, and all of your retirement income does need to come from your personal savings. At the other end of the spectrum, your pensions are sufficient, so that you do not need any personal savings at all. When might the latter occur? This might be the case for those with very generous employer pension plans but also for those who are very low income earners during their working years and CPP/QPP and OAS are sufficient to meet their retirement income needs. When calculating your pension income, don't forget about your hidden pension – Old Age Security. A Canadian resident who does not have any employment earnings during their working years will at the very least be entitled to receive an OAS pension starting at age 65, based on the number of years they were a Canadian resident. The maximum OAS payable is approximately $6,300 per year and, although it is a very small amount, it is a pension that we are not required to contribute to and for which we don't receive a pension statement. This is why I call it your *hidden pension*.

In addition to saving for retirement, don't forget that entering retirement debt-free is just as important, so that you won't have to use your retirement income to make principal and interest payments. When determining how much you need to save for retirement, you need to include all of your sources of retirement income and your cash flow — in other words, look at your savings and your spending.

rescue it!

☐ Using the formula in this chapter, determine what size of nest egg you need — you may not need $1 million.

☐ Do a detailed estimate of your expenses during retirement.

☐ Determine all of your sources of retirement income, such as government and company pensions — don't forget OAS, even for a spouse who is not currently working.

☐ Review your personal net worth statement to get an idea of how much personal savings will be available to you to help fund your savings goal.

PART 5

pensions

CHAPTER 21

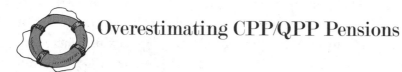 Overestimating CPP/QPP Pensions

What you expect to collect from CPP/QPP may not be what you get.

CANADIANS ARE OFTEN UNSURE about how much of a pension they will be entitled to under the Canada Pension Plan (CPP)/Quebec Pension Plan (QPP). It is important to understand how much you are entitled to, and to include a reasonable estimate in your retirement income equation. Not knowing how much pension income you will receive from CPP/QPP can result in overestimating how much you can spend during your retirement, as well as underestimating how much you need to save personally to fund retirement costs.

Not long ago I conducted a retirement planning seminar for a group of young employees. I asked them how many had started to save for retirement. Not many hands went up — that's when I realized that individuals either forget that they have been saving for retirement by contributing to the CPP/QPP, or they discount the value that this pension will provide. When asked how much they thought they could expect to receive at retirement, most had no idea whatsoever. Older Canadians have the opposite view — they tend to overestimate how much they will be entitled to receive, and to their detriment often make plans and decisions with inaccurate information.

the details

The Canada Pension Plan and the Quebec Pension Plan (CPP/QPP) began in 1966. Which plan you pay into — CPP or QPP — depends on where you **work**, not where you live. If you work in Quebec, you pay into the QPP. If you work in any other province or territory, you pay into the CPP. If during your working years you work in Quebec as well as another province or territory, you will pay into **both** plans, but you will receive only one pension; which one depends on where you live at the time you apply for the pension. If you live in Quebec, you would apply for QPP, if you live elsewhere in Canada, you would apply for CPP. If you live outside Canada at the time you are applying for the pension, you apply to the last province in which you lived before you left the country.

The CPP/QPP is a defined benefit pension plan and falls into the category of what I consider a "true pension" plan, because it pays a guaranteed income for life. It is available to all workers age 18 and over, including those who are self-employed who have made at least one contribution and are at least 60 years of age. Both the employee and employer make equivalent contributions to the plan (if you are self-employed, you will contribute both the employee and employer portion). The pension is designed to replace approximately 25% of the year's maximum pensionable earnings (YMPE). The YPME for 2011 is $48,300, which means you will have reached your maximum contributions to CPP/QPP once you've earned the YPME. However, if you do not work, or if you do not earn more than $3,500 in any particular year, you will be exempt from making contributions, and you will not earn any pension credit for that year.

not automatic at retirement

It is important to note that *you must apply* to receive the CPP/QPP, as it does not start automatically when you retire. If you have forgotten to apply (or think you know someone who might have forgotten), you can apply late and ask for retroactive payments for up to 12 months, or longer if the reason the application was not made earlier was because of incapacity.

getting the maximum pension

Over $62 billion in benefits are paid annually to millions of Canadians. However, not everyone gets the same pension payment. For 2011, the *maximum* pension payable at age 65 is $960 per month, whereas the *average* amount paid in 2010 was $504.88 per month. This reflects the fact that not everyone has earned sufficient pension credits to collect the maximum amount.

The amount of pension you will be eligible to receive is based on how long you contributed to the plan, how much you contributed over those years, and your age at the time you start collecting your pension. The CPP/QPP contributory period starts when you are 18 years of age (or January 1, 1966, whichever is later), and ends when you start getting your retirement pension or disability pension, or when you turn 70, or when you die. Since the CPP/QPP entitlement is based on career average contributions, based on income level, having too many low-income years will reduce what your final pension will be. To compensate for that, there is a "general low earnings drop-out" provision that excludes up to seven low income earning years from the pension calculation. By 2012, new rules will exclude up to seven and a half years, and by 2014, up to eight years are excluded. The low earnings drop out will benefit those who were in school, on leave of absence for a period of time, or had low income for any other reason. If you were out of the workforce to raise children under seven years of age, there is an additional "child rearing drop-out" provision that excludes those years from the pension calculation. These drop-out provisions increase your final pension entitlement.

Not contributing the maximum is one key reason why pensions are lower than expected. This is especially a concern for immigrants to Canada, but it's important to note that Canada has international social-security agreements with many countries that can help you get pensions or benefits from either country. For example, if you did not live or work long enough in another country to qualify under its rules, the time you spent there and the contributions you made may be added to your time and/or contributions in Canada to allow you to meet the eligibility requirements. If you have lived and worked in another country, this is something that cannot be ignored, as it will impact the total income you may be eligible to receive.

Women are another group who may be faced with lower pensions due to having taken time off or reducing work hours to care for aging family members. For them, it would be a good idea to consider adding a few more years of work to build up additional CPP/QPP pensions.

early pension versus late pension

Recent changes to the CPP and proposed changes to the QPP have caused additional confusion over how much your CPP/QPP pension will be. The CPP/QPP pays a normal retirement pension at age 65. Those who wish to start collecting CPP/QPP earlier can receive their first payment as early as age 60, at a reduced amount, and those who wish to delay can start collecting as late as age 70, at an increased amount. Prior to 2010, the CPP/QPP would be reduced by 0.5% for every month before your 65th birthday that the CPP/QPP was started, and increased by 0.5% for every month after your 65th birthday that the CPP/QPP was started. Beginning in 2011, the rules for early or late CPP/QPP will change so that there is an added benefit in delaying CPP/QPP to after age 65. When the amounts are fully phased in, there will be a 0.6% per month reduction for early pensions and a 0.7% increase for late pensions. This means that, by 2013, an individual who starts receiving their CPP/QPP pension at the age of 70 will receive 42% more than if they had taken it at 65.

Example: If you are 66 in 2011 but have not applied to receive CPP, you have an important decision to make. You can either apply for a late CPP pension and receive 6.84% more (0.57% more for the each of the 12 months you are over 65) for the rest of your life, or apply for 12 months of retroactive payments. This decision involves an analysis of longevity — how long you think you will live — because the longer you live, the more attractive the higher pension starting at age 66 will be, as well as income need — whether you need the lump-sum payment immediately.

CPP/QPP Changes

		prior to 2011	2011	2012	2013	2014	2015	2016
Reduction for	CPP	.50%	.50%	.52%	.54%	.56%	.58%	.60%
early pension	QPP		.50%	.50%	.50%	.53%	.56%	.60%
Increase for	CPP	.50%	.57%	.64%	.70%	.70%	.70%	.70%
late pension	QPP		.50%	.50%	.70%	.70%	.70%	.70%

By 2016, once all of the amounts for early and late pensions are fully phased in for CPP and QPP, the difference in the amount that will be received by a 60-year-old taking an early pension and a 70-year-old taking a late pension is significant. Using the maximum CPP/QPP retirement pension at age 65 for 2011 for comparison ($960), by 2016 the monthly lifetime pension a 60-year-old will receive is $614.40, and the pension a 70-year-old will receive is $1,363. Which of the two individuals will collect more total payments during their lifetime will be based on how long each lives and what the 60-year-old does with the early pension. If, rather than spending it, the 60-year-old saves the pension payment, you would need to factor in how much those extra years of payments will grow to. One never knows what the future will bring, so there is no correct answer to the question of whether one should take CPP/QPP early or late.

working while collecting CPP — more new rules

Another twist to starting CPP early has to do with those who start collecting a pension but continue to work. New rules now allow individuals to collect CPP between age 60 and 70, and to continue working and contributing to CPP. Contributions while working are mandatory if you are under age 65, and voluntary if you are over age 65. These extra contributions will increase your CPP entitlement in future years. This change to the rules will not affect those who are already receiving CPP, or those who take their CPP retirement pensions before 2012. People take many different paths to retirement today, and the changes to the CPP better recognize that retirement is often a process that occurs in stages, rather than a one-time event.

other payments from CPP/QPP

In addition to a retirement pension, CPP/QPP pays the following types of pensions:

- a disability benefit — a monthly benefit available to qualified CPP/QPP contributors and their dependent children.

- a survivor benefit — a monthly benefit available for a deceased contributor's surviving spouse or common-law partner and dependent children.

Survivor Benefits

While there are several types of survivor benefits that may be available on the death of a CPP/QPP contributor, not everyone will be entitled to the same amount. If you have a contributory period of more than 9 years, you must have contributed for the lesser of:

- One-third of the calendar years in your contributory period (i.e., a minimum of 3 years), or

- 10 calendar years.

   Survivor benefits include:

- a death benefit, which is a one-time payment of up to $2,500 that is paid to, or on behalf of, the estate of a deceased CPP/QPP contributor;

- a survivor's pension, which is a reduced monthly pension paid to the surviving spouse or common-law partner of a deceased contributor; and

- a children's benefit, which is a monthly benefit for dependent children of a deceased contributor who are under age 25 if they are attending school full time.

In regard to the survivor pension, it's important to note that for a couple where both individuals are collecting the CPP/QPP, the maximum the survivor can collect from their own and a survivor pension is the maximum pension entitlement for an individual. What this means for couples who are both collecting the maximum pension is that after the death of one spouse, the survivor will only collect one individual pension benefit. This can cause a significant shortfall in income for the survivor.

rescue it!

☐ Contact Service Canada or Régie des rentes du Québec and ask for a pension statement; this will give you an idea of the size of pension you may be entitled to receive: www.servicecanada.gc.ca/eng/isp/common/proceed/socinfo.shtml or www.rrq.gouv.qc.ca/en/accueil/Pages/accueil_regie.aspx

☐ Apply for CPP/QPP at least six months before you would like to start receiving your pension.

☐ If you worked in another country, contact Service Canada or Service Quebec to determine if there is a social security agreement that will help increase your pension amount.

CHAPTER 22

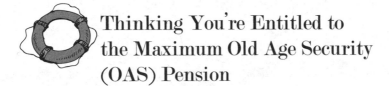 Thinking You're Entitled to
the Maximum Old Age Security
(OAS) Pension

*Well, aren't you? Surprise, you may not qualify for the maximum
payment and, if you do, you may not get to keep all of it!*

CANADIANS ARE GENERALLY FAMILIAR with the Old Age Security
(OAS) pension. Indeed, most of our friends and family over the age of 65
are likely collecting at least some OAS right now. The *Old Age Security Act*
came into force in 1952. Since then, there have been many changes to the act,
such as the introduction of inflation indexing in 1972, and the extension of
benefits to same-sex common-law partners in 2000. The OAS pension is paid
out of general tax revenues — you don't ever make contributions directly into
an "OAS plan" for your retirement. Because it is a social security type of plan
rather than a savings/income replacement plan, eligibility is based entirely
on your age and on Canadian residency, not on income or earnings.

The OAS is another one of those "true pensions" — a certain amount is
paid to you each and every month, starting at age 65, and continues for the
rest of your life. It is inflation-adjusted, which means the pension payment
will be reviewed every quarter and may be increased to reflect an increase
in the cost of living as measured by the Consumer Price Index.

The maximum pension entitlement under OAS is not a large amount,
so don't go planning an exotic retirement. The maximum annual OAS

pension in 2011 is approximately $6,300, so a couple who are eligible to receive the maximum pension would receive approximately $12,600 per year from OAS. While many people believe that they are entitled to the maximum amount, the average individual pension paid in 2010 was less than that — closer to $5,900. It's important to understand how OAS is calculated to better plan your retirement income needs.

rule #1 — your residency

The OAS eligibility is based on 40 equal portions, and to get the maximum pension you need to have lived in Canada for 40 years after your 18th birthday. If you were born in Canada and lived here your entire life, you will be entitled to the full pension amount at age 65. It becomes more complicated if you immigrated to Canada as an adult or, more specifically, any time after age 25, because it will be impossible for you to meet the 40-year residency requirement by age 65. This does not mean you won't get any OAS; you'll just get a smaller amount, based on the number of years you were a resident. Depending on where you lived outside Canada, you may qualify to receive social security from that country as well as from Canada.

Summary of Rules:

To qualify for OAS you must:

- be 65 years of age or older

- live in Canada and be a Canadian citizen or a legal resident at the time your pension application is approved

- have lived in Canada for at least 10 years after turning 18 to get a partial pension

- have lived in Canada for at least 40 years after turning 18 to get the maximum pension

If you have lived in a country that has a social security agreement with Canada, you may be entitled to additional benefits.

Some people do not believe they qualify for OAS, and as a result fail to apply for it. And that's an important thing to note, because you do in fact *have to apply* to receive the OAS pension — it's not automatic once you turn 65. If you have forgotten to apply, or suspect someone you know might have, keep in mind that OAS will pay a retroactive pension for up to one year.

rule #2 — income taxation

Like most things, the OAS pension is taxable, although I still encounter many who believe it is tax-free. Although it's true that there is usually no withholding tax on your pension payment, the pension is taxable as ordinary income. If you prefer to have withholding tax taken at source, you can ask the government to do so; this is not something I would recommend unless you usually have a large income tax balance owing when you file your tax return. The rate of income tax you pay will depend on the total of all your other income. If your income for the year is very low, you might get away with paying little or no tax on your OAS, because the basic personal credit, the age credit, the medical expenses credit (and possibly others), which reduce income tax, may eliminate your tax liability entirely. That's likely the reason why people assume there's no tax on OAS pensions. However, it doesn't take much income to take you above the amounts covered by those credits.

rule #3 — income threshold and clawback

In addition to being subject to income taxes, the OAS is subject to another, more harmful, rule: the OAS clawback, which could also significantly reduce the amount of OAS pension you actually get to keep. How so? Well, for one thing, there's no way to stop the OAS pension from being included in your income tax return. You can't split it with a spouse or partner, you can't have it paid to a trust or corporation, you can't assign it to someone else — so you're stuck with including it in your tax return. And if you have too much other income, such as a company pension, CPP/QPP, rental income, RRIF withdrawals, or interest, dividends or capital gains from your investments, some or all of the OAS pension will have to be repaid to the government (and that's called the OAS clawback). The OAS clawback starts when net income goes above the annual income threshold amount. For 2011 the net income threshold is $67,668. Every dollar of income above that threshold results in a 15-cent repayment of OAS. Go over the income amount by $100 and the clawback is $15. Go over the threshold by $10,000 and the clawback is $1,500, and so on until the entire OAS pension is "clawed back" when net income is $109,607 or more. A detailed discussion of how to keep more of your OAS is found in chapter 36.

rule #4 — retirement outside canada

If you're going to be counting on an OAS pension, and you're planning on ceasing Canadian residency, you might have a surprise in store. Once you start collecting OAS, you'll continue to receive it for the rest of your life, even if you move out of Canada, BUT only if you had lived in Canada for at least 20 years after your 18th birthday at the time you start collecting OAS. If you don't meet that requirement, your pension will only be payable for the month of departure plus six months after you have left Canada. After that six-month period, you won't receive any further OAS payments until you return to Canada and re-establish your eligibility. If you need the OAS pension to help fund your retirement outside Canada, you'll have to start thinking about how the decision to move will impact your eligibility and start saving more today to compensate for the lost income.

Retirees living outside Canada:

- You must be 65 years of age or older.
- You must have been a Canadian citizen or a legal resident of Canada the day before you left Canada.
- You must have lived in Canada for at least 20 years after turning 18.

rescue it!

☐ Apply for OAS at least six months prior to your 65th birthday. If you are over 65 and have not applied, do so immediately, and ask for retroactive payments for up to 11 months.

☐ If you have lived outside Canada, you should determine if Canada has a social security agreement with the country where you lived that might increase your OAS entitlement. www.servicecanada.gc.ca/eng/isp/ibfa/intlben.shtml

CHAPTER 23

 Relying Too Heavily on Your
Company Pension

Only a third of Canadians have an employer pension plan.
Even for them, having such a plan does not guarantee
retirement security.

ARE YOU AMONG THE FEW CANADIANS that have a company pension plan? The lack of access to employer pension plans has prompted the federal and provincial governments to examine and discuss options such as increasing the CPP/QPP and other solutions to make pensions more accessible to small employers and those who are self-employed. But even those with employer pension plans today are not guaranteed retirement security. It's very important to understand and evaluate the kind of pension you have, because relying too heavily on your company pension plan may cause you to under-save for retirement.

what does your pension look like?

What kind of pension arrangement do you have? Is it a Defined Benefit (DB) pension plan, a Defined Contribution (DC) pension plan, or is it a group RRSP? These may all sound similar, but they are uniquely different from one another, and these differences can impact the kind of pension you will be entitled to upon retirement and for the rest of your life.

How can you recognize the difference between a DB, a DC, and a group RRSP — *what is defined or set?* With the DB plan, your benefit — otherwise known as your pension — is determined based on your years of service, your income and a pre-determined *factor* set by your particular pension plan. With a DC plan, the required contribution to the plan is defined, not the ultimate pension payment you will receive — that is unknown. Both DB and DC plans are considered registered pension plans (RPPs) and are regulated by provincial or federal legislation. On the other hand, a group RRSP is not covered by pension regulations, but rather falls under the *Income Tax Act* and is treated virtually the same way as an ordinary RRSP that you might have, except that contributions to this plan may come from both you and your employer. Another clue as to what kind of plan you have has to do with the contributions to the plan. If you are getting a pension adjustment reported on your T4 slip, then you are in an RPP, whereas if you receive an RRSP receipt for contributions at tax time, your plan is a group RRSP. If you're not really sure what kind of pension you have, you need to review your employee benefit book as soon as possible. Without knowing the type of pension plan you have, or the amount of pension you will be eligible to collect, you cannot determine how much, if anything, you need to save on your own.

What kind of pension plan do you have? Here are the basic characteristics of each.

defined benefit pension plan (DB)

A DB plan is what most people consider a true pension plan. Contributions are made into a pool on your behalf. The contributions are invested by the pension fund, and at retirement, a certain amount (i.e., a pension) is payable to the employee for the rest of their life. The size of the pension is calculated using three key variables: income, years of service, and a certain pension factor that can be as high as 2%. Let me give you an example: If you are earning $40,000 per year, you worked for your employer for 30 years, and your employer pension plan uses a pension factor of 2%, you would be entitled to receive a pension of $24,000 per year for the rest of your life. ($40,000 times 30 years times 2%). One thing to note is that even if there are stock market declines that affect the amount of money invested in the pension plan, your employer (and not you) is responsible for making sure there is enough money in the pension plan to continue paying the promised pension to all of the members of the plan. (More on this in the next chapter.)

There are important questions to ask about your DB pension:

- Who contributes to the pension plan? Are you and your employer both required to make contributions, or is your employer funding the entire pension? In some cases, employers fund only a portion of the pension and employees can elect to make voluntary contributions to the plan. If your plan allows you to contribute and you are not doing so, then your final pension will not be as high as you might think.

- What's the maximum pension payable from your employer pension plan? How does this compare to the CRA rules? The CRA has established a maximum pension that can be paid from an RRP. While the maximum amount for 2011 is $2,552.22 per year of pensionable service, your pension agreement may not reflect the most current legislation. High income earners should take the time to review their pension entitlement to determine if they will be collecting as much as they believe they will.

- To get an idea of the pension you might be entitled to, you need to know how the pension is calculated. Of the three factors that determine the pension payment, you have the most influence over your years of service (hopefully) and your average earnings. So let's take a look at how important your earnings are in determining your pension. Is the calculation based on your top earning years, your final years, or some other combination? If the calculation will include any lower income years, then you want to make sure you minimize those lower income years. So if you think you might want to slowly reduce your workload as you ease into retirement, and take a lower pay, you might be jeopardizing your final pension payment.

- Is your pension payment inflation-adjusted, and if so, by how much? Inflation can be the death of your pension — it can result in "the disappearing pension." Even at a 2% rate of inflation, a $2,000-per-month pension today needs to grow to $2,972 in 20 years and to $3,623 in 30 years just so you can buy the same basket of goods in the future as you can today. If your pension is not inflation-adjusted, personal savings will have to make up the shortfall.

- Is your pension integrated with CPP/QPP or OAS, and what does that mean? Pensions that are integrated with CPP/QPP/OAS usually pay a higher amount prior to age 65 and then a lower amount after age 65.

- Is there an early retirement penalty? Normal retirement age is 65, but your pension may allow you to collect a retirement pension before that age. Find out at what age you can start collecting a pension from the plan. If there is an early retirement penalty, how is it calculated? If the penalty is severe, you may want to rethink early retirement, because you may not want to lock in to a lower pension for the rest of your life. Does your pension plan allow you to collect a pension and continue working and contributing to the same pension plan so you can increase your final pension payment? This is a relatively new concept discussed further in chapter 42.

- Survivor pension — who qualifies as a survivor and how much will they be entitled to? The survivor might be eligible to receive significantly less than the employee, which could impact their retirement. Another thing to consider is that if you are separated and not divorced, your spouse or former spouse may be entitled to a survivor pension on your death. This will cause your pension amount to be lower during your lifetime. If you find yourself in this situation, it is wise to seek legal advice to determine what options are available to you.

defined contribution pension plan (DC)

With a DC pension plan, contributions are made into the plan, but rather than pooling the money together, your contributions are invested separately from everyone else's. You may have the option to choose to invest the money however you wish, or your employer may provide you with a few options, including a default investment strategy. Depending on the investment chosen, the value of the DC plan may go up or down with the stock market. Your final pension income will be based on the value of the DC plan at your retirement, and will depend on what maturity option you choose for your plan.

You may decide to use the accumulated funds to create a guaranteed payment for life for yourself that is similar to a DB pension, by buying a life annuity or any other product that provides reliable income for life. These products give you peace of mind that no matter how long you live, you will receive an income. Alternatively, you may prefer to continue to manage the DC money throughout your retirement years in a locked-in version of an RRSP or RRIF and withdraw the required minimum amount from the plan each year. With this option, there is an increased level of uncertainty both while you are saving for retirement and while you are in retirement, because you will be solely responsible for the performance of the investments and ultimately the size of your pension. What if you invest too conservatively and do not earn much of a return? What if you invest too aggressively and there is a stock market decline like what happened in late 2008? One thing to note is that on the death of the employee, any funds left in the locked-in account will be available to a surviving spouse, child or other named beneficiary.

Having an employer pension is certainly better than not having one at all, but having one does not guarantee you'll have enough money in retirement. Pensions rarely provide all of the income a person needs during retirement, and you may find that you do need additional personal savings to fill the gap between the income you need and the income that you will receive. If you are managing your own pension funds, the increased uncertainty of future market performance makes for a less certain retirement, despite the fact that you may be very successful at money management.

other pension options

In addition to registered pension plans such as DC and DB plans, some employers offer their employees an opportunity to save for retirement by using group RRSPs. Contributions to the group RRSP may be made by the employer only, or from a combination of employee and employer contributions. A group RRSP is the same as an ordinary RRSP — meaning you get an annual RRSP contribution receipt for amounts you and your employer contribute to the plan. Because the group RRSP is not regulated by pension legislation, there is no vesting period, so you are entitled to all employer contributions as soon as they are made. At retirement, the funds in the group RRSP can be rolled into an ordinary RRIF — it does not have to be locked-in because the account is not regulated by pension legislation.

In 2010 the federal government released draft proposals to introduce a Pooled Registered Pension Plan (PRPP). Unlike the group RRSP, the PRPP would be regulated by pension legislation and would be similar to a DC plan. At the time of writing, it was still unclear precisely how this plan will be structured; for instance, if the PRPP will adopt the pension rules of the particular province or if it will have its own pension legislation. In March 2011 the Quebec government issued draft legislation that would intro- duce a plan similar to the PRPP called the Voluntary Registered Savings Plan (VRSP). If passed into legislation, the PRPP and VRSP will provide Canadians with additional options for building retirement savings.

rescue it!

☐ Find out whether you are a member of a Defined Benefit (DB) or Defined Contribution (DC) plan or a group RRSP.

☐ Contribute as much as you can to your company pension plan.

☐ If you have a DB plan, know your estimated pension amount. Is it inflation-adjusted?

☐ If you have a DC plan, make sure the money is invested in line with your risk tolerance. If you are unsure about your investment options or how to invest your money, contact your plan administrator or your financial advisor.

CHAPTER 24

 Making the Wrong Choices with Your Defined Benefit Pension on Retirement

If you have the choice of a taking a monthly pension for the rest of your life or taking your money out of the pension plan and investing it yourself, choose wisely!

UPON RETIREMENT, A MEMBER of a Defined Benefit pension plan will be entitled to receive a pension for life based on their years of service and employment earnings. In certain circumstances, employees or former employees may be given the choice to either stay in the company pension plan and receive a lifetime monthly pension at retirement, or take the commuted value of their accrued pension benefits out of the pension plan. This is one decision that should not be taken lightly. Not only is this decision irrevocable, but the wrong decision can have a devastating impact on your retirement lifestyle.

Imagine your employer offers you a choice between a guaranteed pension of $2,000 per month for the rest of your life, or a one-time lump-sum commuted value of $200,000 at retirement. If you choose the commuted value, you have the option of buying a life annuity or rolling the funds tax-free into a locked-in registered account. One key element is that you will be responsible to invest this money wisely and you are solely responsible to ensure that the money will last you the rest of your life. What option would you choose?

In theory, the employee and the employer should be indifferent between choosing the monthly lifetime pension or the commuted value lump sum. This is because the calculation used to determine the amount of commuted value that will be offered to the employee will take all elements of the pension plan into consideration, such as survivor options and inflation protection, and it will also make some assumptions around longevity. But theory and reality don't always mesh. There are many variables to consider that make this a difficult decision. What makes the lump sum offer seem attractive is that for many, such a large amount of money can feel like winning the lottery. Although such a windfall can be tempting, there are several important factors that need to be considered before making this irrevocable decision.

Let's look at what needs to be considered:

- **To what age will you live?** I often stress that without this key number, it's very hard to make important financial decisions around investing, spending, and your pension. Unfortunately, unless you are in ill health, this number is almost impossible to determine. Consider that a guaranteed pension for life means that no matter how long you live, you will be entitled to collect a monthly pension from your employer. There's definitely some peace of mind in knowing that your money will never run out. However, what if you are ill and have a short retirement life? A pension for life might not be that appealing for you because you don't know how much longer you will live and how many pension cheques you'll collect. If you believe in the old saying "A bird in the hand is worth two in the bush," you might opt to take the commuted value rather than the lifetime pension. A large lump sum of money today might seem more valuable to you than the promise of an annual payment for the rest of your life, especially if you're not confident you'll have a long life.

- **Is there a survivor pension?** If you opt for the monthly pension, you need to find out if there is a survivor pension benefit, and if so, how much it is. Are payments guaranteed for a certain minimum number of years, or for the life of the survivor? Survivor pension payments generally continue only to a spouse. So, if you don't have a spouse and your only beneficiary is a child, would the child be entitled to some sort of payment from the pension plan upon your death? The consideration here is, do you wish to leave an estate? If you take the lump-sum commuted value option, any amount left unspent upon your death is available to be paid to your chosen beneficiary, whether it is a child, family member, or charity.

- **What about certainty of payment? Will your company still be around to pay the future pension?** This question might be harder to answer, but you need to think about how secure your employer's business might be in the future. Is the pension fully funded, which means is there enough money in the pension plan to pay pensions for the members? You may never have thought to ask this question, but it's not unusual for a DB pension to not be fully funded. This often happens when the investment returns in the pension plan are less than anticipated and result in a shortfall in the plan. While the employer is obligated to eliminate the shortfall by making additional contributions, some pensions have up to 10 years to fund the shortfall, so as you may imagine, underfunded pensions are not uncommon. During the 2008–2009 market crash, the number of underfunded pensions increased substantially. To better understand what this means for plan members, let's review a well-documented Canadian example. Nortel had an underfunded DB pension plan, and when the company began to experience financial difficulty and eventually filed for bankruptcy, the pension plan did not have enough money to pay the promised pensions to employees and current retirees. Retirees were faced with having their lifetime pension income cut, resulting in a very different retirement than they had anticipated.

- **Are there post-retirement benefits?** In some cases, a former employee collecting a company pension will be entitled to additional post-retirement benefits, such as extended health and dental care, life insurance, and possibly even employee discounts. These types of benefits can be worth thousands of dollars per year, and are not usually available to employees who take the lump-sum commuted value option. However, post-retirement benefits are not guaranteed, and a company can change or amend coverage at any time. Nonetheless, the value of these programs must be factored into your decision to take a lifetime pension or a lump-sum commuted value.

- **Is there inflation protection? Will your monthly pension increase based on inflation?** Inflation protection is often what I consider a deal-breaker when you're making the lifetime pension versus commuted value decision. It's hard to beat a pension that offers full inflation protection when you're investing your own money. Before making any decision, ask if your plan provides inflation protection, and how it is calculated, as some may be quite complex. While some plans offer some inflation protection, it may not be sufficient to ensure your purchasing power remains constant. For instance, a pension that has a maximum 3% inflation protection per year means if inflation is 5%, your pension will increase by only 3% and as a result you are not fully maintaining your purchasing power. Over a 10-year period, a shortfall of 2% inflation coverage per year can reduce your purchasing power by 17%. Inflation protection is a luxury that is hard to replicate, but not all plans provide the same level of inflation protection. Find out whether your pension is inflation protected, and how it is calculated, as this can be a compelling reason to stay in the pension plan.

- **Will there be an excess tax-deferred rollover amount?** In some situations, the commuted value might be so substantial that it exceeds the amount that you can roll tax-free into a locked-in registered account called a locked-in retirement account or locked-in RSP. There are two options for the excess amount. It can be taken in cash immediately, and you'll have to pay tax on it in the year you receive it. This means there will be a lower amount remaining after tax to be invested during your retirement years. Alternatively, if you have unused RRSP room, the excess cash portion can be contributed into your own RRSP.

- **What about investment expertise? If you take the commuted value out of the pension, how will you invest the money? Can you "beat the pension"?** That partially depends on the internal rate of return used by the pension plan to calculate the commuted value. For 2010, the standard internal rate of return used by registered pension plans was 5%. Therefore, if you are a conservative investor, and you don't think you can get more than a 5% return, then you need to think seriously about whether the lump sum is the best alternative for you. You also need to consider whether you have the time and expertise to manage this money in the years leading up to and during retirement. Individuals who took the commuted value option in 2008 found themselves regretting their choice when they saw the bulk of their retirement savings shrink before their eyes. While the market has returned to previous levels, one never knows what the future will bring. Can your retirement savings withstand potential future periods of low or negative returns while you are making annual withdrawals? You have a finite amount of money to last you the rest of your life, and a few years of negative returns during the spending phase can cause your money to run out before you do.

- **Can you buy a better pension?** How much would it cost to replace the lifetime pension with a product that pays a guaranteed lifetime payment? There are products out there, such as a life annuity, that closely resemble your company pension plan. With a life annuity, you give up control of your money but are guaranteed a set payment for life, which can include an option to pay a 100% survivor pension. For additional fees, the annuity can also include perks such as inflation protection or a guarantee period. With a guarantee period, payments will be paid for a predetermined number of years regardless of how long you live. Unfortunately, annuities are not very attractive when interest rates are low. New products have also entered into the "income for life" market with varying payment structures and potential access to market growth, but these come with hefty costs.

The decision to take a lump-sum commuted value of a monthly pension is an important one. In the saving years, you rarely have to make irreversible decisions such as this.

No wonder people are unsure. If you find yourself having to make this decision, don't go at it alone. Get help from a financial advisor who can do some projections and calculations to help you understand the implications of your choices.

rescue it!

Get the facts:

☐ Review your pension booklet to understand how your pension is calculated — check for inflation protection and survivor options.

☐ How secure is your pension? Ask your employer or pension administrator if the employer pension plan is fully funded and, if there is a shortfall, what is the strategy to bring it back to full funding.

☐ Are there any other benefits or perks you will be entitled to as a pensioner, such as health, dental, travel, or life insurance, that you will not get if you take the commuted value?

CHAPTER 25

 Not Considering All the Maturity Options
for a Registered Retirement Savings Plan

*Your RRSP has a limited lifespan, and before long, you're
going to have to make a big decision — how will you turn your
retirement savings into a retirement income? Don't make this
decision without considering all your options.*

I CONSIDER AN RRSP a kind of personal pension plan. In fact, an RRSP
is much more flexible than a pension plan, because you can skip contributions and double up in the future, you can invest in any qualified investment available on the market based on your personal risk tolerance, and
you can make withdrawals at any time, for any purpose, even when you're
still working (you just have to pay the applicable taxes). Locked-in RRSPs
(also known as a locked-in retirement account or LIRA) are very similar
to RRSPs, but the money in these locked-in plans originated from either
DB or DC company pension plans that the employee is no longer part of.
In any case, an RRSP is a savings plan and NOT a "true pension," which
means it will not provide a guaranteed monthly payment for life during
your retirement years. Years of poor investment performance will affect
the amount of money you have in the plan, and thereby reduce the size
of "pension" you will be able to withdraw from the plan. Unlike a regular savings account, withdrawals from an RRSP or any of the maturity
options discussed below are considered fully taxable income in the year of

the withdrawal. So it's very important that you understand how and when to turn your RRSP into retirement income. Otherwise, you might end up with less income than you expect.

when to convert funds

The income tax rules are very specific in this regard. You must close the RRSP by the end of the year (i.e., December 31) in which you celebrate your 71st birthday. (E.g., if you turn 71 on February 13, 2012, you have until December 31, 2012, to close out your RRSP.) However, if you are retired or need to access the money in your RRSP earlier than age 71 to supplement other retirement income, you have full access to the account, as long as the investments are cashable and not in a long-term investment such as a five-year GIC. Access to the funds in a locked-in plan will be determined by pension legislation. How you withdraw money from the RRSP depends on whether you only need a certain amount for a specific reason, or if you are ready to turn on the tap and collect an annual income. If you're only looking to make a one-time withdrawal at any age before 71, you can just make a withdrawal from the RRSP. Note that the financial institution will retain withholding tax: 10% on withdrawals up to $5,000, 20% on withdrawals between $5,001 and $15,000, and 30% on withdrawals above $15,000 (in Quebec the withholding rates are 21%, 26%, and 31%). The withholding tax is not the final tax payable on the withdrawal. Depending on your income for the year and marginal tax rate, you may have additional tax to pay, or you may get a refund of the tax paid. Be sure to ask if there is an administration fee to make withdrawals, because if you do this on a regular basis the fees can certainly add up. One-time withdrawals are generally not permitted from locked-in RSP plans. Once the individual has reached the specific retirement age outlined in their pension plan, the locked-in funds must be rolled into a maturity option such as a locked-in retirement income fund (LRIF) or a life income fund (LIF) and then annual withdrawals will have to be made from the plan.

If you are retired or have had your 71st birthday and are ready to convert the RRSP or locked-in RRSP into a steady income stream, there are several options available.

Choosing the right retirement income option for you is one of the most important financial and estate planning decisions you'll make, especially today, when statistics show that Canadians are living longer, healthier lives, and retirement can last 30 years or longer. You want to be sure your retirement savings will last as long as you do!

RRSP maturity options

There are a variety of options for maturing an RRSP. You may select one or any combination of options to suit your income needs.

- **Cash out the entire account.** A one-time lump-sum cash withdrawal of the entire account balance will be fully taxed in the year you receive it. Unless the value of your RRSP is quite small, if you withdraw the funds all at once you will probably find yourself being taxed at a much higher rate than if you had transferred your RRSP into one of the other maturity options and received smaller payments over multiple years. And what's more, because you have to pay income tax on the entire amount upon withdrawal, you now have a much smaller sum of money left over to invest for the duration of your retirement.

- **Tax-free rollover to a registered retirement income fund.** I like to explain a RRIF by saying it's a backwards RRSP. Rather than making a deposit and getting a tax refund, you make a withdrawal and get a taxable income receipt. Because it is an income fund, a RRIF requires minimum annual withdrawals to be made from the plan each year. Similar to an RRSP, while the money is in the plan, all of the growth and income generated by the assets are tax sheltered until they are withdrawn from the plan. With a RRIF you continue to control your investments, and you should exercise extra caution to make sure you invest your money wisely. Since retirement can last 30 years or more, you can take a long-term view with a *portion* of your money, but remember that you have to make an annual minimum withdrawal, so you will want to leave some money in lower-risk investments that are easily cashable for future withdrawals. Because there is no maximum withdrawal limit, you may withdraw any amount of money in excess of the minimum any time you need it. The risk in taking out large amounts from this plan is that you may run out of money before you run out of time.

If your plan is a locked-in RRIF, the annual minimum withdrawals will be the same as for a regular RRIF, but there will also be annual maximums that must be adhered to that slow down the depletion of the account. The withdrawal limits vary by province and by plan type, but they all reduce your flexibility released how much you would like to withdraw in any given year.

- **Life annuity.** If you want to turn your RRSP savings into something that more closely resembles a true pension, then you might want to consider purchasing a life annuity; these are available from life insurance companies. This product provides a series of periodic payments that you are guaranteed to receive for the rest of your life. The amount of your annuity payments will be determined by the value of your RRSP, your age and sex, current interest rates, and whether you want all or a portion of the payments to continue for as long as your spouse lives. With an annuity, you need to be aware that you no longer own any investments, because they have been exchanged for a lifetime income. On the plus side, you no longer have to watch the stock markets or interest rates, and you no longer have to worry about running out of money if you live to a ripe old age. Plus, annuity payments are taxed each year as you receive them, which means you are spreading the tax over your lifetime rather than paying it all at once, as you would have had to do if you cashed in the entire RRSP at retirement.

  Although a life annuity offers you the security of knowing that for as long as you live, you will receive a fixed income, many people are uncomfortable with the thought that all of their RRSP savings would be gone if they only lived for a short period of time after retirement. One option is to buy an annuity that will guarantee payments for a specific period of time, such as 10 or 15 years, so that if you die within the guarantee period, the payments continue to your beneficiary. Another thing that concerns people is not having access to a lump sum in case of an emergency: because you no longer own any investments, you can't withdraw money from your account to pay for unexpected costs. This lack of control and flexibility is a key reason annuities lack broad appeal. As a result, over the last few years, some annuities have been introduced that not only have a set guarantee period but also provide individuals with access to a lump-sum cash advance of the future guaranteed payments, which provides some of the flexibility individuals are asking for.

Because you lock in the annuity payment for the rest of your life, converting your RRSP into an annuity is best done only after you have given consideration to all of your other options. If you are undecided about whether or not to buy an annuity, because you feel that interest rates will eventually move higher, or you are not quite ready to give up control over your investments, you could consider rolling the RRSP into a RRIF at retirement and then later on, if rates go up, or if you simply become tired of managing your own money, you can transfer the funds from your RRIF into an annuity. You can do this all at once or gradually over several years. One benefit of waiting to buy a life annuity is that the older you are, the higher your lifetime annuity payments will be. Another option is to roll a portion of your RRSP into a RRIF and use the remaining amount to buy a life annuity. This way you can get the best of both worlds.

a RRIF reversal

We already know that if you roll the RRSP into an annuity, you're in it for life. You can't decide later that it would have been better to keep the money in the RRSP or roll it into a RRIF. On the other hand, if you roll your RRSP into a RRIF, you can later roll it back into an RRSP, as long as you're under 71 years of age. This rule also applies to locked-in RRSPs and LIRAs. When would you ever want to have the money go back into an RRSP? The most common situation occurs when someone retires and later returns to work, either full time or part time, and finds they no longer need the income from the RRIF withdrawals. A RRIF reversal is a good strategy for people who return to the workforce after "trying out" retirement for a few years. If the RRIF continues, CRA requires the minimum annual withdrawal to be made whether you need the money or not. In that case, it's best to reverse the transaction. The way to do this is to take the minimum withdrawal for the year (you can't avoid this), and then transfer the remaining funds into an RRSP, where they can continue to grow on a tax-deferred basis. Do not withdraw the money from the RRIF — the transfer has to be done using a special tax form your bank or financial institution can provide you. Since you're rolling funds from one registered plan to another, you do not need any RRSP contribution room. Essentially, you're just putting your money back where it was. Later on, either at age 71 or whenever you need access to a regular income stream, you can roll the RRSP back to a RRIF and start receiving payments again.

So, as long as you are under age 71, maturing the RRSP to a RRIF is not an irrevocable decision. This would not be the case if you retired and started receiving a pension from your company pension plan. You would not be able to start and stop the pension if you no longer needed the money.

minimizing the size of withdrawals

If you find that your RRIF withdrawal is more than you need, you have one of two choices: take an in-kind withdrawal or find a younger spouse or partner. An in-kind withdrawal allows you to take the investments out of your RRIF "as is," so you don't have to sell your investments — so if your RRIF is in stocks, you can continue to own the same stocks, but outside the tax-protected environment of the RRIF. Unfortunately, you will still have to pay the tax on the withdrawal. On the other hand, if you have a younger spouse, then you can base your required minimum withdrawals on the younger person's age. So if you were 75 years old but had a 70-year-old spouse, the minimum withdrawal from your RRIF could be based on your younger spouse's age — the minimum withdrawal based on your age would be 7.85%, versus 5% for a person five years younger. The younger your spouse, the lower the minimum withdrawal percentage. This allows you to keep more of your money in a tax-deferred plan for a longer period of time. Who says there's no tax advantage to having a younger spouse?

how long will your RRIF last?

The minimum RRIF withdrawal is based on two key variables: age and account balance as shown in the chart at the end of the chapter. The older you are, the higher the percentage for the minimum withdrawal. And the bigger the balance, the higher the withdrawal. That is, as long as your account balance isn't shrinking too fast. For instance, at age 71, your minimum withdrawal is 7.38% of the value in the plan. Based on a $100,000 plan, the required withdrawal is $7,380, which leaves $92,620. The next year, the minimum withdrawal rate is 7.48%, and if the plan earned 7%, the minimum withdrawal amount would be $7,412.93, which is slightly less than the previous year's amount. As long as the plan earns 7% each year, annual withdrawals will continue at about the same level.

However, things will be different if the plan earns only 5%. If you still want to keep the withdrawal at $7,380 for as long as you can, or actually increase it each year to compensate for the fact that the cost of goods and services will be going up over time, you will be depleting the account much faster and will run out of money a lot sooner.

Below, I summarize four scenarios.

1. In the first, the plan earns a 7% rate of return and only the minimum withdrawals are made each year. At age 90, there is still $57,732.55 in the RRIF.

2. In the second, the plan earns a 5% rate of return, and only the minimum withdrawals are made each year. At age 90 there is $40,339.05 in the RRIF.

3. In the third, the plan earns a 5% rate of return and the withdrawal is kept at a constant amount of $7,380. In this scenario, the plan is completely depleted by age 91.

4. In the fourth, the plan earns a 5% rate of return, and while the withdrawal begins at $7,380, it is increased each year by 2% to compensate for a minimum amount of inflation. In this scenario, the plan is completely depleted by age 87.

This example assumes a constant rate of return each year of either 5 or 7%. We know from historical data that it is rare that a portfolio would be able to achieve a constant rate of return over a retirement period. A few years of very low or negative returns, especially at the start of the withdrawal period, will greatly reduce the duration of the funds.

RRIF minimum withdrawal chart

Age on January 1	Minimum withdrawal	Age on January 1	Minimum withdrawal
65	4.00%	80	8.75%
66	4.17%	81	8.99%
67	4.35%	82	9.27%
68	4.55%	83	9.58%
69	4.76%	84	9.93%
70	5.00%	85	10.33%
71	7.38%	86	10.79%
72	7.48%	87	11.33%
73	7.71%	88	11.96%
74	7.85%	89	12.71%
75	7.99%	90	13.62%
76	8.15%	91	14.73%
77	8.33%	92	16.12%
78	8.33%	93	17.92%
79	8.53%	94 and over	20.00%

RRSPs and RRIFs provide a huge benefit in terms of tax-deferred growth on the investments in these registered plans, as well as flexibility.

rescue it!

☐ If you want maximum flexibility and are willing to take full responsibility to manage your funds, use a RRIF.

☐ Consider converting a portion of your money into a guaranteed lifetime-income product.

☐ If you are under 71, roll your RRIF back into an RRSP if you don't need the income from the minimum withdrawal.

☐ If you have a younger spouse, consider using the young spouse's age in the withdrawal formula to reduce the required withdrawal.

☐ Make in-kind withdrawals from a RRIF if you don't need the cash from a withdrawal.

☐ Don't wreck your retirement by depleting your registered accounts too quickly and paying too much tax.

PART 6

living in retirement

CHAPTER 26

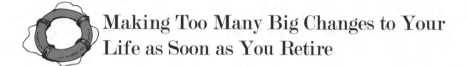 Making Too Many Big Changes to Your
Life as Soon as You Retire

*Congratulations, you're retired! Are you looking forward to
starting a new life or getting your old one back?*

WHAT ARE YOU PLANNING TO DO when you retire? For some,
this is an important life event that they view as a rite of passage. They
plan to make big changes in their lifestyle, just because they feel they
have to, and as a result end up feeling less satisfied about how their life
has turned out. But being retired doesn't mean you leave all aspects of
your current life behind. This may surprise you, but chances are you
will do a lot of the same things after retiring as you did before — we're
somewhat hard-wired after a certain age and it's hard to change us. You
won't likely be a crazy happy-go-lucky retiree unless you were already
that way.

Still, not everyone wants to do the same things in retirement that they
do now. Let's say you have a vision of what your retirement might look
like, and that vision contains many new activities that you've put off doing
until retirement. It could be anything — learning to play the guitar, learning a new language, building a school in Africa, even working part time.
Sometimes the ideas in our vision are our own ideas, and sometimes they're
adopted ideas. You know the kind, the ones that sound really good when
you read about them in a magazine or when someone else suggests them.

As you plan the next phase of your life, consider all your options and think about what they mean to you and what need they fulfil.

now what?

What if you've planned this wonderful retirement, only to find that you're not musically inclined, or much of a builder? Imagine how disappointed you might feel if you waited until your retirement to try these things, and now that you're doing them, you realize you aren't enjoying yourself. You may even ask yourself, "What's the big deal? Why did I look forward to doing this for so long?" Even if you are disappointed, try to accept what you find out, and be flexible. Think over why you wanted to do those activities in the first place. Rather than taking a course to learn a new language, perhaps you can go overseas to teach others a language that you are already an expert in — for instance, English or French. If you are able to teach overseas, you will certainly pick up the local language and culture by virtue of being totally immersed in it. Learning this way can be a more enjoyable option than listening to some language tapes or taking a course. What's more, rather than paying course fees to learn a new language, you may be able to earn enough money teaching in a foreign country to fund the cost of living and travelling overseas, and maybe even add to your savings account.

a very long vacation

Hoping to make your vacation your full-time job in retirement is often a short-lived goal. Although activities you enjoy doing should definitely be continued, retirement is not just about golfing every day, or a permanent move to the cottage, or being on your boat all year long. Some time ago, I delivered an early retirement seminar to individuals who were six months from retirement. I asked everyone to complete a "day timer" exercise — the participants were asked to fill out one week in a day timer with all the things they would be doing one month into retirement. Needless to say, it was a lot of fun, because everyone put exotic and fun things into their week. One person put only one activity in capital letters: GOLF — every day; another listed being on a beach in Hawaii. The next part of the exercise was a little harder to complete, because I asked everyone to think about their activities for an entire week that was one *year* into retirement. As you can imagine, this part was harder. What do you do when you're done with vacation? It became clear to the participants that they needed to plan their life better, and think about the big picture as well as the day-to-day activities in retirement.

We really do enjoy our time off while we're working, and why not? It's a chance to get away from the hustle and bustle and stress of working, and to wind down and relax. Maybe just the thought of getting out of the city is enough to get you packing. We enjoy this time because it's special, it's short-lived, and we want to make the most of it. But how much will you enjoy doing these things when you can do them any time you want? What do you do once you've lived your vacation? And more important, how long can you afford to be on vacation?

It should come as no surprise that travel is almost always the number one thing people say they want to do in retirement, yet when they are retired they don't end up travelling quite as much as they anticipated. It is important to think more broadly about what you want to accomplish if travelling is a high-priority item for you. Do you hope to travel to see and experience new places, to get away from the harsh winters, or perhaps to be able to enjoy more winter activities. Think about how can you "live" your vacation without it costing you a fortune. I met a woman who works part time at the restaurant at her favourite golf course every summer so she can golf for free. There are many similar opportunities to combine work or volunteer with added perks or benefits.

moving to the cottage/cabin

If you own a vacation home, you likely have nothing but good memories of this place, and what could be better than to retire there all year long? But have you ever stopped to ask yourself what it is about this location that you really enjoy? Is it the fishing, the quiet, the fun time you have skiing, the time you spend with your family and especially grandchildren, who visit during school breaks? Will those things you love be there all year long when the kids are at work, the grandchildren are at school, your neighbours have returned to their city homes, and the lake is frozen over? Perhaps while you are working you enjoy the seclusion and quiet, but during retirement, will this make you feel isolated and alone? Consider how far away the neighbours are, and what about shopping and access to medical attention? If you're considering buying a vacation property at retirement, talk to those who already own one nearby. You may learn that it's not as glamorous or relaxing as you may think.

wanting to move to a new location

Moving to a new location may be very appealing to you, especially if you live in a big city. I know a couple who had a time-share in Florida. The family really enjoyed it, so just before retirement they bought it outright and began to spend part of the year there and part of the year back in Canada. They continued to live this way for a few years and then one year, when back in Canada, a doctor's visit identified an illness that required regular medical attention and would prevent the couple from spending too much time in Florida. The couple sold their Florida home and made changes to their lives to accommodate this new situation. Make sure your plans are flexible — it's not only *where* you live, but what you will be doing, that is important. Think about how you will continue to do the things you love in a different location.

take up an exercise program

Maintaining good health is a key factor in being able to enjoy retirement. But don't wait until retirement to join a fitness centre or a golf club. If you join a fitness centre, work with a trainer to develop a program for your level of fitness and minimize the risk of injury from pushing yourself too hard or not using the equipment properly. If you want to golf during retirement but all your golfing buddies are at work, this should not take the fun out of it. Use this opportunity to meet new people by joining other single golfers. This is a great way to combine an exercise program with developing or expanding your social network.

above all, do it now

You may have put off certain decisions or big plans until your retirement. But retirement is not always the best time to try new activities. Why not try out retirement while you're working? Start doing some of the activities you think you want to do in retirement — remember, with everything we do, it might take a few years to become an expert at it.

If you have defined your life by your work, then retirement represents a major life event, a big change, and can cause lots of stress as you sort out and shape this new phase of your life. Create a life plan with your key life goals, and set a timeframe for achieving them. Don't rush yourself; take the time to enjoy this phase of your life. Don't try to do everything at once — do only as much as you want to. Introduce changes gradually, if needed, and most of all, be flexible.

rescue it!

- ☐ What activities do you want to try for the first time? Write them down and set a schedule for when you're going to try them out. Do them now, before retiring, and see if you like them, and then you can just do more of what you like during retirement.

- ☐ Where do you want to live? Try it off-season and without the family.

CHAPTER 27

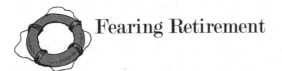 Fearing Retirement

The only thing to fear is fear itself — rather than fearing the unknown, refocus your energies on the things that really matter to you.

WE SPEND THE FIRST PART of our lives preparing for the working years. We spend the next part of our lives working, building, and changing careers, but we don't spend much time at all preparing for the retirement years. Of course, we save money for the future, and contribute to pension plans, but rarely do we plan our lives in retirement. We've all heard that people spend more time preparing and planning for a family vacation or a new car purchase than they do for their retirement. No wonder retirement is something people are wary of.

Take a minute to remember the last social gathering you took part in. Did you meet some new people? Do you remember what the conversation was about? Perhaps the conversation went something like this: "Hello, my name is Richard." "Hi, Richard, I'm Samantha. So tell me, what do you do?" If you are currently retired, or soon to be retired, how would you answer that? Are you excited about this next phase of your life, or are you reluctant to say it out loud?

The reality is that you may be ready to retire based on your age, or just because you're tired of your job, but you may not be ready psychologically to shift gears to no longer working. This is especially true if you have negative thoughts and beliefs about what retirement is going to be like. Some people see retirement as being just one step closer to the end of your life. That's not a very appealing thought. Many go through different emotional stages during retirement.

Seven Stages of Retirement

1. Impatience (I can't wait to retire!)

2. Worry (What if I haven't saved enough to retire?)

3. Relief (I made it!)

4. Fear (What am I going to do with all this free time?)

5. Excitement (I'm going to do it all!)

6. Disappointment (Is this all there is?)

7. Happiness (Life is good, retirement is good!)

Don't sabotage your retirement with negative thoughts. Retirement can be a very rewarding and exciting time. Perhaps it's time to face your fears — retirement is just another phase of life that brings change and a little bit of the unknown, so what are you really afraid of?

loss of routine and structure

From very early on in life, we have routines to follow. Bedtime was set; so was playtime and mealtime. We went to school and then work according to a specific pre-set schedule that we often had little control over. It was a very structured environment, with set duties and responsibilities, a boss to evaluate your work, co-workers to talk to, children to drive to activities. Imagine a time when there is no structure to your day — you can do whatever you want with your time. There are no demands from anyone. If you speak to some retired folks, they'll say they don't even know what day of the week it is — after all, every day feels like Saturday. Imagine the freedom, imagine the choice. Rather than worry about how you will fill the day, look forward to a time when you control the entire 24-hour clock, not just a few hours here and there. And if you are worried that you won't be busy all day long, just talk to your retired friends — I'm certain they'll tell you that they've never been busier. I met up with a former colleague about a year after she retired and asked her how she was adjusting to not coming to the office every day and how she was spending her time. She laughed and said she's so busy that doesn't know how she ever found the time to work.

loss of stature, or no longer feeling important

Do you currently connect your achievements at work to who you are as a person? Some people identify themselves primarily with their jobs, their titles, or their accomplishments. *I'm an entrepreneur, I built a company. I helped thousands of sick people. I taught children how to read.* Years ago, a client of mine, a surgeon, felt retirement would mean he'd no longer be able to call himself a doctor. He knew he was leaving his job, but he felt that he was leaving his profession, his colleagues, and his identity. Will you still be the person you were when you were working? Yes! You just won't be the person it says you were on your business card — and so what? Your business card does not define who you are. Titles are just titles and rarely describe the entire sum of an individual's worth or capabilities. Think about the things that describe you that are not on your business card. Those things are still in you, and now you can accentuate them!

choice and flexibility

The responsibilities of full-time work prevent us from choosing how to spend our time, and limit our opportunities to make changes in our lives. No matter how much you love your job, there are days when you just need a break. Vacations never seem long enough, or frequent enough, and you usually have to schedule and coordinate them with your employer well in advance. What's more, there are many jobs that restrict when you can take your vacation. I recall a conversation I had with a teacher and her frustration at not being able to choose when to take her holiday. It wasn't the number of days that was the issue — it was the lack of freedom to choose to take a different week off. But in retirement, you have the freedom to do what you want, when you want — and you have the freedom to change your mind. You're not tied to your job or work schedule — your entire day is yours, not just the hours after 6 p.m.

small business owners

Many self-employed people and small business owners don't think about retirement very often, and when they do, they are thinking of their next business venture. They can leave their business whenever they want to, and don't have to wait until they reach a specific age or milestone. So for them, retirement isn't viewed the same way. Perhaps that's why it is common for small business owners to retire later than the average Canadian, or never retire at all. They just slow down or pass the reins to a family member, while they continue to play a role in the business.

make it a transition

If you are really feeling unsure about retirement, try easing into it by gradually reducing work hours — or even taking a "mini-retirement." I know someone who did just that. He took a six-month sabbatical from work and tried out retirement — at age 50. He discovered that he was able to do a lot of the things he was hoping to do during his retirement years in a mere six months, because his goals were so short term. When he returned to work, he was able to refocus and plan for the things that really mattered and would bring him joy and fulfilment during his full-time retirement. Like filling out a retirement life plan, thinking about both long-term and short-term goals adds clarity and gives meaning to your plans.

Then there is gradual retirement. If your employer agrees, you can work fewer days per week; this will continue to provide enough structure to your life, while you enjoy *extra long weekends* every week. As those *weekends* get busier, you can reduce work days even more, until you are fully retired.

turn a hobby into a job

Have you ever wanted to convert your hobby into an income and thought, "I'd love to quit my job and do this . . . but I'd never earn enough money to live on." In retirement, you will likely have income from various sources of pensions, so the "extra" income you hope to earn from this activity doesn't need to be as high as it would need to be during your working years.

One retiree I met said he started a Web site for social networking purposes, as a way to continue to keep in touch with his fellow retired employees. This is one way of taking a skill or knowledge base and continuing it in retirement. Find your hidden talent; think about how you can use your talents in a new and innovative way. Think about what motivates you — what are your passions? Look for ways to give back — volunteer opportunities. Educate others, build a playground, provide services for free to a charitable organization, help with fundraising ideas or marketing strategies.

What would you have done if work/raising a family hadn't intervened? What have you always wanted try or be involved in? Remember those old yearbook notes — what did you say you hoped to accomplish in life? Do it now.

rescue it!

☐ Create a retirement life plan with your key life goals and a timeframe for achieving them.

☐ Try a mini-retirement or a gradual retirement. Don't forget to ask your employer about the impact this might have on your pension as discussed in chapter 24.

☐ Start doing activities you want to try now — don't wait until you reach retirement.

CHAPTER 28

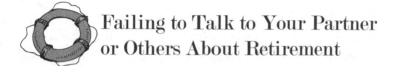 ## Failing to Talk to Your Partner or Others About Retirement

What you are looking forward to in retirement may not be the same things your partner is thinking about. One of the biggest mistakes people make is failing to discuss their views about retirement with those who will be sharing it with them.

THERE ARE MANY IMPORTANT CONVERSATIONS we have in our lifetime — conversations around getting married, buying a house, having children, going back to school, change in employment, or starting a business . . . maybe even retirement. As more and more women have entered the workforce, joint retirement planning has emerged. In the past, retirement was by definition what a man did at the end of his career. There was only one retirement in the household and the household simply adjusted to this expected event. But today, with more and more couples having independent careers, you may have spent 20 to 40 years with the other person, but how much time did you actually spend together? Having kept busy with work, children's activities, and a very full life in general, some couples may find that they are not on the same page when it comes to retirement. Your retirement dream may be to open a bed and breakfast — your partner's may not!

Set aside some quiet time and think about retirement. What comes to mind? Talk openly to your partner about your thoughts and listen to your partner's views in return. If it helps, write your ideas down on paper and share the notes — don't worry if something seems silly, just write it down; you might be surprised how fruitful the conversation becomes. This is a time of self-discovery. Talk to others who you think have retired successfully. They can provide a wealth of free advice.

Consider discussing these topics with your partner:

- Will the two of you be retiring at the same time, or not?
- What activities do you see yourselves enjoying (consider shared and independent activities)? Are you hoping for a leisurely retirement or an active one?
- What will your vacations look like — active or passive, shared or independent, when, how often, with whom and where?
- How will family be part of retirement — will you be travelling to reunite with long-distance relatives? Will you be taking a more active role in caring for grandchildren?
- Friends and social networks — how are you going to continue to develop and grow friendships? Do you have a social network outside of work? Do you expect to inherit your partner's friends? Or worse, your children's friends?
- Role spouses each play in retirement — how will your role at home change once you are retired? Will you take on more of the household chores?

independent activity list

I believe that even in retirement you need to have some independent time. Make a list of activities that you enjoy doing and plan to continue to do during retirement, separate from your spouse or partner. It doesn't necessarily mean you will be doing these activities alone; they can be activities you do with your friends or children, for instance.

Ever wonder why some recently retired people go back to work? Sometimes it's because once they retired, they did everything with their spouse and ended up getting under each other's feet. That's exactly what happened when Simon, a recently retired business owner, decided he would surprise his wife, Julia, by cleaning out the kitchen cabinets. When Julia returned home and started to prepare dinner, she couldn't find anything she needed. Simon had rearranged the entire kitchen.

shared activity list

Shared activities are important too, so start dating — each other! You may find you need to get to know each other all over again.

Develop together a list of activities that you enjoy and would like to share with your spouse or partner. Each of you can prepare a list, and then you can share and discuss. In one of my seminars, a couple completed this exercise and when they read over each other's shared activity lists, the husband had listed fishing as a shared activity. The wife asked, "Why would you think I'd want to go fishing with you during my retirement?" He thought that the reason she was always upset when he went fishing with the boys was that she was excluded — in fact, she was upset because he spent so much time away on weekends that she had to do the bulk of the chores around the house. It was definitely not because she wanted to go fishing!

planning for a co-retirement

When couples dream of retiring, they tend to plan to retire at the same time or within a short time of each other. Individuals are more likely to consider retirement if their spouse has already retired, because they feel pressure to retire too. They may want to share in the same experiences and emotions as they start the journey into this new phase of life. While this sounds good, the fact is, few couples are the same age, so retirement at 65 for one partner could mean early (or really early) retirement for the other. A co-retirement can be a mistake for couples who have an age gap of even a few years, because an early retirement will result in fewer contribution years to pensions and retirement savings, and ultimately a lower income during retirement. This is an issue for women in particular, because women typically spend more time out of the workforce than men, often caring for a young family and then later caring for a parent. Combine that with the fact that women on average earn less than men, and retiring early can result in pensions that are significantly lower. Since women generally live longer than men, and are therefore more likely to become widowed during retirement, it's important for them to build as much pensions and personal savings as they can. The impact of reducing a woman's working years should be considered before any plans for co-retirement are made.

rescue it!

☐ Set aside some time to talk to your partner and other significant people in your life about your plans and vision for retirement.

☐ Make an independent activity list, and make a shared one as well.

☐ Think about the impact that retiring at the same time might have on expected retirement income.

CHAPTER 29

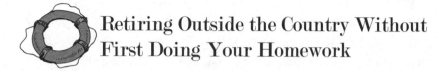 Retiring Outside the Country Without First Doing Your Homework

Vacationing abroad and living abroad are two very different things. Important considerations must be evaluated before you make this a permanent part of your retirement plans.

FOR MANY CANADIANS, THE IDEA OF living in another country after retiring, or at least spending some time as a snowbird, is very appealing. You may have even scoped out a few locations while on vacation, so that by retirement you have a fairly good idea of where you want to settle. But everyone knows that being on vacation and living somewhere permanently can be very different. So before you make any kind of move, ask yourself whether you are considering a permanent move or a temporary stay.

permanent move

There are many reasons why a permanent move abroad is appealing. While it is most common among people who immigrated to Canada and who are considering moving back to their country of birth once they retire, it can also be appealing to those who would like to experience living in another part of the world. For some, wanting to leave Canada also has to do with personal taxation and the potential lower income tax rates payable in other countries. But just because you leave Canada and start living somewhere else does not mean that Canada won't continue to tax you as if you were still a resident. For you to be considered a non-resident of Canada, your move would have to be considered permanent.

Ceasing Canadian residency has many tax and estate implications that need to be considered prior to undertaking such a move, and so it is best to speak to a tax advisor if you think you might want to become a non-resident.

In general, while ceasing residency will not impact your Canadian citizenship, it essentially means that you no longer consider Canada your permanent home. To prove you are no longer a resident, you will be required to demonstrate that you have minimal residential ties to Canada. Evidence could include selling your Canadian home or renting it out on a long-term lease, closing Canadian bank accounts, giving up your Canadian driver's licence and provincial medical coverage, and cancelling golf club and other fitness memberships.

From a tax perspective, ceasing Canadian residency also means that you will be deemed to have sold all of your assets and investments at the time you stop being considered a resident of Canada. This means you might have to pay taxes to Canada Revenue Agency (CRA) if those assets and investments have increased in value. You may also be surprised to find that your chosen country may not welcome you with open arms. For instance, as a retiree, you may not be able to immigrate permanently to the U.S., whereas the rules are simpler if you choose to make Mexico your new home.

impact of non-residency on retirement income and savings

Even if you cease Canadian residency, RRSP/RRIF assets are not considered "disposed of" and can remain in Canada and will continue to enjoy tax deferral from a Canadian perspective. However, these accounts may not be considered tax deferral accounts in your new country of residence, which means you might have to start paying local income taxes on the investment earnings in your RRSP or RRIF. When you make a withdrawal from these accounts, you will pay a flat withholding tax of 25% to CRA. You may find that the 25% tax is lower or higher than you might have had to pay on such withdrawals had you remained a resident of Canada.

In some cases, the withholding tax will be reduced by an income tax treaty between Canada and your new country of residence. For example, RRIF withdrawals that are considered periodic payments (i.e., you don't take all your money out of the plan in under 10 years) will be subject to only 15% withholding by CRA if your new country of residence has an income tax agreement with Canada. There may also be additional income taxes to pay in the new country of residence.

CPP/QPP and OAS

Even if you cease Canadian residency, your CPP/QPP entitlement will continue to be paid to you in your new country. As for OAS, you'll be able to continue to receive it while you are living abroad, but only if you have lived in Canada for at least 20 years after your 18th birthday. If you don't meet this criterion prior to leaving Canada, you will collect OAS for the first six months you're away, and then the payments stop. You can reapply for OAS once you return to Canada and re-establish residency. Again, CRA will take a 25% withholding tax on the CPP and OAS payments made to you while you are not a resident.

temporary move (snowbird)

This is by far the more common situation, especially since the 2009 housing crash in the U.S. has resulted in so many more Canadians buying homes south of the border. With a temporary move, your intent is not to cease residential ties. However, there are still a few things you should know about. For instance, even if you are still considered a resident of Canada, you may also be considered a resident in your host country if you spend too much time there. In general, you want to spend less than 183 days in a particular country. In addition, spending too much time out of your home province can affect your provincial medical coverage.

other considerations

When you are on vacation at a resort, you should remember that the employees there are trained to make your stay as comfortable and memorable as possible. They cater to your every need, bring you drinks, give you fresh towels, and so on. The wonderful time you had on vacation may also have been because you were travelling with family or friends, or at the very least, a bunch of other sun-seeking Canadians. However, a vacation is very different from living some place permanently, or even long term.

Language Barrier

Not every country has English as their native tongue. Will you have to learn a new language? Will you feel isolated or lost if you cannot read the local newspapers or understand the news?

Food Choices/Cost

Vacationing at a resort might shelter you from the local reality that there is a lack of availability of a wide range of food choices. If you are a vegetarian, it can be a challenge to find enough of the kinds of food you need for a balanced diet. Alternatively, in some countries, vegetarian living is part of the culture, and you may find it difficult to find a variety of meat, poultry, and so forth. If you are in a country that has to import the kind of food you enjoy, you will find yourself paying a lot more for those items than you paid back home in Canada.

Housing Options

Few people wander away from the resort to see what kind of housing options there are. You might be surprised by what's available and at what cost. Standard housing options that you are used to at home may be considered "luxury." On the other hand, you might have access to the beach or your own swimming pool or even housekeepers at a very low cost!

Health Care

Canada has one of the best health care systems in the world — and most services are available free of any additional cost. This isn't always the case elsewhere. Find out what options are available, and consider buying private health insurance coverage just in case. Get a checkup before you leave, and take a supply of your medications with you. You may not be able to buy the same ones, or the standard dosage size might be different, and you could end up taking an incorrect amount of medication.

Cultural Isolation

Being immersed in a new culture is part of the appeal of going to live in another country. However, a prolonged visit can result in a feeling of isolation if cultural or religious differences are significant. In some countries, same-sex marriages are not recognized, which may cause same-sex partners to feel uncomfortable or excluded from social gatherings.

Travelling with Pets

Many retirees have pets and they expect to be able to take their pets with them. You may be shocked to find that in some cases your pet will be quarantined, either before or upon entering another country. It's important to check the country's rules around bringing pets in.

rescue it!

If you are considering a permanent move:

☐ Review your personal net worth statement to find out what assets will be considered sold upon your departure and will therefore be subject to Canadian tax.

☐ Prepare to take the necessary steps to prove to CRA that you have ceased Canadian residency.

☐ Do some additional research to determine tax rates in the new country and whether there is an income tax treaty with Canada that might reduce the tax rate on certain payments from Canada.

If you are considering a temporary move:

☐ Review your provincial medical coverage to make sure the length of time spent outside your province won't cause you to lose your coverage.

☐ Review the host country's income tax rules to make sure your stay does not cause you to be considered a resident in the host country while still being considered a resident in Canada.

☐ Learn more about living and travelling abroad by doing some research. A good place to start is www.voyage.gc.ca.

CHAPTER 30

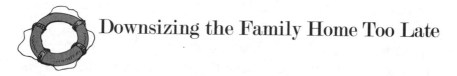 Downsizing the Family Home Too Late

Canadians value home ownership — we upsize during working years and then say we'll downsize once we've retired — but what we say and what we do often don't align.

WHETHER YOUR HOME IS A RETIREMENT ASSET or a personal use asset, one thing is certain, it's one of the largest items on your personal net worth statement. One of the best strategies is to have a fully paid-for home at retirement, so you can spend the rest of your days rent-free. But what if you've spent years paying off the home and don't have much in the way of personal savings — you may find yourself asking whether your home is still your castle.

There are many reasons why you might consider downsizing your home. Perhaps it's just too big now that the children have moved out; maybe you want to move to be closer to children or other family; you may want to move into a condominium to leave behind grass cutting and snow shovelling; you may decide to move to a smaller home to pay off the mortgage before retirement, or reduce property taxes and other costs associated with a bigger home. As we age, living in a one-storey rather than a two-storey home can make a huge difference in comfort and mobility. Your home may no longer be appropriate for you or your spouse, especially if your mobility is restricted. If a wheelchair is required, can it fit through the doorways? Will you need to go up and down lots of stairs? Just as we age, so does our home. Once you've been in a home a number of years, extra exterior maintenance may be needed — painting, a new roof, driveway repairs, window replacements, and the list goes on. Even regular maintenance can become a chore as you get older.

If you think you might want to downsize your home in the future, when is the right time to downsize? Of course, the right time is when you're ready to move. If you're not in a rush to sell, you can wait to get the best price for your home, and you can take your time to find the perfect replacement home in exactly the neighbourhood you want, at the right price. The housing markets do fluctuate, so always leave yourself some flexibility and don't be rushed into selling or buying too quickly.

trends in home ownership

You may have noticed more and more active adult retirement communities and life lease residences popping up in many provinces across Canada. In these communities, residents are usually 55 years of age and older and are still very independent. In addition to added security features, some communities also provide services such as exterior maintenance and snow removal, fitness centres, and on-site health care. The residences come in a wide variety of options to suit your needs, such as bungalows, townhouses, or condominiums. With a life lease, the resident does not own the home, but owns the right to live in the home for the rest of their life. When the time comes to think about moving out of your current home, an adult retirement community may be just what you need.

Another new trend in homes owned by seniors is the introduction of elevators. I recently asked a real estate salesperson about this and he said that many Canadians were finally able to afford their dream home at the age of 50 or older, and were installing elevators because they wanted to be able to remain in the home in their later years, when they might not be able to go up and down the stairs. While an elevator is a practical feature, you don't have to move to get one. Elevators can even be installed in most small two-storey homes.

guidelines to follow

If you have decided you will move, then don't wait too long to do so. It will become much harder to move out of the family home as you get older and especially so if you have lost a spouse. There are many memories that are hard to leave behind when you move from a home and a neighbourhood. You know your neighbours and some may be close friends. Perhaps you rely on each other for care or support. Don't discount the value of that, as it takes time to meet new people and become comfortable with them.

Know the neighbourhood you are moving into. If you have downsized your home, you may find yourself in a neighbourhood of first-time home buyers. Being in a neighbourhood filled with young families has its advantages, but what if all your neighbours are at work during the week and running around town with their young children on the weekends? There may be few people in the neighbourhood that have the same interests as you do.

Don't keep a home that is larger than you need just for when the grandkids come over. And don't put in a swimming pool so that the kids and grandkids can occupy themselves when they come over. How often do they come over, anyway?

When downsizing, there is the question of what to do with all the extra furniture. Don't expect that the children will want it all, so sell or donate it so someone else can enjoy it. In fact, it might be a good time to ask the children to remove their personal belongings and other memorabilia from your home.

When you move, take your memories with you. A home contains many memories, so take some pictures and write notes about activities, parties, and other times that have special meaning for you.

the benefits to downsizing

Once you become an "empty nester," it's time to reap the rewards and downsize. A smaller home will often come with fewer expenses — lower property taxes, lower heating costs. Remember that any capital gain you realize on the sale of your principal residence is tax-free. But be careful not to overspend on your new home. I knew a couple that sold their large home for $525,000 — not bad, since they had paid $220,000 for it 15 years earlier. This was their last big home, and they were ready to downsize, since all the kids had moved out. It was a great idea, and gave the couple an opportunity to access their other retirement "savings" account — their home! So when they bought a smaller home for $450,000, I was more than a little surprised. First of all, it wasn't that much smaller, and once they paid real estate fees on their sale, land transfer tax on the new home, legal fees, and moving costs, they didn't have much money left over to put toward their retirement. If the decision to downsize is prompted by the desire or need to extract equity from your home to help fund retirement, aim to net at least 30% of the value of your home. Moving can be emotionally draining; don't let it become financially draining, too.

how to eat your house

What if you find yourself in a situation where you're house-rich and cash-poor and you absolutely do not want to move? There is an option that allows you to "eat your house," called a reverse annuity mortgage. While this is rarely the best option for individuals, it's worth knowing about.

A reverse annuity mortgage allows you to draw out anywhere from 10 to 40% of the equity from your home and turn it into a lifetime income stream. A reverse annuity mortgage has two main parts.

1. A mortgage that bears an interest rate. Unlike a regular mortgage, no regular mortgage payments will need to be made. Instead, the interest accumulates during the time the mortgage is outstanding, and becomes part of the balance owing.

2. A life annuity that pays a monthly income for life.

On the death of the homeowner, the total mortgage principal plus accumulated interest must be paid back. The home is sold and the proceeds from the sale are used to pay off the outstanding mortgage. If the proceeds from the sale of the home are greater than the outstanding mortgage, the homeowner's estate gets the difference. If the proceeds are less than the outstanding mortgage, then the mortgage is still considered fully paid off, but there will be nothing left for the estate.

The main difference between a regular mortgage and a reverse annuity mortgage is that with a reverse annuity mortgage, you do not have to make any mortgage payments during your life, which means better cash flow management. If you simply take a regular mortgage or line of credit against your home and use it to buy an annuity, or to invest it and live off the income, you would still have to make regular mortgage payments, which would reduce the amount left over for you to spend.

rescue it!

☐ Give some thought to whether you want to downsize your home in retirement.

☐ Have your home appraised to determine the potential proceeds from a sale.

☐ Start looking for opportunities to buy a smaller home, and estimate how much you can save in reduced housing costs, and how much money you can set aside.

☐ Research locations of active adult retirement communities.

CHAPTER 31

 Not Doing Some Research Before
Starting a Business in Retirement

Since the age group that has the highest growth in new business is the over-55 crowd, it's clear that boomers are interested in starting businesses post–full-time work. However, there are some big risks to consider before starting down the entrepreneurial path during retirement.

TIRED OF WORKING FOR SOMEONE ELSE? Why not start your own business? And what better time to do so than in retirement! You have tremendous experience, you've made some good business contacts, you're respected in your field, and now you have the time to dedicate to a new venture. But before you start down the entrepreneurial path, think about what is truly motivating you to start a business in retirement. Is it just to fill a void, or is it because you are truly passionate about your business idea and can't wait to get started?

One thing is certain: as a self-employed business owner, you'll work just as hard if not harder than you did as an employee. In fact, a recent survey found that 32% of self-employed persons worked over 50 hours per week, compared to fewer than 4% of employees![1] When you realize that you,

---

[1]Statistics Canada Labour Force Survey. April 2010.

and only you, are responsible for the success of your business venture — handling the marketing of your business, paying bills, collecting money from sales, and doing the work — the long work hours are not surprising.

The trend to self-employment is not new, and with Canadian baby boomers beginning to turn 65 in 2011 and considering the possibility of self-employment, the trend is likely to rise, and the term *seniorpreneur* will be heard more often. In 2005, seniorpreneurs made up more than 30% of the total workforce over the age of 55, and they are by far the fastest-growing segment in the small business sector.

Statistics Canada found a genuine trend, at least among working men. It studied the employment status of working men aged 55 to 59, and found that 26% of them were self-employed. Five years later, it surveyed a group of men aged 60 to 64, and found that 37% were self-employed; five years later, it surveyed a group of men aged 65 to 69, and 60% of them reported being self-employed.[2] However, men aren't the only ones interested in self-employment. It is estimated that 47% of small and medium-sized enterprises have some degree of female ownership. In addition to *entrepreneur* and *seniorpreneur,* a new term has been coined — *copreneurship*[3] — to describe couples who go into business together.

To create a successful business, you often need more than just a good business idea. Here are several things to consider.

do you have the necessary skills?

Will you require a special licence or certification to run the business? How long will it take you to get it? Do you want to manage the business and hire staff to perform the services? If you haven't run a business before, make a list of all of the professionals, such as an accountant, a lawyer, and a business banker, who you can ask for information or guidance. You may also want to consider taking a course. Many community colleges offer programs specifically tailored to small business management. What's more, you may be able to take advantage of distance or online learning.

---

[2] Statistics Canada 1999 Summer Perspectives, "Working Past Age 65," Mark Walsh.

[3] Statistics Canada 1999 Winter Perspectives 75-001XPE, "Couples in Business."

what capital outlay is needed for the start-up?

Some businesses can be started up with very little initial outlay, while others require much bigger investments to buy machinery or other tools. When a large outlay is required, you need to consider if you will be able to borrow to finance the start-up, or if will you have to dig into your personal savings. Since there is no guarantee that your business will be successful, you need to consider the impact that a bankrupt business would have on your retirement nest egg.

how will the business be structured?

There are three very different ways to structure a business.

1. You can operate as a *sole proprietor,* where you and you alone run the business. Any profit is taxed in your hands personally, which could put you in a higher tax bracket or cause you to have to repay part of your OAS entitlement if your income is above the annual threshold. You will also be personally liable for the debts of the business, which could put your retirement savings at risk if the business fails.

2. You can enter into a *partnership* with another person or persons to share the initial costs to set up the business and day-to-day management. The profit generated will be shared according to each owner's share in the business, and each will report their share of the profit on their personal income tax return.

3. If you decide to *incorporate* the business, it will operate as a separate legal entity. All business profits are reported on a corporate tax return, and tax will be payable at the corporate tax rate. With a corporation, the owner's personal liability is limited to the money invested in the company. Some professionals, including lawyers, architects, engineers, public accountants, and certain medical professionals, can establish what's called a professional corporation. The provinces have different rules around who may create a professional corporation. Unlike a regular corporation, a professional corporation does not absolve a professional of personal liability for his or her own negligence or malpractice.

is there a demand for your product or service?

Even if you believe you have a great business idea, are there people out there willing to hire you or buy your product? Do some market research, either by hiring a company to do this for you, or by talking to potential customers about what they are looking for and what would make them switch to a new provider.

who are your competitors?

Search the Internet for similar businesses and visit their Web sites to get an idea of their products and services, pricing, locations, and how they advertise to potential customers. How do you intend to compete for business? Do you have a better product, a better price, better delivery, or better customer service?

location

Where will your business be located? Will you be renting office or warehouse space? Can you save costs by operating out of your home? Check with your local municipal office about any restrictions, permits, or other requirements that must be met regarding the operation of a home business.

marketing strategy

How will potential customers learn about your business? Do you have a marketing plan and budget? Have you considered costs such as having a Web site, advertising in print media like newspapers or magazines, or sending direct mail marketing, or will you be relying on word-of-mouth referrals?

time commitment

How much time will you need to dedicate to running the business? In analyzing the time commitment required, consider whether you can be absent from your business when you want to take a vacation, and if your employees can handle things while you're away.

franchise option

When you buy a franchise you buy the right to operate a business that may already have a proven brand, and an established system of operation. As a franchisee, you don't build a business from scratch but rather you manage the particular franchise location. In some cases, you can even find a home-based franchise that might be appropriate for you. Your initial costs include an upfront franchise fee and, as part of the agreement, you may receive start-up training and ongoing assistance. You will also have to pay a royalty to the franchisor on all sales you generate.

rescue it!

☐ Take a course — many colleges offer business courses that can help you to understand what it takes to start and manage a business.

☐ Consider forming a partnership or purchasing a franchise — joining forces with someone who has the skills you don't have and can provide additional capital can make the transition to business ownership easier.

☐ Start slowly — perhaps you can start doing some market research and making contacts through your network while you are still working. Depending on the nature of the business, you may be able to try it out slowly and then expand as the business grows.

PART 7

spending in retirement

CHAPTER 32

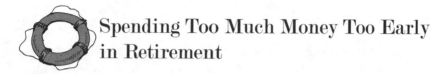 Spending Too Much Money Too Early in Retirement

Despite the excitement you might feel as you enter retirement, dipping into your nest egg too quickly can increase the chance that you will run out of money before you run out of time.

IF THE GOAL DURING OUR WORKING YEARS is to save as much as we can for retirement, then once we get there, it's natural to want to start spending the money. After all, that's all part of the plan. You work, you save; you retire, you spend. The difficult part is that you never know exactly how long retirement will last, or how much money will be needed in the various phases of retirement.

different phase, different spending

We know that retirement can last 30 years or more, and a lot can happen during that time period. Retirement is not one long phase of life — it's better described as several shorter phases that vary in duration and can be very different from each other.

It's common to think of retirement in terms of three phases. In the early phase of retirement, you're active and on the go; in the middle phase you're a pro at retirement and have settled into a routine; in the later phase, you truly slow down and the theory is that your spending decreases significantly. That frame of thinking reflected the norm for previous generations, but looking at today's pre-retirees, we see that retirement isn't the same as it used to be, and the different phases won't be the same either. For instance, rather than reducing spending as the years go by, you may need to increase spending substantially.

Let's take a closer look at each of the three phases.

Early Phase

The first few years of retirement are similar to the honeymoon years. This is because you've been waiting and planning for this moment for quite some time and are anxious to do all the things you've put off doing during your working years. Plus, early in the retirement phase, you are the most healthy and active you'll ever be so you may want to do things that might be more physically challenging, such as training for a marathon or climbing Mount Kilimanjaro. This may also be the first time in a while that you haven't received a steady income from work and have had to rely on accumulated savings to fund your needs. For some, this phase will include an additional sub-phase — one that includes you changing your mind and deciding to go back to work, either for pay or not, maybe full time or maybe part time or perhaps spending some time in volunteer work.

Middle Phase

Although the duration of this phase is different for everyone, it is usually the longest phase. During this phase, you know what you enjoy doing, and you're more realistic about how much time and money certain activities consume. You're clearer on what retirement means for you and you understand what it's going to take for you to be happy. You may still be trying new things, but you've developed a routine. You may spend more time at home, rather than travelling to other countries. You are fully aware of your sources of income, and are accustomed to managing your cash inflows and outflows.

Late Phase

What about the later years — the so-called slow years? There is no set age for when these years begin. It may be your health that prompts you to slow down, or other family circumstances, such as the loss of a partner. While it's true that you might not be jet-setting around the world (or maybe you will be), you will likely be spending more money on things you've never had to spend on before, such as home care or other services, including someone to cut your grass or shovel your driveway. Rather than reduced spending because of a slower lifestyle, costs may be higher because of health-related expenses.

Lack of Pensions

When does your retirement phase begin? The earlier you retire and stop working entirely, the longer your accumulated retirement nest egg has to last. Simple enough, but there's one major concern and that's pensions. The earlier you retire, the less likely it is that you'll have full access to pensions, including CPP/QPP, OAS, and company pension plans, and as a result, you'll be dipping into your savings a lot sooner than you probably had planned. And by a lot more!

To put it in perspective, if you decide to call it quits at age 55 but don't start collecting CPP/QPP and OAS until age 65, you'll be without these pensions for a full 10 years. If you have plenty of other sources of income, then you may not even miss these amounts. However, if you do need the income, you would need to have what I call a Retire Early Fund of approximately $160,000 in savings just to bridge the income gap for those 10 years. Does that sound like a huge amount of money? It isn't, and let me explain why. I'll assume the Retire Early Fund is a RRIF, because withdrawals are fully taxable, as the income from the CPP/QPP and OAS would be. A $160,000 RRIF will provide a full 10 years' worth of annual withdrawals of $17,800 (which is approximately the maximum combined CPP/QPP and OAS for a 65-year-old in 2011), inflation adjusted at 2% per year where the investments earn a 5% rate of return. If your Retire Early Fund is a tax free savings account (TFSA), you can get away with a smaller fund, because withdrawals won't be fully taxable. If you are in a 30% tax bracket, the after-tax amount of the $17,800 RRIF withdrawal is equal to $12,460, so, using that amount as the TFSA withdrawal, the TFSA Retire Early Fund will have to be $110,000.

Withdrawals from either a taxable account or a TFSA are more tax-efficient than RRSP or RRIF withdrawals, so even if you accumulate less money, you may still be able to receive the same after-tax amount.

After 10 years of withdrawals, your entire RRIF or TFSA Retire Early Fund will be depleted, but you will be 65 and eligible to collect full CPP/QPP and OAS.

one-time withdrawals

If you don't have a Retire Early Fund, then you need to consider how making large withdrawals from your current savings will affect how long those savings will last. You can guess the answer — there will be a big impact — but let's do the numbers anyway . . .

Let's take a look at the impact that a one-time withdrawal at the start of early retirement will have on your savings by comparing the value of an RRSP with and without a one-time withdrawal at the beginning of retirement.

Let's say you start retirement and you make a one-time RRSP withdrawal of $20,000 from your $160,000 RRSP. Ten years after the one-time withdrawal, assuming the RRSP earns 5% over this period, the RRSP has grown to $228,045. The RRSP without the withdrawal would have grown to $260,623. The difference between the two account is significant — it's 63% more than the original $20,000 withdrawal. In this example there was only one withdrawal made from the RRSP, but often withdrawals are more frequent in the early phase of retirement. Spending too much early on in the retirement years can easily and quickly wipe away all those years of saving. Often, you are able to do the things you want without it costing too much. Always do a cost benefit analysis when you're thinking about making large expenditures from your retirement savings.

rescue it!

☐ Start a Retire Early Fund.

☐ Find ways to enjoy activities without it costing too much.

☐ Transition into retirement by working part time to fill the income gap until pensions begin.

CHAPTER 33

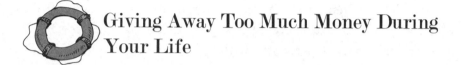 Giving Away Too Much Money During
Your Life

Big caution here — you may live 30 years in retirement — are
you sure you don't need the money?

YOU'VE HAD A GOOD LIFE, AND NOW you want to help your children or grandchildren financially. They'll inherit your money anyway, but helping them while you're alive allows you to see them enjoying the gift! It's perfectly normal for parents to want to help their children succeed and be well-rounded, successful, and confident adults. But at what cost? Decisions around saving and investing often include decisions around paying for children's activities and education costs. One of my colleagues said his rule is that he will pay for the first university degree, but the rest of his savings are for his retirement. I know another person who had to take out a line of credit on her home to pay for post-secondary educations for her three children. For parents who have not saved for education by contributing to an Registered Education Savings Plan (RESP), borrowing or withdrawing funds from their RRSP is becoming more common as tuition costs continue to climb, and more and more children are leaving home and taking up residence closer to campus. Just when you should be saving as much as you can for your future, expenses may increase substantially as you're paving the way for a child's future.

As you approach retirement, you need to start thinking more about *your* future and how much money *you'll* need, rather than how much you should be giving to the kids. If you haven't saved enough and are close to running out of money during retirement, how comfortable would you be asking your children for financial support? Do you want to rely on your kids to help pay for your retirement needs?

gifts as you approach retirement years

Gifts to adult children can be problematic for three reasons. First of all, the gift may result in a taxable event to the parent. Second, you lose control over the funds once they are gifted. Third, giving gifts to adult children exposes your gifts to your child's creditors.

Family Support

Another trend is parents supporting adult children, with or without their own children, after a divorce. There may also be feelings of guilt or possible undue influence from a child causing you to make a gift.

Assisting Kids to Buy a Home

Home prices are high and giving money for the down payment is quite common. Care should be taken when doing this, because giving a child money to buy their family home can create an unintended result should your child get a divorce. A family home has special characteristics in divorce claims and may be split 50/50, which would include any money you've given to your child to help buy the home. As a result, you could find yourself losing 50% of your original gift to an eventual ex-spouse. If you are giving money to buy a home, you should consider registering a mortgage on the home you helped to buy. This protects your loan from creditors and division of assets as part of a divorce settlement.

Charitable Giving

When supporting a favourite charity, large donations during your lifetime may or may not be fully tax-deductible, based on your taxable income. Large donations also impact how much money is left over for you. It is often a better strategy to leave a legacy to a favourite charity directly in your will. If you are concerned that there may not be sufficient assets to leave the kind of legacy you wish, you can also consider purchasing a life insurance policy and naming the charity as a beneficiary. Not only do you get annual charitable receipts for the premiums, you'll be sure the donation will be made in full.

Non-Cash Gifts

Give away personal property or family heirlooms during your lifetime. You'd be surprised how much these gifts mean to children or grandchildren, and they don't have to cost you anything. These items are usually not specifically outlined in detail in your will, but even some of your least valuable possessions can cause some of the most heated battles. Giving them away while you are alive allows you to discuss your decision with family members and minimize family disputes.

impact on your estate

When making a gift during your lifetime, you will want to consider how your gift to one child will impact the total value of your remaining estate, which would be divided among your beneficiaries. Many gifts and loans to children and other family members are not documented. No one may know about the gift or loan other than the person making the gift and the person who receives it. When it comes to estate distribution, it is quite common for parents to want to divide their estate equally among their children. Making a gift or a loan to one child can cause unintended results if the gift is not taken into account in the distribution of assets under a parent's will, or if the loan is not paid back prior to the parent's death. It can also develop into a legal dispute, as the children fight to prove whether the asset transfer was indeed a gift or a loan.

Giving away money during your lifetime so you can see your family enjoy it is wonderful if you can afford to do it. But you need to be certain that you can indeed afford to give away your money and won't need it later on in life for health care, home renovations, or simply because you live a long life.

rescue it!

☐ Rather than cash, give away personal property or family heirlooms during your lifetime.

☐ Grandchildren — if you want to help fund a grandchild's education, open an RESP to benefit from tax-deferred growth and take advantage of free money from federal and some provincial governments in the form of Canada Education Savings Grants and Canada Learning Bonds. One other important feature of the RESP is that you can take back your contributions should you need the money back during your retirement years.

☐ Draft a loan — document the fact that a loan has been given to a family member and ask for a demand promissory note.

☐ Register a mortgage on the home you helped your children to buy.

☐ Document large gifts and amend your will to take the gift(s) into account when dividing up the estate amongst the beneficiaries.

CHAPTER 34

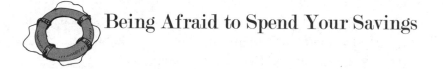 Being Afraid to Spend Your Savings

You've worked hard to accumulate personal savings for retirement and now that you are retired, why should you be afraid to spend the money?

AFTER YEARS OF SAVING FOR THE FUTURE, are you ready to shift from seeing your account grow over time to watching your savings shrink as you make regular withdrawals from your savings to pay for your living expenses? Many people aren't and, as a result, some enter retirement hoping to live off the income and growth while leaving the capital intact for emergencies or to pass on to the next generation.

We've heard that Canadians haven't saved enough, and we've heard that we can expect to live a long time in retirement, so it's no wonder some of us are worried about spending too much money and running out. Calculating how much you can withdraw from your savings on an annual basis is not an easy thing to do, especially when there are so many different factors to consider. Experts have established general guidelines to follow, but those too are full of estimates and assumptions. For instance, the usual thinking is that a withdrawal rate of 3 to 5% of the balance in a particular account will provide withdrawals for up to 30 years. That is, provided the account is invested in a balanced portfolio and you don't make any additional withdrawals.

Another thing that needs to be considered is the type of account that you will be withdrawing from. For instance, withdrawals from registered accounts such as RRSPs/RRIFs and DPSPs (Deferred Profit Sharing Plans) are fully taxable as ordinary income; withdrawals from TFSAs attract no tax whatsoever; withdrawals from non-registered savings and investment accounts may attract taxation if the amounts withdrawn have increased in value since they were purchased. In chapter 32 we saw how a smaller TFSA Retire Early Fund could generate the same after-tax income as a much larger RRIF. Here's another example that illustrates how a $30,000 withdrawal is treated differently depending on the type of account.

Example: Withdraw shares in ABC Company, purchased for $10,000, now worth $30,000, and assuming a 30% tax rate. It compares a fully taxable RRIF, a tax free savings account and a non-registered investment account.

	RRIF	**TFSA**	**Investment account**
Withdrawal	$30,000	$30,000	$30,000
Taxes owing	($ 9,000)	NIL	($ 3,000)
Net proceeds	**$21,000**	**$30,000**	**$27,000**

As this example shows, it is critical to choose wisely when deciding from which account to make the withdrawal.

fear of running out of money

The fear of running out of money can paralyze retirees into living a meagre, circumscribed lifestyle. If the primary concern is the uncertainty around longevity — meaning how long you will live — then a viable solution could be to convert some savings into a stream of payments that are guaranteed for life. With these types of products, regardless of how long you live, you can be assured of receiving a steady, reliable income stream. Whether this strategy is appropriate for you depends not only on your views around longevity but also on your risk tolerance, your desire to leave an estate, and how much flexibility you want. Let me explain. If you have a low tolerance for risk, then your savings may not grow as much as you need them to, and they will be depleted faster during the spending phase. Also, if you wish to leave a legacy, you should revaluate which income for life products work best for you, because many of these products provide little if any estate value to beneficiaries. Finally, if you wish to retain access to and control over your money for emergencies or unforeseen expenses, your choice of income for life products may be limited.

Just as you would do when building an accumulation portfolio, you should also diversify your retirement spending portfolio. You do not need to choose one product or solution for all of your savings. One approach may be to ensure you have a guaranteed lifetime income stream that covers at least your basic needs, and then you can invest the rest of your savings in other products that give you the flexibility for discretionary spending, emergencies, or leaving an estate.

not wanting to spend capital

There is a certain sense of security knowing you have money available should you need it for emergencies, but chances are you will need this capital to help pay for your retirement lifestyle.

It's surprising how many people still believe they can live off the income their savings will generate without having to spend any of their savings. While this may have been possible in previous years when interest rates were in the double digits, it will be next to impossible to achieve that now unless you have a very large capital base, or interest rates increase substantially. You shouldn't be afraid to spend some of your capital, as long as it's done in a steady and systematic way — not spending too much in the early years, and determining the maximum amount that can be withdrawn each year so you don't spend it too quickly. While this may require a reduction in retirement lifestyle, make sure you still actually do some of the things you've been looking forward to doing. Don't wait too long to do those things because you don't want to find that your health prevents you from doing the things you've put off for too long.

wanting to leave an estate

Few people look forward to discussing death and estate planning, but most people agree that they wish to leave an inheritance. Discussions regarding leaving an inheritance should not be approached without a careful analysis of whether leaving an inheritance is a realistic goal. Perhaps you have more than enough money to live on, so this won't be an issue for you, or maybe you don't. But if leaving an estate is a dream you wish to preserve, then you have to face the reality that what's left for you to use during your retirement is going to be less. So it's important to consider whether your children need the inheritance, or if it's something that is more important to *you*. While parents would like to leave an inheritance, most children say they would prefer knowing that their parents are living a comfortable life. The lack of open dialogue around inheritances can lead to financial insecurity both for the person leaving an inheritance and those who expect to receive a larger inheritance than they actually get.

Following are four approaches to decisions around inheritance planning.

1. Use whatever money you need to live the lifestyle you wish, and the children will receive an inheritance if there's anything left.

2. At the start of retirement, deliberately allocate a portion of your savings to an inheritance for the kids and don't use this money for your retirement.

3. Purchase life insurance to create an estate at your death.

4. Buy an annuity to create income for life and use some of the cash flow from the annuity to buy a life insurance policy that replaces the savings used to buy the annuity. This is referred to as an insured annuity strategy.

rescue it!

☐ If you are concerned about outliving your money, consider products that pay a guaranteed income for life. Speak to your financial advisor about the options and costs for these types of products, and build them into your retirement income plan.

☐ Determine how important it is for you to leave an estate, and consider how much you would like to leave.

☐ Assess whether you can afford to leave a legacy and, if not, discuss options with your financial advisor to create an estate by using life insurance products.

☐ Have an open dialogue with your children about your wish to leave an inheritance — you may find your children would rather you use the money during your lifetime.

PART 8

paying too much tax

CHAPTER 35

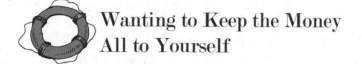 Wanting to Keep the Money
All to Yourself

*Not splitting income could mean paying a lot more tax, now
and during your retirement years.*

CANADA HAS WHAT IS CALLED a progressive tax system with different tax brackets, which means the more income you earn, the higher your tax rate on the income earned in that higher tax bracket. Canadians in the highest tax bracket pay anywhere from 38% to up to 50% tax, depending on the province or territory of residence. On the other hand, Canadians with little or no income pay zero tax. A typical retiree age 65 and over can earn approximately $19,000 of income (assuming at least $2,000 of pension income) before paying any federal income tax.

Because Canadians file separate tax returns from their spouse or common-law partner, there may be situations where one person is paying tax at the highest rate and the other is paying no tax at all. If these two individuals could somehow share or split their income as reported on their tax returns, they could save a great deal of tax. Here's an example of how this could work.

No income splitting:

	Spouse A	Spouse B	Combined
Income	$65,000	$5,000	$70,000
Tax estimate	$13,000	$ 0	$13,000
Net after tax	$52,000	$5,000	$57,000

With income splitting:

	Spouse A	Spouse B	Combined
Income	$35,000	$35,000	$70,000
Tax estimate	$ 5,000	$ 5,000	$10,000
Net after tax	$30,000	$30,000	$60,000

Although this example is a bit of an oversimplification, splitting income saves the family $3,000 in taxes. While this is often impossible to accomplish during working years, when employment income cannot generally be split, it would provide a fantastic opportunity to reduce a family's income taxes. For those who are self-employed, splitting income can be more easily accomplished by hiring a spouse and paying a reasonable salary for the work being done.

The end goal in income splitting is to reduce or eliminate income tax for the family. By reducing income tax, the family increases their net cash available to spend or invest. Reducing income tax has the same result as earning more money — but it gives you more money without having to work more or take on more risk in your portfolio.

The Canadian income tax rules are quite complex, and the rules that deal specifically with income splitting between spouses (called the income attribution rules) are often being tested in the court system.

By wanting to keep the money, and more specifically investment assets, in one person's name, you are forgoing the opportunity to significantly reduce your family's income tax bill, both today and during retirement, when every penny counts. Income tax can impact your cash flow even more than inflation and rates of return. By *sharing* investment assets, you will be sharing the investment income and reducing your income taxes. Here's another example. If Julie, a high-income earner, invests $10,000 and earns $1,000 in interest income, the tax could be as high as 50%, depending on her province of residence. But if John, her lower income earning spouse, had earned the $1,000 interest income, the taxes would have been substantially lower and maybe even zero, resulting in the family getting to keep and use more of the $1,000. So to save some tax, a high-income spouse might consider making a gift to the low-income spouse of $10,000 to invest. The following tax year, the low-income spouse earns $1,000 — who pays the tax? You might think it's the low-income spouse, but due to the complex income attribution rules, it's the high-income spouse who must pay the tax on the $1,000, even if the investment is in the other spouse's name. So what went wrong? The current income attribution rules specifically target actions designed to split investment income with a low-income spouse or minor child the way Julie and John have done. The rules look through the transaction and investment made in the name of the lower income earner, usually as a result of a gift of cash or actual investments, as if the transaction never happened, and taxes the higher income earner. In subsequent years, second generation income (for instance, interest earned this year on the interest income earned in previous years) will be taxed in the hands of the lower income earner. But since second generation income is usually a much smaller amount, it will take many years to achieve significant results from income splitting using this strategy.

However, there are a few efficient and highly effective ways to get around the income attribution rules and do income splitting. Read on . . .

use a spousal RRSP

There are significant advantages of using a spousal RRSP to build retirement assets for a lower income spouse. Since the introduction of pension income splitting, some believe there's no longer any use for spousal RRSPs; however, using this strategy works better than using pension income splitting alone.

We already know RRSPs are great for saving for retirement — you get a tax deduction for your contribution, and your money grows untaxed until it is withdrawn — usually during retirement when you're in a lower income tax bracket. However, when you do withdraw those funds, the money is considered taxable income, and when combined with your pensions and other income, it could put you in a higher if not the highest tax bracket, even in your retirement years. On the other hand, if the withdrawal could be taxed in your lower income earning spouse's tax return, you would be splitting income and could save some tax, as shown in the example above. The way to do this is to build retirement assets in your spouse's name before retirement. But how can you build enough retirement assets in your spouse's name to benefit from income splitting? That's where the spousal RRSP comes in.

As you know, you need *RRSP room* to make a contribution. But you may not be aware that your contribution can be made to your own or to a *spousal RRSP*, even if your spouse is not working and does not have any RRSP room. The higher income earner uses their RRSP contribution room to make a contribution to the lower income earner's spousal RRSP. The higher income earner gets the tax deduction and tax savings now, and the money can grow tax-free in the spousal RRSP. During retirement, withdrawals from the spousal RRSP or spousal RRIF will be taxed in the lower income earner's tax return and at the lower rate of tax. Keep in mind that there is no federal income tax on the first $19,000 of income earned by a 65-year-old.

give your spouse a loan

As mentioned, if you give your lower income earning spouse money to invest, the income attribution rules come into play. However, if you loan your spouse money for him or her to invest, and charge interest on the loan, at a rate not less than the prescribed interest rate as specified by CRA, any investment earnings will be taxable to your spouse and not to you. But one important thing to remember is that you do have to charge interest *and* collect the interest on the loan within 30 days after the end of calendar year. It's important to document the loan as evidence of the arrangement, in case you ever need to prove it to CRA.

Here's how it works.

Julie loans John $50,000 and charges interest at the CRA-prescribed interest rate of 1% (this is the rate as of the third quarter of 2011).[1] John invests the money and earns 10%, or $5,000. Let's see how the taxes are paid:

Julie pays tax on $500 (1% of $50,000) of interest income she received from John as a result of the loan.

John pays tax on investment income of $4,500, which is equal to $5,000 he earned on the investments less the $500 of interest that he has to pay

---

[1] Prescribed rates can be found on the CRA Web site: English www.cra-arc.gc.ca/tx/fq/ntrst_rts/menu-eng .html or French www.cra-arc.gc.ca/tx/fq/ntrst_rts/menu-fra.html

Julie because of the loan. Since the loan was for investment purposes, the interest is tax-deductible, as discussed in chapter 15.

Of all of the strategies discussed in this chapter, this one is the most complex, and so tax and legal advice should be obtained prior to entering into such arrangement.

split pension income

Even if it's too late for you to start a spousal RRSP or enter into a spousal loan agreement and make any significant impact in reducing income taxes, all is not lost. In 2008, the federal government introduced rules that allow spouses to split eligible pension income even when it is being received by only one person. Using the pension income splitting rules, you can split up to 50% of eligible pension income with your spouse. Eligible pension income payments include amounts received from an employer pension plan. If you are 65 years of age or older, it also includes withdrawals from a RRIF or annuity payments where the source of the funds was an RRSP, RRIF, or other registered pension fund, such as a defined contribution plan or locked-in RSP (or LIRA) or LRIF/LIF. Payments that cannot be split under the pension splitting rules are OAS payments, CPP/QPP, Saskatchewan Pension Plan payments, or amounts received under a retirement compensation arrangement (RCA).

By splitting pension income, your spouse may qualify for the pension income tax credit on the first $2,000 of pension income. As a result, both you and your spouse can receive up to $2,000 of pension income virtually tax-free. In addition to the pension income credit, depending on the province of residence, the basic personal exemption and the age credit means the spouse may be able to receive close to $19,000 in tax-free income at age 65.

Example: Albert a sole income earner who earns $50,000 per year retires at 65. In retirement he will collect a $20,000 employer pension as well as maximum CPP/QPP and OAS.[2] His spouse Elaine will be entitled only to the maximum OAS because she never worked.

---

[2]www.taxtips.ca/calculators/taxcalculator.htm

During working years, the family income might look like this:

Sole income	
Employment Income	**$50,000**
Less:	
EI/CPP/QPP deductions	($3,000)
Income tax	($9,000)
Net after-tax income	**$38,000**

At retirement, with pension splitting, Albert and Elaine will each include in their income tax return 50% of the employer pension. As a result of pension splitting the couple will have more net income after tax than during their working years:

Two income	Albert	Elaine
OAS/CPP/QPP	$17,000	$ 6,400
Split pension income	$10,000	$10,000
Total income	$27,000	$16,400
Tax	($2,100)	($0)
Net income	**$24,900**	**$16,400**
= total after-tax income for the couple is **$41,300**		

So while the total gross income at retirement is less than the income during the working years, pension income splitting saves the family additional income taxes, which puts them in a better financial position than before retirement. Albert and Elaine may also be eligible for CPP/QPP splitting, which is explained in the next section.

CPP/QPP pension sharing

The CPP/QPP also permits pension sharing of up to 50% of the pension entitlement between spouses and common-law partners. This pension income sharing is separate from a division of accrued benefits as a result of a marriage breakdown. Pension income sharing just evens out the monthly payments between spouses, with the objective of reducing income taxes for the family unit. The way it works is that pension credits earned during years that you were together are eligible to be shared. To qualify, spouses or common-law partners who are together, who are at least 60 years old, and who receive CPP retirement pensions, can share their pension benefits.

To give you an idea of how this works, let's say Albert is eligible to receive CPP/QPP of $11,000 per year and Elaine is eligible to receive $2,000 per year. Using this strategy, in the best-case scenario, Albert and Elaine would each receive pension cheques totalling $6,500. There would be no change whatsoever in total family income, but because CPP/QPP pension of $4,500 has been shifted from the higher income earner to the lower income earner, there could be substantial tax savings to the family.

a word of caution

Although the rules permit splitting of up to 50% of eligible pension income and CPP/QPP, you may not want to split the full 50%. Recall that the strategy is to split income to reduce income tax as much as possible for the family, but by moving income between spouses, other tax programs and incentives may be affected. For instance, if you currently qualify for a spousal tax credit because your spouse is considered a low income earner, giving your spouse additional income may cause you to lose the spousal credit, if your spouse then earns more than the annual maximum amount. Also, if your spouse is claiming the medical expenses tax credit because his or her income is lower, splitting income may reduce or eliminate the credit. Finally, pension income splitting could result in the lower income earner having to pay back some or all of their OAS entitlement if the additional income puts them over the annual income threshold.

use a tax free savings account (TFSA)

The TFSA provides a new strategy to do income splitting, both now and during retirement, without having to worry about income attribution, loans, and interest rates. With a TFSA, none of the income earned in the account is taxable, so when one spouse gives the one other money to make a TFSA contribution, there is no income to attribute back to the higher income earner. As such, a higher income earner can contribute to both their own plan and to a spouse's plan. That doubles the amount of TFSA room from $5,000 to $10,000 per year, and doubles the amount of money that can be invested to earn tax-free income. During retirement, withdrawals made by the lower income spouse do not affect taxable income and won't impact any income-tested tax amounts, such as the age credit or the spousal tax credit, and won't push the individual into a higher tax bracket.

By using a TFSA, Albert can give Elaine $5,000 each year so she can contribute to his own TFSA. No loan is required and no interest needs to be charged. Plus, if it makes sense, Albert can still make a spousal RRSP contribution into Elaine's RRSP, and during retirement they can also take advantage of any of the other pension splitting techniques we already reviewed.

rescue it!

Pre-retirement years

☐ The higher income earning spouse should pay all of the household expenses so the lower income earner can save most of their income in their own name.

☐ If you and your spouse are in different tax brackets today, build assets in the lower income earning spouse's name by making a contribution to their TFSA, setting up a spousal loan, or if you are self-employed, hiring your spouse and paying them a reasonable salary.

☐ If your spouse will be in a lower tax bracket in retirement, start building assets in their name today by using a spousal RRSP.

In the retirement years, if you and your spouse are in different tax brackets:

☐ As soon as you are eligible to split pension income, make an election on your tax return and claim pension income splitting of up to 50% of eligible pension income.

☐ As soon as you are eligible to share CPP/QPP payments, apply to do so.

CHAPTER 36

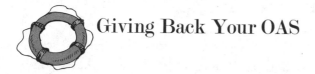 Giving Back Your OAS

Let's face it, OAS isn't a huge sum of money on a monthly basis, but it's there for you if you qualify. The key is to make sure you continue to qualify during your all of your retirement years.

A QUICK REVIEW: OAS IS PAID to Canadians aged 65 and over who have lived in Canada for at least 10 years after their 18th birthday. You get the maximum entitlement after 40 years of Canadian residency (after age 18). While the monthly amount is not significant, if you collect the maximum OAS over a 25-year period, you could receive more than $160,000. Now that we know how much OAS can add up to, it is important to do what we can to keep as much of this income as possible.

Even though there is no withholding tax on OAS payments, the amount you receive from OAS is taxable income and is taxed at your marginal (highest) tax rate. If you have very low income, you may pay very little, if any, tax on this income. This is why most people believe OAS is a tax-free pension. Besides being subject to income tax, OAS is income-tested. What this means is that you may have to give back some or all of your OAS if you have income in excess of the annual threshold amount, which is approximately $67,668 for 2011. At income levels above approximately $109,000, all of the OAS is clawed back. In addition to paying income tax, you effectively also pay another 15% "tax" on income above $67,668 (the 15% is the OAS money you never receive). Most Canadians won't have to worry about the clawback, but just in case you get close to the threshold amount in any given year, here are some ideas that can help you to keep more of your OAS.

withdrawals from your savings

The income threshold is based on income earned in the calendar year. In some cases, you can delay the receipt of taxable income so that it doesn't put you over the annual threshold amount. While most retirement income, such as pension income, is spread out evenly throughout the year, if you will also be making withdrawals from your personal savings to generate additional cash flow, you can time those withdrawals so you don't realize too much income in a particular year. If you ignore the impact that additional income has on your OAS entitlement, you could lose part of your OAS pension.

Here's what happened to Jane. Upon retirement, Jane wanted to rebalance her portfolio to better reflect her income needs. She had done very well on some shares that she had owned for quite some time. When she sold those shares, she realized a sizeable taxable capital gain. This was not a surprise to her, but when she prepared her tax return, she *was* surprised to learn that she had to repay most of her OAS for that year because the taxable capital gain put her over the maximum income threshold amount. Had she split up the transactions and sold some of her investments in December and the rest in January, she would have been able to spread the income over two different tax years and keep most of her OAS for both of those years.

Example: How to reduce the OAS clawback

Let's assume pension and other income in 2011 is $50,000. There is a taxable capital gain of $32,000. The total income for 2011 is $82,000, which is above the annual OAS threshold of $67,668. Therefore the OAS clawback is $2,149.80, which is calculated as 15% of the income above the threshold amount or $82,000 minus $67,668 multiplied by 15% equals $2,149.80. But if the capital gain is realized over two tax years, so that $16,000 is realized in 2011 and $16,00 is realized in 2012, the clawback can be avoided in each of 2011 and 2012 because taxable income in each of those years falls below the threshold amount:

Tax year	2011	2012
Income	$50,000	$50,000
Taxable capital gain	$16,000	$16,000
Total	**$66,000**	**$66,000**

Another way to minimize taxable capital gains is to sell some investments with accrued losses (i.e., investments that are worth less today than they were when you bought them). By selling those shares you trigger the capital loss, and it can be used to offset some of the capital gains. (Of course, you can't repurchase those loss shares for 30 days, otherwise the loss will be denied.) The income tax rules for capital gains and losses are complex, so it's wise to get the proper tax and investment advice before entering into these transactions.

It is best to review your portfolio at least five years before retirement, and if necessary begin the process of rebalancing over time. If you start this prior to age 65, you avoid OAS clawback. Waiting until retirement puts undue pressure on you, and you may find yourself selling in a market decline. Those who retired in 2008 or 2009 may have found themselves rebalancing a portfolio during the worst possible time.

Another strategy to reduce income and maximize the OAS is to make withdrawals from your RRSP or RRIF earlier than age 65, so that once you begin to collect OAS the required minimum RRSP/RRIF withdrawal will be smaller and will have less impact on your total income and the OAS clawback. This may not be appropriate for two reasons. First of all, you want to preserve the tax-deferred growth of your RRSP or RRIF as long as you can. Second, taking RRIF withdrawals early only works if you are no longer working full time and you have low income, because withdrawals while you are still working could put you in a higher tax bracket, resulting in a higher rate of income tax on the withdrawal than you might pay during retirement.

use pension income splitting techniques

There are three very effective ways to split pension income during retirement and with the first two, you don't have to plan for it years in advance. First of all, the pension income splitting rules found in the *Income Tax Act* allow you and your spouse or common-law partner to split up to 50% of qualified pension income. Second, the CPP/QPP benefit splitting rules also allow splitting of up to 50% of pensions.[1] The third method requires some early planning: you can make contributions to a spousal RRSP so that, during retirement, your spouse will be taxed on the withdrawals made from the spousal RRSP, even though you made the contributions. Although most people think of these strategies as ways to reduce total income tax paid by a couple, the fact that the higher income spouse will be reporting a lower taxable income for the year can also result in them retaining a bigger portion of their OAS. Although income splitting can be very tax-effective and help you keep more of your OAS, giving your spouse more income may cause you to lose out on some federal or provincial tax credits, such as the spousal credit and medical tax credit.

minimize income tax on investments

Holding Canadian dividend-paying investments in your non-registered portfolio during retirement is a good strategy for creating tax-efficient income. One word of caution for those with considerable dividend income — be aware of the dividend "gross-up," which artificially increases your net income before adjustments. Dividends from Canadian public companies are grossed-up, which means you include 144% of the actual dividend you receive in your tax return. A $10,000 dividend increases your income not by $10,000 but by $14,400. And although the dividend tax credit reduces the total tax you pay on those dividends, the higher dividend amount counts as income and might put you over the threshold and cause you to lose some of your OAS.

---

[1] Pension income splitting and CPP/QPP benefit splitting are discussed in more detail in chapter 17.

use TFSAs

If you find you need a bit more money in a particular year, you should make the TFSA the first place you look for the cash flow. Withdrawals are tax-free whether you are withdrawing your original contribution or income earned in the account, so they won't affect your taxable income *at all* and therefore will not impact your OAS entitlement. What's more, unlike an RRSP, you can recontribute the money back into your TFSA in future years without it affecting your annual contribution room. You do need to keep in mind that you are not permitted to make the recontribution within the same year that you made the withdrawal or there will be a penalty.

rescue it!

☐ Make an estimate of your retirement income to determine how close you might be to the OAS threshold. Ask your financial advisor to help you with this.

☐ Begin to rebalance your portfolio up to five years before you start collecting OAS, so that there is no spike in income resulting from capital gains.

☐ With advice and proper planning you can reduce the impact that a withdrawal from your savings will have on your income and the OAS clawback.

CHAPTER 37

 Not Taking Advantage of Tax Gifts Such As the Tax Free Savings Account

We all want to reduce the taxes we pay, and there's no better way to do that than with a TFSA, a tax free savings account.

A NEW TYPE OF ACCOUNT WAS INTRODUCED to Canadians on January 1, 2009, which will change the way we approach saving and investing. It is the tax free savings account (TFSA). When making decisions about what types of investments to hold in a TFSA, you will not have to be concerned with how the investment income is going to be taxed. While contributions are made from after-tax dollars, meaning you do not get a tax deduction for your contribution, all investment income, whether it is interest, dividends, or capital gains, is tax-free — both while it is in the account and at the time it is withdrawn. This makes the TFSA unique in Canada, as the money that can be received tax-free makes a very short list: the proceeds from a life insurance policy; lottery winnings; an inheritance (although the deceased's estate might be liable to pay tax before you receive the inheritance); the proceeds from the sale of your home; up to $750,000 of capital gain on the sale of private company shares or farm property — and that's pretty much it. Over the years we've lost the opportunity to earn up to $100,000 in general capital gains tax-free — that was eliminated in February 1994.

So, rather than earning income tax-free, we've been able to defer or postpone tax on investments earned in retirement accounts such as an

RRSP/RRIF, registered pension plan, or Deferred Profit Sharing Plan (DPSP), but payments out of these accounts are fully taxable as ordinary income. So it stands to reason that the TFSA provides a big tax savings opportunity and you should take maximum advantage of it.

TFSA rules

A Canadian resident aged 18 and over (19 in provinces where this is the age of majority) with a social insurance number can open a TFSA. Individuals will receive $5,000 of contribution room each year, regardless of whether they have opened an account or not. If the maximum contribution is not made in the year, the unused room can be carried forward to future years. Some believe that the $5,000 contribution room is too low to make any significant impact on savings and taxes, but the TFSA can grow over time. For instance, since the account was created in 2009, accumulated contribution room to 2011 is $15,000 and by 2012, total contribution room will be $20,000 ($40,000 for a couple).

Another feature is that there is no limit on how long you can have a TFSA. Since the TFSA is not just for retirement, you can continue to contribute for as long as you wish. What's more, there is no mandatory withdrawal amount, so you never have to take money out of the TFSA if you don't need to. If you do make a withdrawal from the TFSA, you can recontribute the amount you have withdrawn back into your TFSA in future years, but no earlier than the following year. This is especially useful if you have contributed to the TFSA, made withdrawals, and later receive a windfall or inheritance. The recontribution amount is over and above any regular contribution room you have. The following example shows how it worked for Martin.

Example:

Year	Contribution room	Contribution (Withdrawal)	Carry-forward room
2009	$5,000	$ 0	$ 5,000
2010	$5,000	$10,000	$ 0
2011	$5,000	($10,000)	$15,000
2012	$5,000	$20,000	$ 0
2013	$5,000	$ 2,000	$ 3,000

Even though the TFSA became available in 2009, Martin doesn't need to have a TFSA to get the contribution room. In the example above, if Martin opens a TFSA in 2010, he can make the full $10,000 contribution, based on his unused room. In 2011 Martin withdraws the $10,000, but he must wait until 2012 if he wants to recontribute the $10,000. He can then also make a regular contribution based on his room for that year. This example assumes no income was earned on the TFSA contribution, but if Martin's original $10,000 contribution had grown to $25,000 and he withdrew the entire $25,000, then the recontribution amount would be $25,000 and not $10,000. The entire amount of a TFSA withdrawal can be recontributed.

investments

Although the TFSA contains the word *savings*, it does not mean that the account should be used as you would an ordinary savings account. The TFSA is like a shopping cart that can hold a wide range of investments: guaranteed investment certificates, mutual funds, publicly traded securities such as stocks and bonds, and certain shares of small business corporations. Any investment that you can hold in your RRSP/RRIF can be held in a TFSA. This provides an excellent opportunity to build a portfolio that meets your risk tolerance and investment goals.

in-kind contributions

In some cases, rather than making a cash contribution, you may have some investments that you would like to contribute directly to your TFSA. While your financial institution may be able to accommodate the in-kind contribution, this transaction will result in what CRA calls a *deemed disposition at fair market value* and it will treat the transaction as if you had sold the investment prior to contributing it to the TFSA. As a result, there may be capital gains taxes due, if the value of the investments being contributed exceeds the amount you originally paid. If you are contributing investments that are in a loss position, meaning they are worth less today than what you originally paid for them, then the loss is denied and cannot be used to offset any other capital gains you might have.

TFSAs grow retirement savings

The TFSA is being hailed as an ideal savings vehicle for young investors who are in a low tax bracket and won't get a large tax saving from making an RRSP contribution, and who may need to access their savings for other things, such as a down payment for a home. However, a TFSA provides everyone with an unmatched opportunity to save tax-free, and therefore provides an excellent savings vehicle to accumulate retirement savings, no matter what stage of life you might be at. While Canadians are accustomed to using RRSPs for retirement, a TFSA can be used in addition to making regular RRSP contributions. And since the $5,000 contribution room accumulates each year regardless of whether you are working or not, you can continue to make contributions to the TFSA well after you retire.

why continue to have TFSAs during retirement?

1. To minimize income tax on investment income.

2. To maximize OAS entitlement, since income earned and all withdrawals from a TFSA are not considered income.

3. To continue to shelter future growth on your RRIF withdrawals — if you do not need the cash from your RRIF withdrawal, you can contribute it to a TFSA and continue to shelter future growth on your contribution.

4. To give you the flexibility to pay for unexpected costs without increasing your taxable income, which could reduce the age credit or medical tax credit.

5. To preserve the tax-free status of an inheritance you have received, since growth is not taxed in a TFSA.

6. To maximize the value of an inheritance you are leaving, because the account can be closed and passed to the next generation without paying any taxes.

income splitting

For couples where only one person is working, a TFSA can be used to create investment assets in the other person's name. Again, there are very few ways to do income splitting with a lower income spouse, and the TFSA provides a simple way to accomplish income splitting without having to be mindful of complex tax rules. For a couple, the combined TFSA contribution is $10,000 each year, which can certainly add up to a significant amount over time.

Everyone should absolutely open a TFSA and contribute the $5,000 maximum each year. If you have a child who is 18 or over, if they start early enough, they may never pay income tax on any investment income they earn!

rescue it!

☐ Open a TFSA today and contribute as much as you can.

☐ Double up on tax-free savings by opening an account for a spouse or common-law partner.

☐ Don't just save—invest. Review your investments and make sure they reflect your personal situation and investment goals.

CHAPTER 38

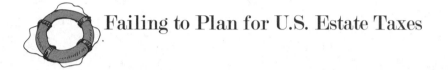 Failing to Plan for U.S. Estate Taxes

Without proper planning, Canadians who own property in the U.S. may find themselves having to pay substantial estate tax to the U.S. government at death.

MANY COUNTRIES IMPOSE AN ESTATE TAX or succession duties. In Canada, although there is no estate tax, Canadian estates may be subject to tax at death in one of two ways. Individuals are deemed to have disposed of all of their assets at the time of death, which may result in taxable capital gains on property, as well as income tax on the value of their RRSP and RRIF accounts. In addition, estates may be subject to probate fees, which are fees levied on the value of assets that must pass through a will to be distributed to the beneficiaries. Quebec is the only province that does not levy a probate fee.

Canadian estates may also have to pay U.S. estate tax on U.S. property owned at the time of death. In 2010, the U.S. estate tax was repealed, which meant anyone who died in 2010 did not have to pay any U.S. estate tax regardless of the size of their estate. But for deaths that occur in 2011 and 2012, the estate tax can be as high as 35% of the value of the U.S. property. Assuming there is no change in current U.S. legislation, the tax rates will be as high as 55% for deaths in 2013 and beyond. For now, the best approach is to plan to minimize U.S. estate tax and wait to see what the legislation will be in future years.

This may come as a surprise to most Canadians, but the U.S. imposes an estate tax on *all individuals,* including Canadian residents, who own certain U.S. assets at their death. U.S. estate tax is imposed on ownership of assets and does not depend on whether you live in the U.S. or spend any time there. However, if you are a U.S. citizen or green card holder, your U.S. estate tax will be based on your worldwide assets, not just your U.S. property.

are you exempt?

All non-resident aliens of the U.S. are permitted a basic estate tax credit of US$13,000 against the U.S. estate tax. This basically exempts the first US$60,000 of taxable U.S. property. Another important thing to note is that the Canada-U.S. income tax treaty gives Canadians a credit against the estate tax, so that Canadians with a worldwide estate valued at less than US$5 million (or US$10 million if the spouse inherits the entire U.S. estate) will not have to pay the U.S. estate tax. So if the value of your assets falls below either of these two thresholds — $60,000 of U.S. property or a worldwide estate of less than US$5 million — you don't have to worry about having to pay any U.S. estate tax when you file the U.S. estate tax return. It's important to know that if you are relying on a treaty exemption to reduce or eliminate your U.S. estate tax, then you have to file a U.S. estate tax return to claim the exemption.

Upon your death, the deemed disposition rules in Canada may result in capital gains tax or it may not. For instance, if at the time of your death the fair market value of your investments is below the price paid for those investments, there will be a capital loss, not a capital gain. In that case, no tax would be payable by the estate. In fact, if there have been capital gains in the three prior years, the capital loss can be carried back to offset those capital gains and the estate would be entitled to a tax refund. In contrast, U.S. estate tax is imposed on the fair market value of the property at the time of death, rather than on the cost or appreciation of the property. As a result, there may be U.S. estate tax payable on an estate that has net losses.

what is considered U.S. property?

From a Canadian perspective, U.S. assets include real property (such as a vacation home located in the U.S., as well as any furniture, a boat, or even a car that is in the U.S.), and stocks or options to acquire stocks issued by a U.S. corporation, even if held in Canadian brokerage accounts, including RRSPs and RRIFs and TFSAs. If U.S. assets are owned within a Canadian corporation, including a Canadian holding company, there is no U.S. estate tax. Fortunately, not all U.S. investments are subject to the estate tax.

what is NOT considered U.S. property?

- Shares of Canadian companies, even if acquired on a U.S. stock exchange
- U.S. treasury bills
- Personal bank accounts in the U.S.
- Some publicly traded U.S. bonds issued after July 18, 1984
- American depository receipts (ADRs)
- Canadian mutual funds that own U.S. securities

tax relief in detail

The Canada-U.S. tax treaty outlines three very important factors that reduce U.S. estate tax for Canadians.

Basic Unified Credit

The U.S. will allow a Canadian resident's estate to claim a *portion* of the unified credit available to U.S. citizens against the estate taxes that are otherwise payable. For deaths occurring in 2010–2012, the amount of the unified credit available to Canadian residents is $1,730,800. The credit is pro-rated, based on the ratio of the value of U.S. assets to the value of the worldwide assets. As mentioned, Canadians with worldwide assets of less than US$5,000,000 should not have to pay U.S. estate tax. However, the way the formula works, Canadians with larger estates who hold only a small portion of their wealth in the U.S. will have access to a smaller fraction of the unified credit and as a result may have a large U.S. estate tax liability. So if you own US$3 million of U.S. assets and your total world-wide estate is US$10 million, the credit available is $519,240 (30% of the $1,730,800). The U.S. estate tax on $3 million is $680,800, less the credit of $519,240, for a net tax payable of $161,560.

Credit for Surviving Spouse

An additional credit is available under the treaty, effectively doubling the unified credit as determined above in certain situations where the surviving spouse inherits the U.S. property.

Elimination of Double Taxation

Since a Canadian resident may have to pay both U.S. estate tax as well as Canadian income tax on the same U.S. property, double taxation may result at death. The treaty specifically deals with such situations and allows U.S. estate tax payable by Canadians to be claimed as a foreign tax credit on their Canadian tax return for the year of death. Depending on the amount, the foreign tax credit may reduce or eliminate the Canadian income tax on the U.S. property that was subject to U.S. estate tax.

Joint Ownership

In Canada, joint ownership with a spouse or common-law partner avoids probate and, because investments can be inherited by a spouse on a tax deferred basis, it postpones the *deemed disposition* until the death of the surviving spouse. However, under U.S. tax rules, it is assumed that the first person to die contributed 100% of the purchase price of the U.S. property unless there are good records showing the ownership structure. This could result in a deceased Canadian's estate having to pay U.S. estate tax on U.S. property even when there is no Canadian tax on the same property because of the tax-free rollover.

Life Insurance

Insurance proceeds, while non-taxable upon receipt in Canada, do form part of the worldwide value of the estate for U.S. estate tax purposes, so, for instance, a $1 million insurance policy gets added to the denominator, reducing the amount of exempt U.S. assets.

rescue it!

☐ Review your net worth to determine your potential exposure to U.S. estate tax.

☐ Ask your investment advisor how to invest in U.S. securities through Canadian mutual funds.

☐ Get tax advice on whether it is appropriate for you to hold U.S. investments in a Canadian holding company.

☐ Don't wait to sell the U.S. vacation property until after the death of the owner. If it is not being used, sell it and move furniture and other belongings to Canada.

CHAPTER 39

 Paying Too Much Tax on Investments

If you don't consider the after-tax rate of return when selecting your investments, you may be making inappropriate investment decisions and paying too much tax.

THERE ARE TWO THINGS THAT CAN IMPACT your after-tax rate of return: your personal marginal tax rate, and the type of investment return you earn. The more income you earn, the higher the marginal tax rate, and the one thing that is consistent at all levels of income is that the tax you pay on investment returns will vary significantly, depending on the *type* of return those investments earn.

With the introduction of the Tax Free Savings Account (TFSA) in 2009, taxation of investment income may eventually become a moot point. But for now, there are millions of dollars saved in ordinary investment accounts, and so the rate of income tax that is payable on investment returns is something that cannot be ignored. When comparing investments, looking at the expected rate of return without factoring in the potential income tax payable is a mistake, since it gives an inflated view of the expected return. Failing to manage personal income tax both before and during retirement can have a significant impact on how much you can accumulate for the future.

Although there are virtually thousands of investment options available today, there are only *three types* of investment returns: interest, dividends, and capital gains, and as mentioned, *each type* of return is taxed differently.

interest income

Interest income is received on investments such as guaranteed investment certificates (GICs), government and corporate bonds, and certain mutual funds such as money market or bond funds. Interest income is taxed as ordinary income at your marginal tax rate. Keep in mind that for long-term investments that do not pay income annually, such as a five-year GIC, interest income is taxable each year on the anniversary date of the investment, even though it is not paid out to you until maturity. This may cause significant cash flow problems for investors, especially during retirement years, who must pay the tax liability each year without having received the corresponding income. From a tax perspective, interest income is the most expensive form of investment return, and leaves you with the lowest net after-tax amount. For that reason, it is often recommended that interest-bearing investments be held in accounts that either allow you to delay the taxation for as long as you can, such as RRSPs and RRIFs, or avoid tax completely by holding them in a TFSA.

dividend income

If you invest in Canadian companies, either directly by buying shares or indirectly by purchasing a mutual fund or other product that holds shares of Canadian companies, you'll find that some of those companies pay out part of their profits to shareholders in the form of a dividend. When you receive dividends from Canadian companies, these payments are made from after-tax dollars, so to eliminate double taxation when the dividend is received by the shareholder (you), the income tax rate applied is significantly reduced. This is a two-step process, which includes a gross-up of the dividend, which means you include in your tax return 144% of the actual amount received and a dividend tax credit. For lower income earners, the dividend tax credit can eliminate the tax on dividends altogether. In most provinces, if you have no income other than eligible Canadian dividends from public companies, you can earn approximately $50,000 of dividends ($30,000 in Nova Scotia and Quebec) without paying any income tax at all on the dividend. But with the dividend gross-up, instead of including $50,000 of actual dividends in your tax return, you include $72,000 because of the gross-up. This amount of income now puts you over the OAS threshold for the year. (So while you may not pay any income tax, you will lose part of your OAS payment because of the clawback.) The actual amount varies by province, but the result is clear: earning dividend income instead of interest income can greatly reduce the taxes you pay and so you should take this into account when making investment decisions. Even at the top marginal tax rate, if we compare interest income to dividend income, you must earn approximately $1.25 of interest income to receive the same after-tax return as only $1.00 of dividend income. Keep in mind that this rule *only applies to dividends from eligible Canadian companies*. If you receive dividends from a foreign corporation, even if you bought the shares on a Canadian exchange or hold them in a Canadian mutual fund, the dividend is taxed the same way as interest income, and no dividend tax credit is available to reduce the income tax. What's more, there may also be foreign withholding tax on the dividend. Depending on the rate of foreign withholding tax, and your personal marginal tax rate, you may end up paying a higher rate of tax to the foreign country than you would have to pay had you earned the return from a Canadian source.

capital gain/capital loss

When you invest in shares of a company, or in any other asset that may go up or down in value, you will realize a capital gain or a capital loss if the investment is not in a tax-deferred or tax-free account. Capital gains are taxable and receive preferential tax treatment on the tax rate applied to the gains. In Canada, only 50% of a capital gain is taxable; the other 50% is tax-free. While the actual amount will differ based on your province of residence, if we compare interest income to a capital gain, you must earn approximately $1.46 of interest income to receive the same after-tax return as only $1.00 of capital gain income.

What's more, since capital gains are taxed only when realized, you are able to defer the taxation of the annual growth to when the investment is sold. (Unlike the example of the interest on a five-year GIC, which you must pay tax on every year.) In the case of capital gains, if you purchase a $10,000 investment that grows at a rate of 6% per year, and sell the investment after five years for $14,186, the $4,186 capital gain will be taxed only in the year you sell the investment and not annually. One exception to the tax deferral is capital gains distribution from mutual funds, which would be taxable when received. This is because the individual investments in a mutual fund may be bought and sold throughout the year, and any net capital gains at the end of the year are distributed to the unit holders and taxed when in their hands, rather than at the trust level.

If an investment is sold for less than the original purchase price, there is a capital loss. A capital loss is not deductible from other types of income you earn in the year. It is only deductible against capital gains. If you don't have any capital gains to offset a capital loss realized in a particular year, the loss can be carried back to reduce capital gains from up to three previous tax years, or carried forward to reduce future capital gains. Only in the year of death can capital losses that cannot be deducted from capital gains in the previous three years be deducted from all other types of income.

tax-deferred plans

The investments held in tax-deferred registered plans, such as RRSPs and RRIFs, as well as their locked-in counterparts, DC plans and DPSPs, are not subject to income tax on any of the income earned while the money remains in the plan. However, when the funds are withdrawn from these plans, they lose their specific characteristics and the withdrawal is taxed at the same rate as interest income. This is the case even if all of the income earned in those plans was from Canadian dividends or capital gains. While this may deter some people from holding equities in registered plans, individuals need to consider their appropriate asset mix first, and then decide which account should hold the different investments.

return of capital (ROC)

In some cases, investments pay a return of capital to the holder. This is exactly what it sounds like: you are getting part of your original investment back and as a result it is not taxable income. However, if the investment is not in a tax-deferred plan or TFSA, you do need to keep track of the ROC amount and deduct it from your original cost. When you sell the investment, the difference between the selling price and your remaining cost is considered the capital gain.

Comparison of after-tax return: Ontario top marginal rates (June 2011)

	Interest	Dividend (Cdn)	Capital gain
Return	$10,000	$10,000	$10,000
Taxable amount	$10,000	$14,400	$ 5,000
Tax payable	$ 4,641	$ 2,819	$ 2,321
Net after tax	$ 5,359	$ 7,181	$ 7,679

Comparison of after-tax return: British Columbia top marginal rates (June 2011)

	Interest	Dividend (Cdn)	Capital gain
Return	$10,000	$10,000	$10,000
Taxable amount	$10,000	$14,400	$ 5,000
Tax payable	$ 4,370	$ 2,391	$ 2,185
Net after tax	$ 5,630	$ 7,609	$ 7,815

rescue it!

☐ Review your investments to see exactly what kind of income you are earning and how it is taxed.

☐ Keep investments that pay interest income or foreign dividends sheltered in a tax-deferred or tax-free plan.

☐ If you have capital gains, consider selling investments with a capital loss to offset the income taxes.

PART 9

new realities about retirement

CHAPTER 40

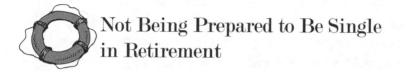 Not Being Prepared to Be Single
in Retirement

So what's wrong with planning a joint retirement? Statistics show that there is a very good chance you will be single in retirement, and your retirement income may be much lower than expected.

IF YOU ARE PART OF a couple right now, your retirement plans likely include both you and your partner. There may be two distinct retirement dates, and two sets of pensions and retirement savings. Still, most of your discussions and plans are based on being together during the retirement years. So you might be surprised to hear that 43% of Canadians aged 65 and older are single. Some never married, but 88% of those singles are widowed, separated, or divorced. Being single at some point in retirement is a new reality that few Canadians have planned for. Whether as a result of a divorce, or the death of a partner, becoming suddenly single at some point during retirement is a reality for many people, and will result in a new set of challenges for the survivor — from both a financial and an emotional perspective.

grey divorce

Divorce is not new. According to a 2006 Statistics Canada survey, a third of marriages in Canada will end in divorce before a couple's 30th anniversary.

However, the general belief has been that if a marriage survived the early years and the middle years (dealing with financial stress and children), the later years were pretty much guaranteed. The assumption was that couples weren't likely to divorce later on in life. How many of us can recall grandparents divorcing? That was then. In Canada, the only age group that is seeing a rise in divorce is people over the age of 50. So it's not a surprise to see the term *grey divorce* beginning to surface around the world. There are many reasons for this. Imagine a couple who spends most of their married life separate and apart from their spouse for 8 to 12 hours a day due to working or managing children's or grandchildren's activities. Then suddenly, during retirement, they find themselves spending the entire day together, day after day, and they realize that they are no longer compatible and have grown apart. Having to face a division of property at a point in time when there are few years to recoup can result in a very different retirement than originally planned. It is much more costly to manage two households than one.

will you be a survivor?

Although we're living longer, many will face retirement alone. There's a 50% chance that at least one member of a couple aged 65 today will live to celebrate a 90th birthday, and a one in four chance that one will live to age 94. The odds are that that person will be a woman. What's more, the loss of a spouse doesn't only happen in old age — the average age for widowhood in Canada is 56.

There are many implications around not being prepared to be single during retirement. The results can be devastating for the survivor, who will need to live on less money than they were living on before the death of the spouse.

impact on women

Although the average total income for a Canadian woman has increased over the years, women typically continue to earn less than men during their working years. Part of the reason for this is that women simply earn less. But that's not all. Women are more likely to work part time and thus not have access to company pension plans. They are also more likely to take extended leaves from work to care for children or aging family members. Taken together, these result in lower savings capacity during working years, and lower government and company pensions during retirement. What's more, since women have a longer life expectancy than men, a few years of funding a man's ill health can quickly erode accumulated savings, leaving much less for a woman to live on during her much longer retirement years.

loss of income

For couples, retirement planning factors in combined savings and dual pensions. However, when the couple are no longer a couple because of either a divorce or death, there can be a substantial loss of retirement income without much decline in expenses.

Let's examine what happens to a retired couple's financial situation in two situations, (1) if they were to become divorced, and (2) if one of the individuals dies. For simplicity, let's assume both of the individuals will be collecting the maximum amount from CPP/QPP and OAS, as well as the same amount from a company pension.

The first scenario looks at the impact of a divorce. If we assume that none of the pensions is subject to division, each person's retirement income is kept intact, but when you look at the impact on total income, each individual has to live with half of the income they were accustomed to having as a couple.

In the second scenario, we look at the impact that a death has on family income. Based on the assumptions that each was collecting the maximum CPP/QPP pensions, the death of one of the partners means a 100% loss of that person's pension entitlements — that's right, there is no survivor pension if the survivor is already collecting a maximum pension. In addition, the survivor options available to a spouse or common-law partner under a company pension plan may be less generous than you think. In fact, most plans provide a surviving spouse with only a fraction of the pension that was paid to the employee. Another thing to consider is that the survivor's higher income may cause other tax concerns. For instance, it may push them into a higher tax bracket, resulting in more tax to be paid, and it may cause OAS clawback if the survivor's total income is above the annual threshold, and it may also reduce other income-tested income tax credits.

Incomes	Couple	Survivor	Difference
CPP/QPP	$23,040	$11,520	
OAS	$12,600	$6,300	
Company pensions (Self)	$48,000	$24,000	
Company pensions (50% survivor)		$12,000	
Total annual income	**$83,640**	**$53,820**	**$29,820**

In this example, the survivor's retirement income drops by more than one-third.

A survivor will end up with less total income than when they were in a couple relationship, but more than someone who becomes divorced.

Without any advanced planning, the survivor will face having to make big changes in lifestyle to deal with the loss of income. Even couples who feel they have saved enough for their retirement, or at least have managed to make do with what they have accumulated, need to consider how a death will affect the survivor. Part of retirement planning that cannot be overlooked is an analysis of survivor income. It's essential to consider investment, insurance, and pension options that will provide maximum income for survivors.

lack of investment knowledge worsens the situation

Many of us think financial matters are just too complicated and happily relegate financial decisions, such as saving and investing, to a spouse who is more knowledgeable and confident. While this may seem to some as a viable solution, in reality it's a disaster waiting to happen. Not knowing how your money is invested, how much income you are receiving, or how your expenses are impacting your total savings can cause you to be totally unprepared to take on this responsibility later in life should you suddenly become single. This is more often an issue with women, who are more likely to lack confidence in their own financial knowledge, and to take a back seat when it comes to making financial decisions. When such a woman is forced into financial decision making in the early stages of grief, whether after a death or after a divorce, she may find herself having to make decisions that she is not entirely sure about and that end up doing more harm than good. When preparing for retirement, both members in the couple should take an active role and understand the family finances to ensure a successful retirement.

rescue it!

☐ Review all of the family's sources of retirement income and figure out what the survivor income will be. Make sure you calculate this for each spouse as a survivor.

☐ Consider options such as life insurance coverage to provide for the survivor.

☐ Get to know your family's financial advisor and make sure you understand how your money is invested.

CHAPTER 41

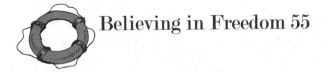 Believing in Freedom 55

What age is the right age for retirement? It might be later than you think.

THE CONCEPT OF RETIREMENT was first introduced in Canada in 1927 with the introduction of an old age pension[1] that was payable to Canadian citizens who were at least 70 years old. In 1966 the Canada Pension Plan (CPP) and Quebec Pension Plan (QPP) were launched, and at the time paid a retirement pension starting at age 70.

The gradual shift from retirement at age 70 to retirement at age 55 is one that evolved with hopes and dreams of leisure and freedom from work. The concept of early retirement was symbolic of a successful working career. Being able to retire early signalled good personal financial management and wealth. Even today, pension legislation in Canada, defines "normal" retirement as age 65, but you can have access to your pension money as early as 10 years before "normal" retirement age (i.e., age 55), and with some plans even earlier than that.

But *should* you retire simply because you have reached a specific age or have access to a company pension?

---

[1]The *Old Age Security Act* was announced in 1951 and the pension could be started at age 65 but was means-tested.

Although the concept of early retirement did catch on for a while, the majority of Canadians have never actually retired at that age. Statistics Canada reported that the average retirement age in Canada reached an all-time low in 1998, with an average retirement age of 60.9. Coincidentally, this was during a time when offering employees early retirement packages was the norm. These days, the *evolution* is taking an interesting turn — the average retirement age is around 61.5 and there are clear signs that it will continue to rise, as more and more Canadians have a different view as to when they want to retire. The elimination of mandatory retirement at age 65 in virtually all parts of Canada may have encouraged people to express more defiant sentiments, such as — *I'll retire when I'm ready — which might be never.* Does age even matter anymore? Is it not more important to have the freedom to choose when to retire, rather than be forced to retire at a particular age?

While in the past it may have been a social status symbol to retire early, now it is viewed negatively and may be seen as an admission of the end of usefulness. This is quite possibly because we don't look or feel old, but the word *retirement* certainly sounds old — that's a good enough reason not to want to have anything to do with it.

Only *you* know when is the best time for you to retire, but for most people, retiring early can be a mistake.

when is early retirement a mistake?

Too Few Saving Years

One of the top reasons people give for delaying retirement is not having saved enough money, and with good reason. Only a third of Canadians belong to a company pension plan, and while 6 out of every 10 families in Canada held savings in Registered Retirement Savings Plans in 2005, these plans had a median value of only $25,000.[2] Let's put it in perspective: if you start working at age 25 and retire at age 55, you've worked for 30 years. Given longevity stats, you may live another 30 years in retirement. This represents 30 years of work, during which you are maintaining

---

[2]Perspectives on Labour and Income, Statistics Canada, February 2008.

your lifestyle, while at the same time you are trying to save enough money to maintain your lifestyle for another 30 years during which you will not be working. If you start a family later, or buy a home later, there may still be obligations such as education costs for children and a mortgage to pay, which makes it even more difficult to save for the future. Retiring early is even more problematic for women, who may have been out of the work-force to raise children and are more likely than men to reduce their working years later in life to care for aging family members, including a spouse or common-law partner. Fewer years in the workforce will result in lower pensions and less personal savings for these women.

too many retirement years

Good news: we're living longer; bad news: we're living longer. Increased longevity means the earlier you retire, the longer your retirement savings need to last. If retirement is expected to last only a few years, there's no need to worry about building a large pool of savings for the retirement years. However, that is no longer the case — by retiring early you could end up living 30 or more years in retirement. Life expectancy estimates of a couple who are age 65 today show a 50% chance that one of them will live to age 90. So leaving work at age 55 means a 35-year retirement. Some financial advisors have started to use age 100 as a target for retirement planning, but this may be too long or too short a time period. Statistics Canada reported there were 6,530 centenarians in Canada as of July 2010 and of those, 5,196 were women. In April 2011, the world's oldest man died at age 114[3] — at the time, the world's oldest woman was also 114 years old. Next time you're out with friends, ask them how old their oldest living relative is.

old isn't old anymore

Fifty-five is the new 40! Since people are looking and feeling younger, why would they want to retire? You may believe that retirement is for old people. You may feel there is still a great deal to learn and accomplish in your

---

[3]"World's oldest man dies in Montana at 114," *Globe and Mail*, April 14, 2011.

career, and not want to retire because you simply enjoy working. It's a fact that work is a great place to stay mentally active and be connected with others, and good mental health is a positive factor in overall health.

You Could Be in Your Peak Earning Years

These years may represent your highest income-earning years; in fact, you may just be entering the senior management ranks and be entitled to additional perks or benefits. Plus, if you've taken care of most of your other financial obligations, this may be the one time in your life when you can devote much of your disposable income to building retirement savings. What's more, if you are a member of a defined benefit pension plan that determines your final pension entitlement based on your highest income earning years, you can increase your lifetime pension by working a few more years. For instance, if you have 30 years of service with an average salary of $60,000 per year, you could receive a lifetime annual pension of $30,000. If you work five more years at a higher salary, so that the average salary used for the pension calculation is, say, $80,000, and you have 35 years of service instead of 30, your lifetime annual pension would be $56,000.

Why adopt someone else's frame of mind regarding when the best time to retire should be? Don't feel pressured to retire at 55 or any age if you feel you can't afford to or you simply don't want to.

rescue it!

☐ Think about the age that you might want to retire.

☐ Ask your employer if early retirement will impact your pension and other benefits.

☐ Review chapter 20 to help you determine how much you need to save for retirement.

CHAPTER 42

 ## Believing That You Have Only One Retirement Date

More and more, people are not looking at retirement as one set date, and it shouldn't be.

RETIREMENT USED TO BE MORE EASILY DEFINED. It happened once; you saw it coming and felt it when it happened. Today retirement is more like a journey. Even if you might be retired right now, it may not necessarily be permanent. It is not uncommon to retire several times in your lifetime. Comments such as, *I'm starting my second retirement — I've already retired once — this time it's for good,* are no longer the exception. These days it's not unusual for people to move in and out of work, school, and retirement. It's quite normal.

Here is a typical lifeline. In the past, life was simpler:

school → work → retire

Now the path can go in many directions:

school → work → school → work → retire → school → work → retire

early retirement packages

In some companies, employees are offered early retirement packages: in some cases on an opt-in basis, while in other cases, employees have no option. Depending on years of service, and how many years you are from retirement age, early retirement packages often provide additional incentives to retire early. For instance, some employers will give severance in the form of salary continuance for the duration of the severance period. The benefit to this is that you continue to earn pension credits, and continue to participate in all employee benefit plans, until the salary continuance ends. Although you may not be going to work every day, in many ways, you continue to be treated as an employee.

assessing your options

Whether you have chosen to leave your current job, or the decision has been made for you, do you need to find a replacement job? Is it time to start something new? What kind of job are you looking for, and what are your transferable skills? Are you attracted to a company because of the employee benefits, or the prospect of earning income?

With an imminent workforce crisis as the baby boom generation enters full-time retirement, demands for employees with skills, knowledge, and expertise will increase. If you've already retired once and are collecting a pension, you have one added feature that employers might be looking for — you may be able to work flexible hours and enter into job-sharing arrangements. Perhaps you want to be off in the summer so you can travel — not a problem, because that's when all the students are looking for work. Will your former employer hire you back part time or on a contract basis? There may be more options for you to continue working than you think. Many things influence a retirement date, such as paying off a mortgage, the birth of a grandchild, your age, your health, whether your kids are still in school, when you can start receiving your company pension, whether you have saved enough money, your spouse's retirement date, how much you enjoy your job, when your friends are retiring, and so on. That's why the best time to retire is different for everyone.

transitioning in and out of work

Have you ever considered working for six months, then being retired for six months? This type of work schedule is no longer unheard of, as Canadians are examining alternative working conditions that will allow them the flexibility to do the things they want to do, while continuing to work and earn income.

If part-year retirement is not possible or appealing to you, working part time may be more in line with your lifestyle. Transitioning into retirement has financial and emotional benefits. The emotional benefits are clear — working gives you a goal and a sense of purpose. However, it's the financial benefits that can make a difference to the kind of retirement lifestyle you can live. By earning income while transitioning into retirement, you can delay withdrawals from your personal savings and pensions. Even though you may not save any more money during the transition years, your accumulated savings will benefit from continued growth and also allows you to slowly adjust your portfolio to accommodate your retirement income needs over a period of time rather than all at once.

While not always necessary, you may find that during those transition years your employment income may be more than you need and as a result you can continue to accumulate savings. That would boost your retirement nest egg even more.

phased retirement

The concept of phased retirement is that you are retired from your full-time job and collecting a pension from your employer, but also working part time for the same employer. While this isn't a new concept, what is new and appealing to would-be transitioners is the ability to collect a partial pension and continue to accrue pension credits in that same pension plan. Additional pension credits will result in a bigger pension in future years.

In 2007, the federal budget announcement contained changes that allow employees to have their cake and eat it too. The new rules permit employees who are at least 55 years of age and entitled to an unreduced pension to start to receive up to 60% of their accrued benefits while continuing to work for the same employer, and also continue to participate in the employer pension plan. Before rushing out to start your phased retirement, however, it's important to know that even though the *Income*

Tax Act, the federal *Pension Benefits Standards Act,* and some provincial pension legislation, have all been amended to provide for this type of phased retirement it is up to each employer pension plan to amend their agreements to specifically allow it. When in doubt, ask your employer if the pension plan has been amended to allow phased retirement.

CPP pension rules allowing collecting and contributing

Until 2011, you can collect a reduced CPP as early as age 60, but only if you can show that you ceased working for the month the CPP is to start and the following month. This rule provided some opportunity for those who wanted to start collecting CPP before age 65 and also continue to work. Once you started collecting CPP, no further contributions could be made. Starting in 2012, these rules will change significantly. First, you will no longer have to show that you are no longer working to begin to receive a pension between age 60 and 65. Second, if you collect an early CPP pension and continue to work, you and your employer will be required to continue to make CPP contributions until age 65. After age 65, if you are still working, you can continue to make contributions but then your employer will also have to continue to contribute. Contributions while collecting the CPP will count toward your future pension entitlement.

QPP

The QPP contains two provisions that aid in transitioning into retirement.

If the employer agrees, those employees between age 55 and 70 can reduce working hours and continue to contribute to QPP at the same level as they did before they reduced their hours. This provision is advantageous for those who wish to reduce work hours without a simultaneous reduction to their contributions, because it will not increase the number of low contribution years — which can reduce their final pension entitlement.

In addition, employees age 60 to 65 can apply for early QPP pension while continuing to work, provided employment earnings for the first 12 months of receiving the QPP do not exceed $12,075 (for 2011). Because

QPP contributions will continue during this time, the QPP pension entitlement will be increased in the following year.[1]

rescue it!

☐ Don't wait — start thinking about your exit plan and how work will fit into your retirement plan.

☐ Talk to your employer about options for working past retirement age.

---

[1]Retirement section of www.rrq.gouv.qc.ca

CHAPTER 43

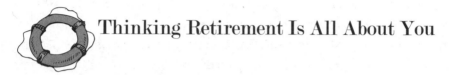 Thinking Retirement Is All About You

Here's some news — it's not! These days, more and more Canadians will find themselves responsible for caring for their parents or others.

IF YOU'VE STARTED TO VISUALIZE YOUR FUTURE self in retirement, you may see yourself with friends and family doing a wide variety of activities in all sorts of places. Even if your retirement vision is more traditional and low key, one thing is certain: in your vision everyone is happy and healthy. Unfortunately, for many this will not likely be the case, as they will be sandwiched between the demands of their children and their parents. What is becoming more prevalent is spending some of our retirement years caring for a parent (or parents), a spouse, a friend, or other family members.

sandwich generation

The term *sandwich generation* has been used to describe baby boomers who are "sandwiched" between supporting children and caring for parents, while at the same time trying to save for or enjoy their retirement. As your children grow up and eventually become independent, the idea is that you'll have more time to yourself. Gone at 18 — not anymore; gone at 21 — keep dreaming. We have seen that children are moving out of the family home at later ages and parents are financially supporting children over 18. And when they do leave, they boomerang back, often with their own children. These are the "boomerang kids," who receive financial assistance, and sometimes childcare services, from their parents. They are gone for a while, then come back for a while, and so on. On the other hand, boomer parents are living well into their 80s and are needing care for a longer period of time. In fact, the sandwich generation has been the subject of many studies, and a new term has emerged — the *club sandwich* — to describe boomers who are caring for parents, children, and grandchildren. As a result of our gradually declining birth rate, the reality is that you may spend 20 years caring for a child, and another 20 years caring for aging parents, other family members, and sometimes even friends. You may have raised two (or fewer) children but may find yourself caring for four parents (or more, if your parents or your in-laws have remarried).

While seeing three or more generations living under the same roof is not new, what's making this a bigger issue than before is that, these days, both partners are likely to be active in the workplace, whereas in previous generations, the woman was not employed and so caregiving did not impact the family's total income. Given that the first of the Canadian baby boomers turned 65 in 2011, the number of people who consider themselves part of the sandwich generation will continue to grow.

nature of caregiving

Caregiving for a parent ranges from simple tasks, such as cutting the grass, paying bills, and driving the person to doctor's appointments, to providing support for daily activities, such as dressing, bathing, and administering medication. Much of the caregiving that takes place is not even considered caregiving by those who are providing it.

positive impacts of caregiving

For many people, caregiving has positive aspects. In some cultures, caregiving is a natural and, in some ways, expected stage of life. Caregivers often feel they are giving back some of what they have received during their lifetime. Some have natural caregiving instincts and are truly fulfilled with their role. Some also say that caregiving has strengthened their relationship with a parent or other family member. It adds purpose to your life and you may find it very rewarding to be able to help someone and bring a smile to their face.

how caregiving impacts retirement savings

Almost three-quarters of the time spent caring for a senior is done by a network of family and friends. These family and friends are also likely to be part of the paid labour force, working hard to pay off debts and save for their eventual retirement. It's easy to see how caregiving might impact earning during the working years if the caregiver needs to reduce working hours, take time off, or use vacation days to provide care. In some cases, job opportunities that involve job relocation, additional responsibilities, or a heavier workload may be turned down because they don't mesh with current family obligations. Reduced earnings, and perhaps reduced contributions to CPP/QPP, will have a negative effect on eventual retirement pensions. What's more, if it is impractical, or you are not qualified to perform the caregiving yourself, you may find that you are responsible for funding part of the care costs, because previous generations are not financially prepared for this type of expense — leaving you with less disposable income to allocate toward your own retirement savings and debt repayment. It's easy to see how caregiving can have a negative impact on your finances.

caregiving can cramp your retirement lifestyle

Overall, the caregiving period has increased substantially. Statistics Canada reported that in 2007, family and friends between the ages of 45 and 64 years had been providing care for an average of 5.4 years. Caregivers 65 years and older had given assistance for an average of 6.5 years.[1] As you think about your retirement vision, you need to consider how the added responsibility of caregiving might alter that vision. Are your retirement

[1] *Eldercare: what we know today.* Statistics Canada. October 21, 2008.

plans still achievable, or will you need to make alternate plans? Your plans for extended absences from home may no longer be possible if you are the primary care provider for a family member. Some people have remarked that we are entitled to a vacation from work, but we do not get a vacation from caregiving. Retirement planning should include discussions around potential caregiving situations, including plans around extended vacations and even downsizing the family home. For instance, a plan to sell your home and move into a smaller condominium might not be possible if an elderly parent will be moving in with you. It's impractical to ignore the real possibility that you will be responsible in whole or in part for the care and financial support of others during your retirement years. What's more, because we are often thrust into being a caregiver with little advance notice or preparation, and we rarely incorporate this possibility into our retirement plans, we find we are totally unprepared.

caregiving can impact your health

Not surprisingly, being thrust into caregiving can cause anxiety and stress. Caregivers ignore their own health and well-being while focusing on the needs of the care recipient. According to a Statistics Canada report, caregivers who perform nine hours or more of caregiving per month reported feeling more stressed (76% versus 67%) and experienced a higher incidence of changes in their sleep patterns (22% versus 9%) compared to caregivers who performed fewer than nine hours of care per month. Caregiving gives a new meaning to work-life balance.

caregiving support

There is also support available for caregivers that can help ease the workload of caregiving. First of all, there is no need to feel you must do all of the caregiving. This is especially true if you have siblings who can share the duties of caregiving. In addition, respite care services provide short-term temporary care for a family member so that the primary care giver can take some time away from full-time caregiving. While this is a short term solution, a few days off can help relieve a caregiver's stress and anxiety.

In some cases there may be workplace programs that provide flexible work hours, information about community or government resources, or general information on health and aging. While workforce programs specifically tailored to elder care are not as prevalent as other programs such as childcare, even if they are offered, studies show that they are not often used either because the programs are not sufficient to meet the needs of the care giver or because the care giver would prefer to keep their caregiving responsibility private for fear it may impact their career progression.

rescue it!

☐ Have a care strategy in place.

☐ Ask family members for help — take a "divide and conquer" approach.

☐ Establish set vacation days from caregiving and stick to them.

☐ Investigate workplace support for elder care services.

PART 10

protection planning

CHAPTER 44

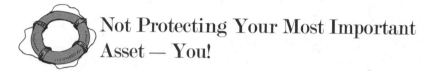 Not Protecting Your Most Important Asset — You!

The best-laid plans can go astray if you don't take the proper steps to protect your earning capability during your working years, and your income and assets during retirement.

YOU SPEND YEARS WORKING AND PLANNING for the next phase of your life — your retirement. Retirement planning is centred around one very important thing — your ability to work today and save money for the future. During the early working years, you likely had few financial assets and, in fact, may have had a negative net worth at some point, meaning you owed more than you owned. However, you had great non-financial assets, such as knowledge and energy, and were eager to get into the workforce. There were many years ahead of you to take these non-financial assets and translate them into financial assets (money in the bank, a mortgage-free home, retirement savings). Economists have a term to describe those non-financial assets — *human capital*. However, being able to translate human capital into financial capital requires time and effort. As you work and earn income, you pay off debts and build assets, and so it is important to protect your ability to continue to work. This enables you to convert human capital into a financial net worth that you can use to provide income and cash flow when you are no longer working.

life insurance

Consider this question: Why do you buy life insurance during your life? The answer is simple — because you think you might die and you want to insure against that. Insurance purchased during your working years is meant to protect your human capital. If you die, the life insurance is used to replace the income that would have been earned over the rest of your lifetime had you lived to retirement. The closer you get to retirement, the lower your human capital becomes, because you have fewer years to continue to work and earn money. By retirement, your human capital has generated physical capital in the form of money, investments, a home, an accumulated pension plan, and other assets. It's a common misconception that you no longer need any life insurance during your retirement years. Children are grown up and independent (hopefully), and many pensions provide a kind of automatic insurance policy in that pension payments may continue to a surviving spouse or partner. However, everyone's situation is different, and there are still viable uses for life insurance even during the retirement years, to protect the lifestyle of a survivor or to create an estate without feeling guilty about spending your life savings.

Life insurance can provide liquidity to your estate, which can help pay for immediate costs such as funeral expenses, and can delay when investments or the family home must be sold by the survivor. It can also be used to fill the income gap that a lower survivor pension income may cause for the survivor.

Life insurance can also be purchased for estate planning purposes, either to make a large charitable gift or to leave an inheritance to family members that your estate might not otherwise be able to make. It can also be used to pay any income tax liability and other estate administration costs at death, so that the estate can remain whole.

A single person without any dependent beneficiaries is better served forgoing life insurance and selecting insurance that will provide money for a disability, a critical illness, or even long-term care in their later years.

If you're a member of a professional association (such as chartered accountants or engineers) or are self-employed, your association or union may have negotiated insurance programs at a group price — this might be the preferred route, because you don't have to continue to be employed by a specific employer to maintain coverage. In fact, if you change jobs later in life, you may be asked to take a physical exam and be required to wait a period of time before being eligible for the coverage under a new plan, which means there may be a gap in coverage. Or your health may have deteriorated since you last applied for coverage and you may be denied the coverage you want or have to pay very high premiums. For instance, let's say that while covered by a very generous employer group plan, you are diagnosed with an illness that requires expensive medication, but the cost is fully covered by your current plan. You may find yourself in a position where you cannot leave your current employer without jeopardizing your coverage.

Those employers that offer life insurance coverage to employees may also offer some form of continued coverage to retirees. More often than not, the retiree coverage is for significantly less than what it was during the working years, and may only continue to a certain age. Individuals should check their benefit booklets to determine how much life insurance might be available to them as a retiree. If life insurance coverage ends upon retirement, or at some specified age, there may be an opportunity to convert the insurance into a private policy, usually within a 30-day timeframe of when it ends, without a health assessment being required.

disability insurance

What if you live, but cannot continue to work? Perhaps there are medical bills on top of all your other daily expenses. How do you pay for day-to-day expenses and save for retirement when your income-earning ability is gone? Disability insurance is a solution used to provide income to you if you can no longer work. It is important to have disability insurance, especially if you are self-employed or are the main income earner. Your employer may offer a group policy, which might be a short-term plan or a long-term plan. These plans are designed to replace a portion of your employment income for periods of time when you are unable to work due to a disability. Some policies require that you wait a certain number of days (or months) before collecting, and may only pay for a certain number of years.

Professionals might want to consider disability insurance that protects the ability to continue to earn income *doing their own occupation,* rather than any occupation.

In addition to disability insurance under group or private disability insurance plans, you may also be entitled to CPP/QPP disability payments.

long-term care insurance

As we live longer in old age, there may come a time when we will need assistance when it comes to our personal care. Canadians often believe that their health care costs will be covered by the government during retirement. Although some costs will be covered, many others are not.

Long-term care insurance benefits provide cash to help cover either home care or the costs of a long-term care facility. Rather than insuring against this health risk, some feel they have enough savings to pay for these costs should they arise. Costs for long-term care range from several thousands of dollars per month to tens of thousands, and in-home nursing care can be double those costs. It's easy to see that retirement savings can be eroded very quickly when one is faced with paying these costs. This is especially a concern if one member of a couple requires long-term care for even a few years. Based on the average costs for care, even three years of care can wipe out the family's entire savings, leaving the survivor with nothing. Some people believe that they can sell the family home to pay for the care, but this isn't always a practical solution when only one person in the couple needs the care.

critical illness insurance

A critical illness can arise at any age, including in retirement. Unlike life insurance and long-term care, critical illness insurance pays a lump-sum cash amount if the insured person is diagnosed with a critical illness. The lump-sum payment is tax-free, and can be used for any purpose. Some policies offer a return-of-premium feature, which pays back premiums if the person does not make a claim on the policy. This feature tends to substantially increase the cost of the insurance.

rescue it!

Before retirement:

☐ Review your disability insurance policy. Make sure you have the appropriate disability coverage, and enough of it, to protect your human capital.

☐ Review your life insurance policy. Is the coverage enough, and can you continue the policy in retirement?

☐ Consider long-term care and critical illness insurance to help cover the costs that may arise.

In retirement:

☐ Incorporate the potential costs for long-term care or a critical illness into your retirement plan, and figure out what impact these would have on your retirement. Consider long-term care and critical illness insurance to help cover the costs that may arise.

☐ Consider life insurance to pay estate costs and income taxes or to create an inheritance.

CHAPTER 45

 Bad Decisions Around Joint Accounts

Are you sure you know what you are getting yourself into?

MANY PEOPLE OWN PROPERTY AND INVESTMENTS jointly with another person, most commonly a spouse or common-law partner, as a way to give the other person the ability to access the money during their lifetime and even to simplify the distribution of their estate. But when joint accounts are used with people other than a spouse or common-law partner, there are considerable risks that need to be understood and managed to prevent financial disaster.

First of all, let's clarify two terms: *joint tenants with rights of survivorship* (which I will call joint ownership for brevity) and *tenants in common*.

joint ownership

This is the most common type of ownership. Each owner has an undivided and equal legal interest in the account. Each owner can withdraw money and make investment decisions without the other's consent.

tenants in common

With this type of ownership, the owners may each own an equal or unequal portion, but the key element is that each owner retains rights to *his or her share* of the account.

which is better?

So the question is: Which is the better way to hold property? Unfortunately, there is no simple answer that can be used in all situations. It depends on the circumstances around why the account was opened and the intent of the owners. The biggest difference with the two forms of ownership is what happens on the death of one of the owners. I'll use an example to illustrate:

Jack and Jill are spouses and have an account that is considered joint ownership. Unfortunately, Jack dies, which leaves Jill as the sole owner of the account. Because of the joint ownership, the account now belongs entirely to Jill. She can access the account to pay for the funeral or other costs, and does not need to show a copy of the will to prove that the entire account belongs to her. In addition, since she automatically owns the entire account, they also avoid provincial probate fees.

Let's take a look at another situation. Fred and Steve are roommates and share their living expenses. They are not considered common-law partners for tax purposes. They open a joint account to pay for rent and other costs. Fred dies, and the entire amount in the joint account now belongs to Steve. This might not be what was intended, and Fred's family and Steve might have to go to court to decide who owns the money in the joint account. Had Fred and Steve opened the account as tenants in common, then Fred's portion of the account would belong to his estate and be distributed according to the instructions in his will, or by the intestacy rules of his province if he does not have a will.

tax consequences of making an account joint

There are two things to consider: *legal* ownership (the names of the owners on the account) versus *beneficial* ownership (who is the real owner?). If there is a change in the beneficial ownership at the time the account is made joint with someone, it results in a "deemed disposition," which is treated by CRA like a sale of half of the account to the other person at the fair market value at the time the account was made joint. If the investments in the account have increased in value since they were originally purchased, a capital gain is realized (even though the investment is not sold), and tax has to be paid by the original account holder.

legal and estate consequences of making an account joint with a child

We've already reviewed what happens on the death of one of the account holders, depending on whether the account is considered joint or tenants in common. But oftentimes a parent makes an account joint with a child, when the main purpose of doing so is to give the child access to the money or to make investment decisions on the parent's behalf, but the parent does not intend to give the child any real ownership interest.

Two recent cases illustrate the issues when a parent has made a child a joint owner on certain accounts. As can be seen, the resulting legal and estate consequences vary between the two.

In the first case, Mr. Sayler named one of his three adult children (his daughter) as a joint owner of his investment account. The father kept paying tax on the earnings in the account. On the father's death, the account passed to his daughter, who was the joint owner on the account. The other two children claimed their sister was only holding legal interest, and not beneficial interest, in the account. Therefore, they argued, the money in the account should form part of their father's estate.The siblings won and the money was distributed according to the father's will.

In a similar case, Mr. Pecore transferred money to joint accounts with his daughter. On his death, his daughter took over the accounts. Soon afterward, the daughter's marriage ended and, during the divorce proceedings, the question of the joint accounts was raised. Interestingly, the soon-to-be ex-husband had been named a beneficiary in his father-in-law's will. However, since the joint accounts (which formed the bulk of the estate) passed directly to Mr. Pecore's daughter (his soon-to-be ex-spouse), they were not part of the estate. As a result, he received a very small portion of his father-in-law's estate. He commenced an action claiming his share of the joint accounts on the basis that the accounts were not true joint accounts with rights of survivorship but rather just a way to make it easier for the daughter to access her father's account. In this case, the daughter was able to prove that the father had intended to make a gift of the accounts to her, and so the joint accounts were not part of the estate. These cases demonstrate the importance of clearly documenting your intentions when you make an account joint with a child.

issues with making your home joint with a child

A home is most often held jointly with a spouse or common-law partner. In some cases, a parent will decide to include a child on title of his or her home to simplify the estate distribution on death and also avoid probate. This too can have unintended consequences. Similar to the concerns with making an investment account joint with a child, the joint ownership of the home puts the asset at risk of the child's creditors, as well as of claims of the child's spouse. In addition, one must keep in mind that any capital gain on the sale of a home that is considered a principal residence is tax-free. An individual is permitted to claim only one residence each year as his or her principal residence. If the parent owns the home, then any gain on the sale or deemed sale that would occur on the parent's death would be tax-free. Note that since 1982, you can only designate one home per family unit as a principal residence for the capital gains exemption. However, when an adult child is added as a joint owner on a parent's home and the child has his or her own home, then there is a risk that the child will be liable for capital gains tax on the portion of the home he or she own with their parent, since the principal residence exemption may not be available to them except for those years they lived in the home with the parent and had no other principal residence.

rescue it!

- ☐ If you will be making or have made an account joint with a child, clearly document whether your intention is to gift the amount to the child.

- ☐ If you are considering adding a child as a joint owner on your home, it is best to seek legal advice to determine if this is the best course of action.

- ☐ Consider using a power of attorney for property, or in Quebec, a mandate, to give a child authority to act on your behalf without transferring legal or beneficial title.

CHAPTER 46

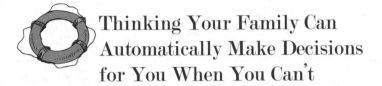 Thinking Your Family Can
Automatically Make Decisions
for You When You Can't

It may come as a surprise to you, but family members are not automatically authorized to act on your behalf should you need them to.

IMAGINE IF YOU WERE TO BECOME incapacitated and unable to make financial decisions for yourself or communicate the kind of care you would like. Who would manage your financial affairs, such as paying bills, cashing cheques, and making investment decisions, and who would make personal care decisions, such as making decisions about your health care? Although typically associated with aging and retirement, incapacity can occur at any time; the key is to address this issue early on in life before an incapacity occurs.

Across Canada, each of the provinces set out their own rules around who would be able to step in and act on your behalf. Many of us assume that a spouse or common-law partner can automatically step in and take care of all of our financial affairs. While this is true in some cases, it is not true for every decision. A spouse or common-law partner can access all joint accounts but cannot sell the family home or any other real property, even if it is owned jointly. In addition, a spouse or partner may not have the financial acumen to manage complex financial matters, and so sometimes it's better to have someone else make those decisions. Therefore it is best to prepare a document in advance to give this authority to either your spouse or another person.

Although the rules differ from province to province, there are some general rules and key considerations to take into account when granting someone this sort of authority. For example, in all provinces, you need to have a legal document that specifically gives the person named the authority to act on your behalf or to carry out your wishes. This form is called a *power of attorney*, except in Quebec, where it is called a *mandate*.

power of attorney

A power of attorney is a legal document authorizing another person, or an organization such as a trust company, to manage your personal financial affairs and/or your personal care should you become incapable of doing so on your own.

A power of attorney can be for a *specific* purpose and for a set period of time. For instance, you can give your adult child the authority to cash your cheques and pay your bills while you are away on an extended vacation or if you are living out of the country for a portion of the year. A power of attorney can also be *general,* and grant your adult child authority to manage all of your financial assets. Although a power of attorney usually takes effect as soon as you grant it, in most cases it stops being valid if you become incapable of making decisions for yourself. If you want the power of attorney to continue during incapacity, you can grant a *continuing* or *enduring* power of attorney for property that authorizes the attorney to continue acting on your behalf should you become incapable of doing so. In Quebec, a court must determine that the power of attorney or mandate can continue.

who can be an attorney?

The word *attorney* does not imply that the person you choose must be a lawyer. The person you choose should be trustworthy and be able to handle your personal finances. You can choose a spouse or other family member or a friend. If you don't feel there is anyone you wish to appoint, or you wish to avoid a family conflict, you may want to consider naming a trust company as your financial power of attorney.

You can also name multiple attorneys, but then each must agree on all decisions that need to be made, which can delay taking action. Alternatively, you can specify that any one of the named attorneys or a majority of the named attorneys may make the required decisions.

Because a power of attorney is separate from your will, you do not need to name your attorney as your executor. However, it is acceptable to name the same person to act under these two separate documents.

authority of the attorney

A power of attorney document allows the attorney to step into the shoes of the person who appoints him or her, and make all decisions as outlined in the document. Unless you restrict your attorney's powers, he or she will be able to do virtually anything you can do concerning your finances. That includes cashing in or selling your investments, selling your home or buying property, and making investments in your name. There are some automatic restrictions built into the power of attorney that prevent the attorney from making, changing, or revoking your existing will, or changing any beneficiary designations on plans such as your RRSP, RRIF, TFSA, and life insurance documents.

For business owners, you may want to have two simultaneous powers of attorney — one for your personal affairs and one for your business so that you can appoint someone familiar with your business to manage it if you are unable to do so. Since this adds an additional layer of complexity, business owners should seek legal advice about how to create two simultaneous powers of attorney.

power of attorney for personal care

A power of attorney for personal care is typically only effective if you were to lose mental capacity and become unable to make decisions for yourself. Depending on which province you live in, this document might also be called a living will, a health care directive, or a mandate. If you want to have both an enduring power of attorney for your personal finances and a power of attorney for personal care, it is best that these be kept as two separate documents. This is because you might want to choose different attorneys to act under each of these powers, and your instructions under each document would be different.

Regardless of the type of power of attorney you have given, the authority of the attorney to act ends on the death of the grantor and at that point the instructions in the will take over.

Because of the magnitude of the powers that are given with a power of attorney, you should think very carefully about who you wish to appoint, as well as how much power you are prepared to give the attorney. Although there are kits that can be used to prepare power of attorney documents, it is wise to speak to a lawyer about how best to structure the documents. When prepared, they can give you the security and peace of mind of knowing that your affairs will be taken care of should you become incapable of acting on your own behalf.

At the risk of stating the obvious, bear in mind that a power of attorney can only be granted by someone who has the mental capacity to understand the implications of doing so. If you wait too long, you run the risk that diminished mental capacity will prevent you from being able to put these documents in place, or will result in legal disputes over your actual capacity at the time authority was granted.

rescue it!

☐ Review your personal net worth statement and decide who you would like to name as your attorney to manage your financial affairs.

☐ Have a discussion with your spouse, common-law partner, or others about your personal care wishes, and decide who you would like to name as your attorney to carry out those wishes.

☐ Notify your chosen attorney or attorneys about your desire to name them on these documents.

☐ Prepare both a continuing/enduring power of attorney for property and a power of attorney for personal care. Although there are kits and fill-in-the-blank forms, it is best to obtain legal advice and assistance when preparing these legal documents.

CHAPTER 47

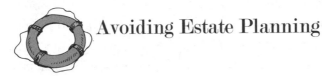 Avoiding Estate Planning

Many avoid this difficult task, but that only serves to impact the lives of those they love and leave behind.

HAVE YOU THOUGHT ABOUT WHO you would like to leave your assets to when you die? Whether you've just given this a brief consideration or you've been thinking about it for some time, thinking about it and doing something about it are two very different things.

An estate plan has many different components. Estate planning involves determining not only who will inherit but also what is being inherited, in what format (for instance, Johnny inheriting the vintage corvette versus the cash proceeds from the sale of the corvette), whether the inheritance is to be received immediately or some time in the future (such as when the grandchildren attain a certain age), as well as considering tax savings opportunities.

When you are developing your estate plan, there are three basic ways to distribute your assets on death. You can name a specific beneficiary on each of a variety of accounts and plans, as discussed in chapter 48; you can hold certain assets with joint rights of survivorship as discussed in chapter 45; or you can have the assets form part of your estate and be distributed in accordance with the instructions in your will. These methods of estate distribution need to be aligned and work together for you to achieve the results you desire.

Often with simple estates, where each spouse names the other as beneficiary of his or her retirement accounts or insurance policies, or where most of
the assets are owned jointly, the presumption is that there is no need to create
a will. When one of the spouses dies, the entire estate will pass to the surviving spouse. But even in circumstances where an estate is considered "simple,"
if both spouses die at the same time, or there are children from a previous
marriage, not having an estate plan or a valid will to deal with estate distribution can cause financial distress for the surviving spouse and family strife if
children are excluded from inheriting, and can result in estate litigation.

There are special (but not uncommon) situations that need to be considered when developing an estate plan.

multiple children/blended families

These days it's not uncommon for people to be in a second (or more) marriage and for there to be multiple children in the family unit: your children, your spouse's children, and children you have together. When you
are preparing an estate plan and deciding who gets what, you may want
to give some extra thought to when each of the children will inherit. For
instance, if you have children from a prior marriage, leaving everything to
a surviving spouse will not guarantee that your children will inherit any of
your assets. Of course, a surviving spouse may make provisions to leave
something to your children upon his or her death, but things might not go
as you would have intended. In any case, this might not be something you
want to leave to chance.

use of trusts

A properly drafted will can be used to establish a testamentary trust for
children or a spouse. A testamentary trust carries certain benefits, such as
being taxed as a separate individual, which will provide income splitting
for the survivor. This is particularly important for a surviving spouse. For
instance, if the surviving spouse were to inherit all of the investments, the
related investment income could put them in a higher tax bracket or cause
them to exceed the annual OAS threshold amount, causing them to lose
some or all of their OAS entitlement.

A trust also provides additional control over how and when the assets will be used for the beneficiaries of the trust. A trust established for the benefit of a spouse (known as a spousal trust) has a unique advantage in that the assets in the trust can be used to support the surviving spouse during his or her lifetime, but on the death of the surviving spouse, the remaining assets can be passed directly to your children without requiring any special provisions in the surviving spouse's will and without any probate fees.

But to get the maximum advantage out of using a testamentary trust, you need to co-ordinate which assets will pass directly to the spouse or others outside of the will, and which assets will form part of the estate and can be placed into the testamentary trust. It is possible that the will establishes a spousal trust, but in an effort to minimize probate fees, all of the assets pass directly to the surviving spouse outside of the will through joint accounts or beneficiary designations and as a result, the spousal trust will have few if any assets in it.

why you need a will

It's clear that an important part of an estate plan is a will. It has been estimated that approximately 50% of Canadians die without a valid will. But if the purpose of a will is simply to outline how your estate is to be distributed, then one can argue that nobody in Canada dies without a *will*. This is because if you have not drafted your own will, then upon your death, your estate will be distributed according to the intestacy rules of your province of residence. This is about as close to a will as you can get if you didn't prepare your own. So why would you need to have your own will? Perhaps you want your province to determine how your estate should be distributed, but perhaps not. You see, the provincial intestacy rules are not exactly as you might think. For instance, your spouse does not automatically inherit everything on your death. Depending on the size of your estate and your province of residence, and if you have children, the intestacy rules will give an initial portion of your estate to your spouse and then divide the balance between your spouse and children. This could significantly reduce the size of the estate that is left for the surviving spouse to live on for the rest of his or her days. While every family is different, there is no guarantee that a child will give any of his or her inheritance to the surviving parent. Another important consideration is that same-sex partners don't automatically inherit under provincial intestacy rules. Without a valid will, your partner may not be entitled to any part of your estate.

There are many situations where people have gone as far as speaking to a lawyer and drafting up a will, paying the legal fees, but then never got around to signing it. It is also important to know that even if you have a valid will there are certain circumstances when a will can be revoked by subsequent life events. For example, a marriage nullifies a pre-existing will, unless the will states specifically that it was prepared and signed in anticipation of the marriage. So when the will is not signed or when a will is signed but the person marries, there is no valid will at the time of death, and the estate would have to be distributed under the intestacy rules. Dying without a valid will also leads to delays in distributing the estate assets, and can result in additional costs and taxes, leaving much less for the heirs.

Estate planning (or lack of it) can impact a surviving spouse or partner's retirement in two ways. First of all, lack of proper estate planning can result in the estate paying a large amount of income taxes, and second, it can cause a premature distribution of the estate to children when this is not the intention and is not in the best interest of the survivor. In both cases, the result is a much smaller amount left for the survivor to live on for the rest of his or her retirement. A bereaved spouse's retirement can be seriously compromised by decisions and actions you never had the gumption to make while you were alive.

rescue it!

☐ Spend some time thinking about the distribution of your estate on death.

☐ Review your personal net worth statement to determine which assets will pass directly to the survivor as a result of beneficiary designations and joint ownership, and which assets will form part of your estate and be distributed in accordance with your will.

☐ Determine if the three methods of estate distribution as currently arranged are appropriate, based on your wishes.

☐ If you don't have a will, speak to a lawyer about preparing one and don't delay signing it.

☐ Review your will whenever there is a life event such as a death or marriage to ensure your will is still appropriate and valid.

☐ Make sure the instructions in your will mesh with your beneficiary designations and joint accounts.

CHAPTER 48

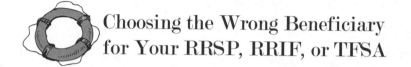

Choosing the Wrong Beneficiary for Your RRSP, RRIF, or TFSA

These accounts allow you to name a beneficiary who will inherit the value of the account on your death. The important message here is "Choose wisely!" because selecting the wrong beneficiary can have unintended results.

IN ADDITION TO PREPARING A WILL to distribute your estate, certain accounts provide one more option by allowing you to designate a beneficiary for those accounts, so that upon your death, the named beneficiary will receive the assets in the plan without the need for specific directions found in your will. Naming a beneficiary results in the asset passing directly to that individual and not having to go through a court process called probate, which depending on the province could save the estate and your beneficiaries thousands of dollars.

In Canada, plans such as RRSPs, RRIFs, and TFSAs allow you to make a beneficiary designation directly in the account documentation. Quebec is the only province where these types of designations can only be made in your will and not directly in the account documentation. Because of the nature of these accounts, there are certain rules that you need to be aware of when deciding who to name as a beneficiary.

Naming a beneficiary simplifies estate planning, because you can change your beneficiary designation on one or all of your accounts at any time without having to draft a new will. Although a will is not required to distribute the assets in these accounts, in some cases the financial institution will want to see a copy of the probated will to verify that the beneficiary designation on the account documentation is valid and was not revoked by a later designation made in the will. For instance, if you signed an RRSP beneficiary designation form in 1990 but then prepared your will in 2010 and included different instructions as to who would inherit the RRSP, the later instructions would prevail.

reduce probate fees

If a beneficiary is named, the funds in the plan do not form part of the estate assets that require probate because they pass directly to the beneficiary. Probate is a legal process whereby the provincial courts confirm a person's will. There are fees associated with the probate process that vary from province to province and which can be as high as 1.5% of the assets distributed under a will in Ontario and British Columbia and as low as $400 in Alberta. In some provinces, avoiding probate on registered plans can result in significant savings. Quebec is the only province that does not charge probate fees or other fees for a notarized will but does charge a small fee ($64 in 2011) for common-law wills.

how to name a beneficiary

A beneficiary designation is usually made in writing directly on the account application form, and can be changed only by the plan holder. A plan holder can make a change to the beneficiary designation whenever the current designation is no longer appropriate or consistent with their estate wishes. The designation should be made in writing, and all you need to do is provide a letter to your financial institution indicating who the new beneficiary will be, or you may make the new designation directly in your will. As noted above, the most recent designation is the one that will prevail. This is especially important in situations where there is a dispute as to who should inherit an asset.

If you have named a beneficiary but later transfer the account to another financial institution, you need to make sure you name a beneficiary on the new account. You do not have to choose the same person as you had named previously, especially if circumstances have changed. In general, you should review your designation whenever there is a change in your life, such as marriage, divorce, death, or birth, to determine if your selection of beneficiary still reflects your wishes. For example, if you are married, you have likely named your spouse as the beneficiary of your plan. Should you become separated or divorced, the beneficiary designation on your account will not automatically change unless you provide a written request to make a change. Recall the story from chapter 5, where the surviving spouse finds that the former spouse is named the beneficiary instead of her. You may also want to ask if you can name a contingent beneficiary. A contingent beneficiary only inherits if the primary beneficiary cannot, for instance if the primary beneficiary does not outlive the account holder. An example of where this might be beneficial is when an account holder names a spouse as primary beneficiary and a child or children as the contingent beneficiary. If both spouses die at the same time, then rather than having the assets go into the estate and be subject to probate fees, the contingent beneficiary will inherit the assets.

rolling an RRSP over to a RRIF

Another important point is that if you have converted or are in the process of converting your RRSP into a RRIF, the RRIF is considered a separate plan, so you should ensure you have named a beneficiary for the RRIF when you set up this account. Do not assume your RRIF beneficiary will be automatically the same as the one named on the RRSP. If you do not name a beneficiary on the new account, the default beneficiary will be your estate, which means the proceeds will be distributed according to the instructions in your will, or without a will, the intestacy rules of your province. As a result, the funds may not go to the intended beneficiary and since the assets must pass through the will, there will be probate fees, which will reduce the final amount available for distribution.

tax consequences of beneficiary choices for RRSPs and RRIFs

Naming Your Estate

If you name your estate or if no beneficiary is named, the plan is considered to be collapsed and will be included in your final income tax return and taxed as ordinary income. No withholding tax will be applied to the payment, but this does not mean the amount is tax-free. Depending on the amount of other income in the final income tax return, tax of up to 49% may have to be paid, leaving a much smaller amount for the heirs.

Naming a Spouse

If your spouse is the beneficiary of the plan, the proceeds may be taxed as part of your spouse's income and not yours. If the proceeds are rolled into the spouse's RRSP, RRIF, or an annuity, no tax will be payable until the funds are subsequently paid out to the surviving spouse.

A RRIF provides an additional form of designation where there is a surviving spouse or common-law partner. You may decide to name your spouse a successor annuitant instead of a beneficiary. As a beneficiary, your spouse will receive the proceeds from the RRIF (once the minimum withdrawal for the year has been made), and may take the money in cash, roll the funds over to their own RRSP or RRIF, or use the proceeds to buy an annuity. Where there is a beneficiary designation, there are special tax forms that will be required by the financial institution, and the beneficiary will receive additional income tax slips showing both the receipt of the RRIF proceeds and the subsequent rollover/contribution to their RRSP/RRIF. On the other hand, where the account names a successor annuitant, the person simply takes over the deceased person's existing RRIF. All withdrawals from the plan will continue as before, and there are no additional tax slips or forms to worry about. If the surviving spouse is planning to continue to receive the same regular withdrawals from the plan, then from an administrative perspective, it's best to name them as a successor annuitant rather than a beneficiary.

Naming a Financially Dependent Child

If you name a financially dependent child or grandchild, the proceeds may be taxed in their hands rather than as part of your estate. A minor child or grandchild may purchase an annuity that would make payments until the child reaches age 18, which allows the child to spread the payments and related taxes over a period of years. However, if your will establishes a trust for your child, you should name your estate if you want the plan assets to be part of the trust.

Naming a Disabled Child

A financially dependent child or grandchild of any age who has a mental or physical disability may roll the proceeds into their own RRSP or RRIF and defer the taxation until the amounts are withdrawn by the account holder.

Naming a Charity

If you name a charity as the beneficiary, the payment will be considered a charitable donation and your estate will be entitled to a donation credit equal to the value of the plan, which will reduce or eliminate all of the taxes payable on the account.

Naming an RDSP

New rules now allow the deceased person's RRSP or RRIF to name a Registered Disability Savings Plan (RDSP) of a financially dependent disabled child or grandchild and allow for a tax-free rollover up to the maximum RDSP contribution room available.

Naming Others

Naming anyone else as a beneficiary results in the estate paying income tax on the value of the account, while the beneficiary receives the proceeds on a pre-tax basis. This can result in an unintended distribution of the estate. For instance, let's say you name your adult son (who is not financially dependent) as the beneficiary of your RRIF and your will indicates that your daughter (also an adult) will inherit all of your other assets. To simplify the example, we'll assume both the RRIF and the total of the other estate assets are worth $300,000 each at the time of death. At first this seems like a fair and equitable division. But once you take income tax into consideration, you realize that the son gets the full $300,000 RRIF and the daughter gets the value of the remaining estate assets once all of the taxes and other estate fees have been paid. Since the estate pays income taxes on the RRIF, the daughter's inheritance will be considerably less than the son's.

tax consequences of a tax free savings account (TFSA)

The rules for TFSAs are similar to those for RRIFs, in that there are two types of designations that can be made: you can name either a beneficiary or a successor account holder.

Beneficiary

A spouse, child, sibling, or any other person can be named a beneficiary of the TFSA. A beneficiary will receive the amount in the TFSA in cash or, where possible, in kind (i.e., they inherit the investments directly), but essentially the TFSA ceases to exist. Unlike the situation where there is a successor account holder, the tax-free status of the TFSA ends at the date of death and any further income earned in the account will be taxable to the beneficiary. There is no opportunity to roll over the inherited funds into a TFSA. However, if the beneficiary is 18 years of age or older and has unused TFSA room, the money can be used to make a contribution into their own plan.

Successor Account Holder

Only a spouse or common-law partner can be named a successor account holder. As a successor account holder, the survivor takes over the deceased's TFSA and can continue to keep the account separate (but cannot make any further contributions to the account), or can combine it with his or her own TFSA. Inheriting a TFSA will not affect any TFSA contribution room the survivor may have.

One of the biggest mistakes people make around beneficiary designations is failing to name a beneficiary other than the estate. Another mistake is failing to update an existing beneficiary designation so that it properly reflects the individual's wishes. Although failing to name the most appropriate beneficiary for your accounts doesn't impact you personally, it will impact the retirement of your spouse or partner.

rescue it!

- ☐ Review your beneficiary designations to understand who you have named and to determine if they are still appropriate.

- ☐ Always consider naming a spouse as primary beneficiary on RRSPs and RRIFs, and a successor account holder on TFSA accounts when appropriate, and then others, to minimize income tax.

- ☐ Ask your financial institution if you can make a contingent beneficiary designation — the contingent beneficiary only inherits if the named beneficiary pre-deceases you or does not live a minimum number of days after your death.

CHAPTER 49

 Sharing Too Much Personal
and Financial Information

*One of the biggest risks that can impact your retirement
nest egg is the risk of financial fraud and scams.*

CANADIANS OF ALL AGES SHOULD DO what they can to protect
their personal and financial information. In 2003, a survey reported that
approximately 9% of Canadians, or 2.7 million people, had fallen victim to
identity theft at some point in their lives.[1] Our financial lives have never
been more complex, and financial products and services have adapted to
meet our changing needs. We hold multiple credit and debit cards, make
online purchases for virtually anything we want, and have access to mobile
technology that gives us 24/7 access to our money. With all of this convenience comes risk — the way we conduct our financial affairs has led
to many new types of frauds and scams. After managing your personal
finances and saving for retirement, your top priority should be to protect
what you've accumulated.

While there is nothing that can guarantee you will be free from risk,
you can take some basic precautions to increase your safety by learning
about the most common approaches that fraudsters take, and knowing
how to recognize and prevent them from happening to you.

---

[1] www.priv.gc.ca/id/primer_e.cfm—Ipsos Reid survey, 2003.

overpayment scams

This typically occurs when you advertise something for sale and the buyer agrees to buy the item, and then deliberately overpays you by writing a cheque for more than the sale price. You are then asked to send them a wire for the difference, and by the time you find out that the original cheque that was given to you was non-sufficient funds (NSF), they have your money.

fraudulent investments

We've already discussed in chapter 3, if it sounds too good to be true, it usually is. Always buy your investments from licensed investment advisors who work with regulated firms or, if you buy investments online, only deal with reputable companies that are regulated.

phishing

This is a term to describe a scam where a perpetrator sends authentic-looking e-mails, appearing to come from legitimate companies, that send you to legitimate-seeming Web sites in an effort to "phish" for personal and financial information. While the sites may look authentic to an unsuspecting individual, they often have an unusual Web address and may not look exactly the same as the authentic site. Once on the fraudulent site, the e-mail recipient is asked to enter personal and/or financial information that is later used to commit fraud.

credit and debit card fraud

One of the most common ways to make a purchase is to use a credit card or a debit card. Credit card fraud comes in several forms. Criminals can steal your actual card; they can obtain your credit card number; they can produce counterfeit cards; or they can get credit cards issued to them by making false applications using your identity. For debit card fraud to occur, a criminal obtains your debit card information and personal identification number (PIN). Without your PIN, the debit card is useless, so if your card is stolen or duplicated, the criminal must try to find out your PIN. That's why protecting your PIN is so important.

vishing

This term describes a technique that combines "voice" plus "phishing." The fraudster uses telephone communications to contact you, either by recorded phone message or by e-mail, and you are instructed to call a telephone number or proceed to a Web site, where you are asked to update your information.

grandparent scam/emergency scam

This is a scam that aims to trick the elderly. It involves the scammer calling and claiming to be a grandchild who has been in some sort of accident and needs money to be wired to them. The grandparent claims to be embarrassed about the situation and ask that nothing be said to the parents.

computer hackers

A personal computer is a standard home accessory these days, but it can be a minefield for leakage of personal information. There are a whole host of software programs that can be purchased to protect hackers from getting into your data, such as antivirus software that protects you from potentially damaging viruses, anti-spyware that will help protect your computer against unwanted software and pop-up advertising, and anti-spam software to prevent unwanted e-mails. There are also personal firewalls that work as a barrier against intrusion into your computer. Rather than just relying on software, common sense should also come into play. Don't reply to or open suspicious e-mails or pop-ups, especially those that indicate that your computer is under attack and ask you to purchase software to protect your information — this is another one of those scams that people fall victim to, called malware or scamware. Finally, if your computer doesn't do this automatically, remember to disconnect from the Internet when you are not using it.

identity theft

Identity theft occurs when someone uses your personal information without your knowledge or consent to commit a crime, such as fraud or theft. Identity thieves steal key pieces of your personal information and use it to impersonate you and commit crimes in your name. They may physically steal important documents, such as your SIN card, driver's licence, or health card, or they may find out your personal information from a single piece of your mail that you threw away. These pieces of identification can allow an identity thief to apply for credit cards and loans, and to open bank accounts in your name. Identity thieves also pose as homeowners and forge documents that they then use to either sell a home or obtain a second mortgage — without the real owner realizing what is happening until it is too late.

In chapter 5, we discussed why it's important to review all your statements REGULARLY. One of the easiest ways to spot if someone is trying to steal your identity is to review all of your statements. Here is a summary of some of the things you should look for.

- Your chequebook, passbook, credit card, or piece of identification goes missing.

- Your statements show transactions on your accounts that you do not recognize.

- There have been debit card withdrawals from your bank accounts that you know you did not make.

- You receive credit card statements for cards that you did not apply for, or other bills for items you did not purchase.

- A collection agency informs you that it is collecting for a defaulted account that you never opened, or bills that you have paid.

- Your legitimate bills and account statements don't arrive when they are supposed to.

- You are informed that you have been denied or approved for credit that you have not applied for.

- You are denied credit that you have applied for, even though you believe you have a good credit record.

- Your credit report shows debts that are not yours.

If you think you might be a victim of identity theft, contact your financial institution, your creditors, and other companies, such as telephone, cable, and utilities companies, the post office, and other government agencies if any of your government-issued identification has been stolen. You may have to close your bank accounts, and cancel debit or credit cards.

Perhaps you are a trusting person by nature, but everyone needs to learn to ask questions about why certain personal information is being collected, how it will be used, and how it will be protected. When in doubt, don't provide what is being asked for, and contact the company that is asking for the information to find out whether the request is valid or not. Remember, reputable organizations and financial institutions will NOT ask you to confirm personal information they should already have on file.

rescue it!

☐ Protect your personal information: shred mail that has your name, address, or any other personal information on it.

☐ Always keep your PIN and other passwords secret, and memorize them instead of writing them down. Be creative with your passwords — don't use birthdays or names.

☐ Never share credit card information with anyone unless you have entered a trusted Web site.

☐ Never carry your SIN, birth certificate, passport, or other documents in your wallet or purse unless you need them.

☐ To check your credit or report a possible fraud, contact Equifax at www. consumer.equifax.ca or toll-free at 1-800-465-7166; or TransUnion at www.transunion.ca or toll-free at 1-877-713-3393 or at 514-335-0374 (Quebec residents), 1-800-663-9980 (Canadians outside Quebec) or 1-800-916-8800 (U.S. citizens).

PART 11

not asking for help

CHAPTER 50

Not Doing the Math: Mortgage Versus RRSP Versus TFSA

If you have a lump-sum amount of cash, you need to do some calculations to determine your best strategy.

FOR AS LONG AS I CAN REMEMBER, Canadians have wondered what their best strategy would be for building net worth — paying down the mortgage or making an RRSP contribution? Today there is one more variable to consider — contributing to the tax free savings account (TFSA). The benefits of paying off a mortgage sooner are clear: lower total interest costs and a shorter amortization period. In chapter 16, we saw how making accelerated payments results in paying off your mortgage years sooner.

So, if you had some extra money this year, what should you do with it? Is it best to direct it toward a mortgage, or should it be invested?

Here are things to consider.

- If you are not going to be able to pay off your mortgage before retirement, consider allocating the lump sum to your mortgage — entering retirement mortgage-free will reduce your fixed costs and help manage cash flows.

- Interest rate uncertainty — who knows what future mortgage rates will be? With rates at record lows, the presumption is that they will increase over the next few years, so paying down the mortgage in a low-interest-rate environment means there will be a smaller outstanding mortgage amount when it comes time to renew at a higher interest rate.

- How do you feel about having debt? Perhaps you can't sleep at night because of the size of the mortgage — in that case you should pay down the mortgage.

- What interest rate are you paying on the mortgage, and how does it compare to the expected rate of return on your investments? Consider the benefits of investing the money and earning compounding growth over a long period of time.

- An RRSP contribution has an immediate impact on net worth. While you won't increase your assets by making an RRSP contribution (you're just moving money from your bank account into an RRSP), you get additional funds as a result of the tax savings from the contribution. A $10,000 RRSP contribution could mean a $4,000 tax refund if you're in the 40% tax bracket. So your net worth goes up by an extra $4,000.

- A home is an illiquid asset. Using the extra cash to pay down the mortgage rather than investing it means that if you need access to the money some time in the future, you can't easily access it. Consider if you are out of work for a period of time and need some cash to pay for expenses; would you be able to increase your mortgage or borrow the funds? On the other hand, if the money was invested in an RRSP or TFSA, withdrawals could be made from these accounts to supplement cash flow.

- Saving with an RRSP or TFSA creates a diversified balance sheet. Your home is usually your biggest asset, so changes in the real estate market will have a big impact on your net worth. By adding other assets you are spreading your risk across different investments.

Because numbers tell this kind of story better than words, here is a comparison of the results from making different decisions with your money.

The assumptions used in the following scenarios are: A one-time lump-sum amount of $10,000; a current mortgage of $150,000 at 5.5% that will be paid off in 15 years; and an RRSP or TFSA investment that will earn a 5% rate of return.

1. Pay down the mortgage. This saves **$11,801** in interest. The mortgage is paid off in 13 years and six months rather than 15 years.

2. Contribute to an RRSP. The RRSP contribution will result in a $4,000 refund, which I assume will be contributed to a TFSA. Investment funds in the RRSP grow to $20,789, and the TFSA grows to $8,316, for a grand total savings of **$29,105.**

3. Contribute to an RRSP. In this case, the $4,000 RRSP refund is used to pay down the mortgage. The RRSP grows to $20,789, and $4,778 in interest is saved on the mortgage. The grand total of savings is **$25,567**.

4. Contribute to a TFSA. The investment grows to **$20,789**.

The winner here is the RRSP/TFSA combination described in scenario 2 with total savings of $29,105. But remember that when money is withdrawn from the RRSP, it will be taxable, whereas withdrawals from a TFSA are not. If the individual's marginal tax rate is 40% (the same as when the RRSP contribution was made), then there is no difference between the RRSP/TFSA combination or just the TFSA. However, income is usually lower in retirement, which means a lower tax rate. In that case, the RRSP/TFSA combination comes out ahead.

rescue it!

Which is the best way to invest a lump sum?

☐ If mortgage rates are much higher than you could be earning on your RRSP or TFSA, then the mortgage wins. In the example shown, with 15 years left on the mortgage, an interest rate differential of approximately 3.5% or more gives the opposite result. So if you are paying 8.5% or more on the mortgage and earning only 5% on your savings (earning 3.5% less), then paying off the mortgage would be the better choice.

These days, with relatively low mortgage rates, using the lump sum to pay down the mortgage rarely comes out ahead.

☐ If you are currently in a low tax bracket, then contribute to the TFSA and not the RRSP, because you won't get much in tax savings from the RRSP tax deduction. A TFSA is also the better choice if you will be in a higher tax bracket at the time you withdraw from the RRSP than when you made the contribution.

CHAPTER 51

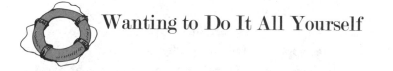 Wanting to Do It All Yourself

As a result of adopting a do-it-yourself approach to retirement planning, you may be headed in the wrong direction without even knowing it.

THESE DAYS WE HAVE ACCESS TO experts who can help in so many different aspects of our lives — we seek the advice of fitness coaches, career coaches, life planners, naturopaths, physiotherapists, marriage counsellors, and more. These people help us to pinpoint what's wrong, and then set us on the right path. They are with us along the way to support and guide us, but also to motivate us to stick to the plan. There are also experts who can help us with our family wealth strategy — building wealth, managing wealth, and protecting wealth. So why don't we feel we need to get help with our finances? A common misconception is thinking you don't have enough money to see an advisor, or that your finances are relatively simple and you can manage on your own.

Thanks to the Internet, we live in an age of information that is available 24/7, and this has led to a "do-it-yourself approach" trend in personal wealth management. While access to information on a wide range of personal finance topics is a step in the right direction, the real issue is, how do we properly diagnose the problem if we don't know there is a problem in the first place? When you adopt a do-it-yourself approach to retirement planning, you may not know what you don't know. Another important consideration is time — how can we possibly find the time to read every-thing that's out there, make sense of what we're reading, and apply general information to our specific circumstances?

how financial advisors can help

There are qualified experts out there who can help identify the barriers to and opportunities for building wealth. Advisors can provide an objective view regarding budgeting and saving, can help determine your investment strategy, and can provide appropriate strategies for building and protecting your wealth. In 2010, the Financial Planning Standards Council released survey results indicating that 64% of clients who receive comprehensive, integrated planning said they feel prepared to manage through tough eco-nomic times, compared with 33% of those with no financial planning. What's more, those who dealt with a certified financial planner reported feeling more on track with their financial affairs and having greater peace of mind than those who had no advisor.

which advisor is right for you?

With a wide variety of financial advisors available, it may be difficult to decide who to go to for help. How do you find the right advisor for what you need? What do all those initials after a person's name stand for? Did the person take a one-day course, or is he or she a member of a profession or association that is regulated, has a code of ethics, and takes disciplinary action against members who do not adhere to certain standards?

Some individuals are specialized in a particular field, while others have broader knowledge but work with other experts to provide a fully inte-grated service. There are different aspects to personal wealth management that are interrelated and, as a result, advisors often have expertise in more than one area. Paying close attention to key words in their business title or the way they describe themselves will help you identify their area of expertise. For instance, words such as *financial* or *wealth* suggest a focus on personal finances, including budgeting, saving, investing, debt manage-ment, income tax minimization, estate planning, and insurance; the word *investment* suggests a focus on portfolio strategy, using investment prod-ucts, managing rates of return, and asset allocation; the word *estate* implies leaving a legacy, wills, trusts, risk management including insurance, and powers of attorney. This is just a guideline to get you started: you need to do your own research. Not everyone who works in the area of estate planning is a lawyer, so if it's a lawyer you need, make sure you ask for one. The following list can help you to understand the different types of advisors you can work with, and the services they provide.

Initials	Definition	Description	Web site[1]
CFP®	Certified Financial Planner	The CFP is an internationally recognized financial planning designation that identifies those who are experts in all areas of financial planning. The Financial Planning Standards Council (FPSC) administers the CFP exam and grants the CFP certification. There is an established code of ethics that guides the conduct of CFPs, and the FPSC reviews complaints against CFPs and may take disciplinary action, including revocation of the rights to use the CFP mark. CFPs must meet annual continuing education criteria.	www.fpsc.ca
R.F.P.®	Registered Financial Planner™	The Institute of Advanced Financial Planners™ (IAFP) grants the R.F.P designation. The IAFP can take disciplinary action, which can include expulsion.	www.iafp.ca
Pl. Fin.	Planificateur financier	The Institut québécois de planification financière (IQPF) is the only organization authorized to grant financial planning diplomas in Quebec.	www.iqpf.org

---

[1]Note: The information in the chart has been compiled based on information found on the association Web sites as shown.

Initials	Definition	Description	Web site
PFP®	Personal Financial Planner	The Canadian Securities Institute (CSI) is the educational body that provides instruction and the PFP designation. PFPs must meet annual continuing education requirements and follow a code of ethics.	www.csi.ca
CFA	Chartered Financial Analyst	The CFA institute is the world's largest association of investment professionals. A CFA must adhere to global standards and professional codes of conduct.	www.cfainstitute.org
IA	Investment Advisor	Investment Industry Regulatory Organization of Canada (IIROC) is the national self-regulatory organization that oversees all investment dealers and trading activity on debt and equity marketplaces in Canada. IIROC registered investment advisors are qualified, trained, and regulated, and meet high standards of conduct to ensure they provide investors with the best possible service to meet investor needs. IIROC sets and enforces rules regarding the proficiency and business and financial conduct of dealer firms and their registered employees.	www.iiac.ca/welcome-to-the-new-iiac-ca
IC/PM	Investment Counsel/ Portfolio Manager	The Investment Counsel Association of Canada (ICAC) — now called the Portfolio Management Association of Canada (PMAC) — is the representative organization for Investment Counsel and Portfolio Managers in Canada. Member firms are only in the business of managing investments for clients in keeping with	www.investment-counsel.org

Initials	Definition	Description	Web site
		each client's needs and objectives and risk tolerance. All PMAC members subscribe to a code of ethics.	
CIM™	Certified Investment Manager	The Canadian Securities Institute provides a series of courses and examinations that lead to the CIM designation, which is needed to be licensed as a discretionary portfolio manager in Canada.	www.csi.ca
CA	Chartered Accountant	The Canadian Institute of Chartered Accountants grants the CA, which is a professional accounting designation. CAs are trained in accounting, auditing, and taxation. They must adhere to a strict code of conduct, are subject to disciplinary actions, and must meet annual continuing education requirements.	www.cica.ca
TEP	Trust and Estate Practitioner	The Society of Trust and Estate Practitioners grants the TEP designation. A TEP must adhere to a code of professional conduct and meet annual continuing education requirements.	www.step.ca
CLU®	Chartered Life Underwriter	The Institute for Advanced Financial Education grants the CLU to identify those who are experts in risk management and wealth transfer. A CLU must adhere to a code of professional conduct and meet annual continuing education requirements.	www.iafe.ca

Initials	Definition	Description	Web site
CPCA®	Certified Professional Consultants on Aging (CPCA) (formerly CSA)	CPCAs are professionals who have taken a comprehensive 24-module course about the health, social, and financial aspects of aging, and agree to abide by a rigorous Code of Professional Responsibility overseen by an independent Board of Standards.	www. cpcacanada. com

Questions to ask an advisor:

- What's your strategy for building a retirement plan?

- What is your area of expertise?

- What designations or licences do you hold?

- What other experts do you work with?

- How do you get paid?

- Describe your client base — how many clients do you have?

- How did you attract those clients?

- How often do you meet face to face with clients?

- How do you communicate with clients, and how often?

- What's your investment philosophy?

The key is to work with an advisor who you trust and respect, one who has the same values and beliefs you do, and who you feel comfortable working with. The best advisors ask the right questions about you, your family, and your goals; they communicate regularly, or at least when they say they will; they look out for your best interests, and are knowledgeable and reliable; and they are open about fees and how they are compensated. Once you find an advisor you trust and would like to work with, then it's a match made in heaven. If not, then it's time to find another advisor.

There are so many things to consider when planning for and living in retirement, that it makes sense to have a team of experts who specialize in different areas helping us along the way.

As you've learned in this book, there are many different aspects to building a sound retirement plan.

rescue it!

☐ Review your personal net worth statement and, based on the information in this book, identify the areas where you could benefit from working with an advisor.

When you are looking for an advisor:

☐ Use the list of questions provided above when interviewing a potential advisor.

☐ Ask friends and family how they found their advisor and if they would recommend that person to others.

☐ Contact the professional organization that regulates the type of professional you are looking for, and ask for a list of members in good standing in your city.

CHAPTER 52

 Substituting a Retirement Calculator
for Retirement Advice

*A calculator can provide a quick snapshot, but it's just one
aspect of a retirement plan.*

THERE ARE CERTAINLY A LOT OF financial calculators available today.
Once these were available only to financial planning professionals, due to
their high prices and complicated questionnaires; today the Internet is a
haven for financial tools. If you do an Internet search for the words *retirement calculator,* you'll find hundreds of free calculators that you can use to
start to paint a picture of what your retirement finances might look like. By
answering a few simple questions, they produce a snapshot of how much
your savings will grow over a number of years, or give you an idea of how
much you should be saving in order to retire when you want to. Calculators
are ideal if you just want a general idea of how you're doing, but they do
not address the many different aspects of a comprehensive retirement plan
that are needed to make important financial and non-financial decisions.

are the inputs and assumptions reasonable?

Calculators are simple projections based on a series of pre-set inputs and
assumptions — a few changes to the assumptions result in a very different
result. If you've used a retirement calculator and it indicates that you don't

have enough money to retire when you want to — simply increase the rate of return, and voilà, you can reach your goal. Even a small change in the rate of return assumption, say from 5 to 7%, means you'll have 46% more savings (based on $100,000 invested for 20 years). But how reasonable is the rate of return assumption that you are using? Based on your risk tolerance, time horizon, and the current market environment, is it possible for you to achieve a 7% rate of return in the future, or are you overestimating what you might be able to earn? Another assumption that has a big impact on how much you need to save so that you can live a certain lifestyle in retirement is the inflation assumption. Increasing the inflation assumption from 2 to 3% during a 25-year retirement means you'll need to accumulate more savings, because inflation erodes your purchasing power. Rate of return and inflation are two assumptions that you can change in the calculator but, in reality, you cannot control. What about the amount you have input for retirement expenses? It's easy to underestimate how much one might spend during retirement and, while using a low expense estimate may indicate that you need to accumulate a smaller nest egg, it too may not be realistic if you haven't done a thorough job at coming up with your expense amount. One must be careful when changing the inputs just to produce the desired results. On the other hand, being able to change the inputs allows you to see how some simple tactics, such as working a few more years, can impact your overall results. Using calculators to run "what if" scenarios can be valuable, and can motivate you to take action when you see what the results could be.

In some cases the assumptions are embedded into the calculator, and you can't see what they are. If you use calculators with different assumptions, you'll come up with different results. I searched the Internet for a calculator that could show how much my money would grow over a 20-year period. While there were a number of different calculators I could have used, not all of them did exactly what I was searching for. I finally found two calculators that would give me the answer I needed, or so I thought. While I input the exact same information into the two calculators, the results were different. One of the calculators indicated that my money would have grown to $104,185 and the other said $102,042.66 (input: 20 years of savings of $200/month earning 7% rate of return). Which one is correct?

other important considerations not addressed by the calculator

While a calculator may offer some ideas to help get you to your goal, it provides no personal advice. Not only are you limited to what you can input, but the solutions and strategies provided are very generic and can apply to everyone, whether or not they used the calculator at all. But as we know, when it comes to retirement planning, one size does not fit all. Calculators tend to oversimplify things and miss many important things that need to be included in a retirement plan, such as whether you have a financially dependent child, whether your investments are appropriate for you, whether you have an up-to-date will, who will take care of you if you become disabled, what happens if you lose your job or your spouse pre-deceases you. What if maximizing your RRSP isn't the best option for you? Perhaps a better alternative would be to contribute to a spousal RRSP or a TFSA?

It's true that many financial advisors also use financial calculators to prepare retirement plans, but they can identify problem areas that others cannot. They know how to connect the dots, and also ask a lot of other questions that uncover potential issues and opportunities not usually identified when using only a calculator.

But remember that for a retirement plan to be valuable, it has to reflect all of your goals and personal circumstances, and you also have to actually follow the plan. A plan is not a crystal ball about what will happen in the future — it's a trajectory. It's rare that even after one year, your financial circumstances are a 100% accurate match to the plan. Our lives are constantly changing, and while you don't need to change your retirement plan daily, it should be updated at least once a year, or more often if there is a major change in your personal situation. The key to success is that once you have a plan, you stick with it.

A retirement plan can be a powerful tool for both you and your advisor. It can identify gaps or issues so that they can be addressed before retirement, and it can show you different paths you can take by presenting different scenarios. It also provides a clear view of what the future may hold, if the assumptions you've made in the plan turn out to be correct, that is.

rescue it!

☐ Use quick tools and calculators to get an idea of whether or not you're on the right track to achieving a particular savings goal.

☐ If you would like to have a comprehensive retirement plan, don't use simple tools and calculators that only show one aspect of your retirement, but work with a financial advisor who can provide the written plan as well as the critical retirement planning conversation that addresses all of your goals and personal circumstances.

☐ Follow the guidance in this book to rescue any part of your retirement plan that needs rescuing.

ACKNOWLEDGEMENTS

I HAVE BEEN PRIVILEGED TO BE PART of the financial services industry and to have worked with so many Canadians planning for and living in retirement. This book is a result of those retirement planning conversations and based on some of the most common mistakes that are made.

A big thank you to all of my family, friends, and colleagues whose collective enthusiasm and encouragement for the book gave me the energy to complete it.

I would also like to acknowledge the many professionals who graciously reviewed the draft manuscript and provided their thoughtful comments and ideas. The book is better because of it. I would like to extend my gratitude to the following individuals for sharing their time, knowledge, and expertise: Jeffrey Hlynski, Associate, Moody's LLP Tax Advisors; M. Elena Hoffstein, Partner, Fasken Martineau DuMoulin LLP; Dianne White, Principal, Nexus Investment Management Inc.; Ted Patterson, Director, Humber College Centre for Employee Benefits; Cherise Berman, Senior Consultant, National Bank Financial; and Grace Lam, BMO Financial Group.

I would also like to thank the entire staff at John Wiley & Sons who have been involved in the production of this book. I am especially grateful for your support and encouragement to take an idea that had been germinating for so many years and helping make it a reality.

Above all, thank you to my biggest fans — my husband Sergio and children, Anthony and Stephanie, for their love and for being with me every step of the way.

ABOUT THE AUTHOR

 **TINA DI VITO** is a Chartered Accountant (CA), Certified Financial Planner (CFP) and Trust and Estate Practitioner (TEP). With more than 20 years of experience helping Canadians plan for and live in retirement, Tina has worked with families and run workshops and seminars for Canadians of all levels of prosperity. She is widely quoted in national and international media such as the *Globe and Mail*, the *Financial Post*, the *Toronto Star*, the *Wall Street Journal* and has been on *Canada AM*, Global Television, BNN, and CNBC. She has also been consulted by Canadian Parliamentary committees on a variety of wealth management topics. As Head of the BMO Retirement Institute she leads retirement strategies and directs the research and creation of industry-leading white paper reports on retirement issues facing Canadians.

INDEX